DISINFORMATION

AMERICAN MULTINATIONALS
AT WAR AGAINST EUROPE

By the Same Author

OAS — Histoire d'une organisation secrète, Fayard, 1986.

With Roger Faligot:

Au cœur de l'État, l'espionnage, Autrement, 1983.
Service B, Fayard, 1985.
KGB objectif Pretoria, PM Favre, 1985.
Kang Sheng et les services secrets chinois, Robert Laffont, 1987.
Porno Business, Fayard, 1987.
Les Résistants. De la guerre de l'ombre aux allées du pouvoir, Fayard, 1989.
Le Croissant et la croix gammée, Albin Michel, 1990.
As-tu vu Cremet ?, Fayard, 1991.
Éminences grises, Fayard, 1992.
Histoire mondiale du renseignement, t. 1 (1870-1939), Robert Laffont, 1993.
Les Maîtres espions (Histoire mondiale du renseignement,
    t. 2, de la guerre froide à nos jours), Robert Laffont, 1994.
Le Marché du diable, Fayard, 1995.

RÉMI KAUFFER

DISINFORMATION

American Multinationals
At War Against Europe

Algora Publishing
New York

Algora Publishing, New York
© 2001 by Algora Publishing
All rights reserved. Published 2001.
Printed in the United States of America
ISBN: 1-892941-50-3
Editors@algora.com

Originally published as *L'arme de la désinformation. Les multinationales améri-caines en guerre contre l'Europe* © *Editions Grasset & Fasquelle, 1999.*

Library of Congress Cataloging-in-Publication Data 00-013108

Kauffer, Rémi.
  [L'arme de la désinformation. English]
  Disinformation : American multinationals at war against Europe / by
Rémi Kauffer.
      p. cm.
Translation of: L'arme de la désinformation.
Includes bibliographical references.
  ISBN 1-892941-50-3 (alk. paper)
  1. Corporations, American—Corrupt practices—Europe—Case studies.
2. Propaganda, American—Economic aspects—Europe—Case studies. 3.
Competition, International. I. Title.
  HD2944 .K3813 2000
  338.8'897304—dc21
                        00-013108

Algora Publishing
wishes to express appreciation
to the French Ministry of Culture
for its support
of this work through the
Centre National du livre

New York
www.algora.com

"Your bait of falsehood takes this carp of truth;
And thus do we of wisdom and of reach,
With windlaces and with assays of bias,
By indirections find directions out."

Shakespeare
Hamlet, Act II, Scene 1.
(Dialogue between Polonius and his valet, Reynaldo).

CONTENTS

INTRODUCTION

Our world has changed. From simple and Manichean, it has become complicated, ambiguous. Yesterday, there were two systems competing, bloc against bloc. Now there is only one superpower. Sure of its geo-economic supremacy, the United States confronts two less-homogeneous entities, the European Union and Asia, that immense and chaotic continent.

This is not the end of History; it is only the beginning of a new chapter. A page has been turned. Nothing will be the same as before, but what will it be like, this century that is just starting out? The broad outlines of force are being drawn, through industrial, technological and commercial confrontations that will continue to intensify between nations as well as between great international companies. The American penchant for hegemony is growing. The future of our societies will depend to a great extent on Europe's capacity to thwart this new world disorder. This is what is at stake: a world under one influence, or indeed a multi-polar, balanced planet. And even though many have already laid down their arms, the show isn't over — yet. In Europe as in America, we like suspense. . .

When we talk about conflict, we think of strategies, tactics, and weapons. You would have thought that the Cold War had been put away, in the prop room somewhere backstage; instead, it is returning to center stage by means of one of its most pernicious legacies, the organized lie, psychological conditioning. In a word, disinformation.

After the collapse of the Eastern bloc, the techniques of mental encirclement changed in nature. Having proven its excellence as a weapon in the great East-West ideological confrontation, it has morphed into a frightening instrument of industrial and commercial war. This migration from one sphere to another, from the political toward the economic, is the subject of this book.

Disinformation. The term is recent. Some American specialists say that it first occurred in the jargon of the intelligence services during the First World War.

The German military staff used the term to indicate certain fake radio communications intended to mislead the enemy. After the October Revolution, under the name of *Dezinformatsia*, the Soviets conceived a far more ambitious plan: to apply this technique in various ways, targeting the masses, the intelligentsia and the leading elites with different messages, for the global subversion of the "capitalist societies". After decades of use by specialists alone, the noun "disinformation" fell into the public domain during the 1970's.

The practice goes far back in time. A contemporary of Confucius, Sun-Tzu, the Chinese codifier of *The Art of War*, ascribed a decisive role to the "36 stratagems", subtle variations of traps cleverly conceived to mislead the political and military chiefs of the opposing party:

"The art of war is based entirely on deception. That is why, when you are able, you should feign incapacity; when you are active, feign passivity. When you are near, make him believe that you are far, and when far, that you are near. Bait the enemy, lure him into a trap: simulate disorder, and strike him", wrote this warlike intellectual, six centuries BC. Nowadays, Master Sun remains the inspiration of certain adherents of "Hypercompetitive Rivalry", who see economic war as a simple alternative to war itself.

One writer follows the other. 200 years ago the Frenchman Beau-marchais — well-acquainted, through the vicissitudes of his own life, with secret missions, with undercover attacks, with covert blows — displayed remarkable lucidity in connection with the thousand and one ways of inducing others to err. Son of a clock- and watch-maker, he knew as well as anyone how to assemble the mechanics of disinforma-tion. If you need convincing, just recall these revealing words from his *Barber of Seville*: "Believe me, there is no malicious rumor, no horror, no absurd tale that you cannot get the idle folk of a big city to believe, if you really try."

The idle. . . and the others, too, if they have the least bit of credu-lity! The art of war and the air of calumny go well together, and that affinity is exploited by any competent disinformer, who fires his shots in clusters of complex, well-considered volleys. No disinformation suc-ceeds unless the intended "targets" (consumers, decision-makers, the media, the public authorities, associations, the general public) has a propensity to swallow the lies that are concocted for them. No brain-washing succeeds unless groundwork has been done, with well-defined goals, predisposing the audience to accept the message.

Calumniate, criticize, insinuate; some residue always sticks. Con-vincing means relentlessly hammering away on well-prepared brains with inaccurate facts. The recommended proportion: 90 to 95% of truth for 5% or 10% of invention. Any more truth, and the message risks being ineffective; any less and it would be too conspicuous. Such is the fundamental principle of the strange alchemy of the lie.

But if you act with the necessary skill, the noises will fuse to-gether in powerful gusts: Company X is in trouble. . . its chairman is ill. . . its shareholders are dissatisfied. . . its finances are shaky. . . the tax department is investigating it. . . and so are the Japanese, who are thinking about buying it. . . it isn't paying its suppliers on time. . . its input costs keep going up. . . its warehouses are full of unsold goods. . . its products are too expensive. . . the quality is shoddy. . . they are dan-gerous to our health (or to the environment). . . the company has a bad record on human rights (alternatives: trade-union rights or consumer rights)...

This kind of aggression is effective and inexpensive, but it bears inherent dangers for the attacker as well. Without a coherent plan, the attack will not work; without sufficient precautionary measures, it can be turned against the perpetrator. The disinformer who is caught red-handed not only misses his goal, he damages his own cause. By losing credibility, the unskillful attacker gives strength to the opposing party. "Good" disinformation is not reversible, as the saying goes. It should only work in one direction.

Brainwashing is good (if one can call it so). Not letting oneself be "traced" is better yet; essential, in fact! The many episodes reported in the current work show that it is easier to locate and describe such and such a disinformation maneuver than it is to determine who carried it out. And it is harder yet to draw out of the woodwork the real master-minds. They are wolves, but prudent wolves. And while one can often tell who benefits from the crime, the tangible evidence is cruelly lack-ing. If that were not the case, the law courts would collapse under the burden. However, charges are rarely brought, and the companies that are under attack generally deny it — for fear of aggravating an already bad situation. There is an industrial and commercial *omerta* wherein the victim "covers" for its attacker and is forced to become its accom-plice.

That is how it goes in the opaque world of modern disinforma-tion, where nothing is clear, where everything is vague. Except for the ultimate goal: the conquest of markets. Win or perish, that is the di-lemma. On the ground, this war results in manipulating public opin-ion, brainwashing consumers, casting discredit upon competitors. In short, shaping people's minds. And what better means than to apply to the latest virtual technologies the tried-and-true methods from the olden days? And so the newspaper and television industries, computer-ized data banks and the Internet have entered the fray.

Such are the battlefields of a permanent offensive that is not as gentle as people may think. European and American multinationals confront each other, with the British — recognized masters of psychological games, hallowed by their successes over the Nazis during the Second World War — playing sometimes on the side of the former, more often with the latter. This is a war that is carried out with an arsenal of myths and symbols, for these are also the implements by which are founded, today, the economic power of tomorrow. It is played out via manipulation and propaganda coups.

Because it is high time to shine a light on these obscure ambushes, I chose to open a series of explosive files that reveal the multiple facets of today's disinformation.

The first of these files deals with the series of attacks on the petroleum concern, Total, in connection with its construction of a gas pipeline in Burma, since 1995.

This initial contact with the turbid universe of economic disinformation calls to mind other cases, cases that have a clearer impact on our daily life. We will delve into the mysteries of the drug industries: three cases add up to a failure. The failure of the Europeans, stumbling and then slipping down the slope that was greased especially for them by Anglo-American competitors, powerful, crafty and none too scrupulous.

Such mishaps, however, are not inevitable. The chapters on aeronautics show how, after having learned the rules by which their rivals across the Atlantic play, the European manufacturers (English included) were able to find ways to work together. Thanks to this pugnacity, Boeing and Airbus have divided the skies almost equally, the New World and the Old Continent finally clashing with equal weapons in a key sector.

Not all the conflicts are so wide in scope. The final chapter offers various examples to illustrate how fertile a terrain the ecologists and consumers represent (generally without their own knowledge) for contemporary ploys of disinformation and demoralization. And they are even more vulnerable to the maneuvers that we will see tomorrow.

The future is yet to come. To those who hope to get by without seriously reflecting on the modern forms of brainwashing, good luck.

Playing the "global village idiot" is tantamount to giving up when the road before us is wide open. And this time, there will be no second chance! In a world where information has became the principal raw material, avant-garde technologies which ensure its almost instantaneous distribution are the same ones that transform it into an arena of virtual combat. Here comes the day of cyber-brainwashing. Largely controlled by our American friends and competitors, the Internet is laced with lures, snares, booby-traps, and intelligence agents. There are more than "hackers", "crackers" or "freakers" roaming the network. There is also an army of hard disk borers, tweakers of read-only memory, phantom consumers and bad Samaritans. In short, disinformation specialists.

This promises to be the beginning of a stormy century. Press "Enter". Here we go...

CHAPTER ONE

IN A BURMESE MUD HOLE

May 1996. What a shock for British television viewers, flicking over to ITV and seeing a spectacular report on Burmese children work-ing under terrible conditions to construct a railway line!

Against a backdrop of scenes from a modern slave system, a voice *off* blamed the company, Total. The French petroleum firm was appar-ently an accessory to the military junta of Rangoon, which was orches-trating the railway work. An amalgam of two distinct elements, this subtle juxtaposition of sounds and images gave off a whiff of scandal: that Total was trading with the Burmese generals, men who were capa-ble of such dictatorial predilections.

That, clearly, was the desired effect. Which leads to the question: who was trying to arouse the British collective unconscious at the ex-pense of a French industrial group? Indeed, these TV images recalled others, crueler still. Those of *The Bridge Over the River Kwaï*, David Lean's masterpiece.

The Kwaï River Syndrome

"Sixty thousand Englishmen, Australians, Dutchmen and Americans gathered in several groups, in the least civilized area in the world — the jungle of Burma and Thailand — to build a railway there, connecting the Bay of Bengal to Bangkok and Singapore. "

Millions of us have read this sentence that comes from the pen of Pierre Boulle, author of the eponymous novel that served as the basis for the screenplay of *The Bridge Over the River Kwaï*. To build the Bangkok-Rangoon railway line, the Japanese enslaved not 60,000 but 45,000 Western prisoners of war. One third of these unfortunates, 16,000 men, found their death along this infernal construction site. At their sides, it is often forgotten, fell 100,000 of their Asian companions in misfortune, many of whom were Burmese.

"Only" 45,000 men among the Allies, it is true. But Boulle was on the trail of a truth that was less abstract than that which emanates from the statistics. He wanted to testify to the human sacrifice perpetrated here more than half a century ago between Thailand and Burma: one death for every two railroad cross-ties.

The survivors never forgot. Another great novelist of international fame, James Clavell, died without having forgiven the Mikado's soldiers for the degrading treatment to which he had been victim in their camps. One day, my own path crossed that of another survivor, a Dutchman this time. Klaas Kooy had been in the camp of Changi, in Singapore, then at the building sites along the Kwaï River. This 86 year old man preserved a clear memory of the insults, the blows, the tropical diseases, and the hunger. Intact as well was the memory of a great pit, dug by the men who were still able; and into it, the day's or the night's dead would be thrown: ten, twelve, fifteen skeletal corpses.

Who would let such images fade in the depths of a dimming memory? Not the English veterans. In May 1998, tossing aside the legendary British impaasivity, several hundred of them openly turned their backs to Emperor Akihito during his official visit to London. This was a posthumous homage and a protest in the memory of their comrades, martyrized by the Japanese war machine. The survivors of the Hell camps whistled *Colonel Bogey's March*, from the movie sound track. "Nissan-Blair", the most resolute of them howled, during the British Prime Minister's address. A Nipponese flag from the war years was burned. A few brief but violent scuffles broke out between the demonstrators and the "bobbies".

This is the yardstick by which we have to measure the impact of the televisual equation France + Total + junta soldier + Burma railway + Japanese war crimes. The ITV report was not a single broadcast, in fact it was part of a series, all along similar lines. Images of Burmese workmen chained to tubes from the pipeline were broadcast on several occasions. The commentaries "overlapped" two distinct elements: the gas pipeline works, run by French construction engineers, and the building of a north-south railway line between the towns of Ye and Tavoy, at the behest of the Burmese authorities and implemented under their leadership, under scandalous conditions (50,000 workers mobilized by force, whole villages emptied of their inhabitants).

What was the point of this campaign? The will to have human rights triumph, at the price of manipulating sounds, images, situations and concepts? Were there strategic interests at stake? No one can answer these new questions without playing back an even more complicated film: that of Total's engagement in a country with such a bloody and disturbed destiny.

The Burma Road

The French oil group's Burmese adventure really begins in 1990. Like its Anglo-Dutch rival, Shell, and the American Unocal, Total had its eye on the Yadana offshore deposit, in the Gulf of Martaban — a particularly promising gas field discovered eight years earlier by the Burmese national group, MOGE (Myanmar Oil and Gas Enterprise).

A military dictatorship has prevailed since June 1989 in Burma — renamed Myanmar. This is the provisional result of a long history, including British colonization following a debate at the House of Commons in 1886; a dockers' riot in 1930; the rebellion led by Saya San (crushed the following year); professions of nationalist faith by Aung San, the Secretary of the Union of Students in Rangoon (the father of the future Nobel Peace Prize laureate); his exile in Tokyo, his return to Burma; the interested support of the Mikado's intelligence services, who also coveted the 1.5 million tons of oil produced annually in Burma. These same Japanese would provide technical training in clandestine activity to the core group of Aung San's faithful followers, called the "thirty comrades".

In 1942, the Nippon army invades the British colony. The soldiers of the Rising Sun cut the Burma Road, by which the Allies supplied China. Controlled by Aung San, the Burma Independence Army is set up under Japanese control.

Orde Charles Wingate is then charged with sowing chaos along the Irrawaddy, the 1375 mile long river that irrigates Burma before it dives into the Sea of Andaman — a suitable task for this forty year old English general whom one might believe came straight out of the pages of a Hugo Pratt album. A friend of the Zionists in Palestine, then the organizer of an astonishingly effective guerrilla unit (the Gideon Force), Wingate infiltrated his "Chindits", commandos trained in jungle combat, in the Burmese depths.

Man sometimes remains incorrigibly naïve, even when he is familiar with the worst treachery. Thus Wingate, the genius of unconventional military action, was ignorant of the unwritten laws that govern economic combat. To initiate him into the mysteries of this universe, whose indirect offensives are at least as effective as those of his "Chindits", it would take nothing less than the new episode that I am about to reveal, 56 years later.

Back in the early days, in 1943, the first American officers arriving to prepare the reopening of the Burma Road disembarked in India. In accordance with his superiors' orders, Wingate's Intelligence Officer, Colonel Steve Wood, had his indigenous agents "search" the newcomers' bags. He discovered a disloyalty greater than his own: the Allies had arrived with their luggage stuffed full of detailed files analyzing every aspect of the structures of the great Indian companies: Tata, in the iron and steel industry, manufacturing engines, trucks, and buses, plus textiles, chemistry, the hotel trade, mechanical engineering, and cement factories; and Birla, with its coal mines, car and bicycle factories, sugar refineries, earthenware, porcelain, and electricity, along with the press and foreign trade.

Obviously, these "American friends" had set their sights far beyond the horizon of Burma! Beyond the anti-Japanese war, the U.S. strategists sought to manage the reorganization of Asian industries to the benefit of American companies, as soon as the former colonizers could be gotten out of the way — a lesson that struck Wood and Wingate, but not their seniors in rank. Met, and even exceeded, by their American pupils, the subjects of His Gracious British Majesty were thus no longer the privileged wielders of the basic strategic axiom: economic war is only the continuation of war. . . by different means.

The Hour of Dictatorship

Let us return to Asia. The Second World War opened new prospects there for the colonized countries: the capture of Rangoon in May 1945, the general strike in September-October 1946; the assassination of Aung San and seven ministers of his government — at the order of his rival, U Saw; the Treaty of Independence (October 17, 1947) and the official birth of the Burmese Union, three months later.

In October 1958, faced with the persistent disorder generated by factional fighting and the parallel development of the Communist and Karen guerrillas (an minority nationality of Chinese origin, influenced by Christian missionaries and considered by the Burmese ultranationalists to be "collaborators" of the former English colonizers), Prime Minister U Nu asked the House of Commons to grant General Ne Win, former pupil of the Japanese and an emulator of Aung San, extended powers in the capacity of head of a national union government.

Initially, Ne Win reestablished a semblance of order in the country. He organized quasi-democratic elections. U Nu became Prime Minister again. In a theatrical twist, in March 1962 the General overthrew the civilian government that he had contributed to restoring! On April 30, 1962, the putschist proclaimed "a Burmese path toward Socialism", which little by little isolated the country and reduced it to poverty. This "path" was inspired by the Maoist "Great Leap Forward" that killed some 30 million Chinese.

Starting in 1964, all political parties were prohibited — except that of Ne Win, who was no longer called anything but "Number One". Consequently, the Chinese model (in Burmese hues) took on all its glory. Ten years later, in March 1974, "an assembly of the people" named the General the first President of the very new Socialist Republic of the Burmese Union. Now he had the opportunity to consolidate the dictatorship and to further repress the national minorities, the Shan, Kachin, Rakhin, Môn and Karen. Insufficiently "socialist", insufficiently "patriotic", they would have to "melt" into the mass of the 30 million inhabitants of the Union (today 45 million), or perish.

The word *perish* must be taken literally, along with economic isolation, imprisonment and political, social and anti-minority repression in the name of Burmese interests. The country sank into destitution, the more so as the aging "Number One" began adding misguided occultist practices to the socialist dimension (of Chinese inspiration). He was surrounded by a cloud of astrologers. . . to suppress inflation, in 1987, they persuaded him to reorganize the entire system on the base of 9 — a propitious number, according to the shamans.

The result: a greater crisis than ever. Bankruptcy, coed strikes, democratic agitation, demonstrations. Blood soon began to flow. The army's intervention killed 2,000 to 3,000. On September 17, 1988, the chief of the general staff, General Saw Maung, removed Ne Win — who nevertheless continued to play an influential role, for a long time, as the father-founder of the regime.

Saw Maung then assumed the chairmanship of the SLORC (State Law and Order Restoration Council). The SLORC was less personalized; it presented itself in the form of a collective structure of about thirty men, practically all of them officers. The dictatorship claimed to be "more rational", but in fact it was only looking for ways to persist, in another guise. This was a farce that did not succeed past the legislative elections of March 1990. The National League for Democracy, led by Aung San Suu Kyi (the daughter of "the father-founder" of the Burmese Union), emerged victorious. No problem: the government, furious at being thus repudiated, immediately canceled the verdict of the ballot boxes.

Anxious about the international stakes (the USSR was on the verge of collapse and post-Tiananmen China turned its back on any hope of political liberalization), the SLORC then set out on a narrow and hazardous route. By attracting Western investors to Myanmar, the military sought to break the isolation of a regime that was weakened when the democracies spurned it. But they did not loosen the police grip on civil society and they sought to keep open what was, in their eyes, the principal economic pipeline: drugs, the "real" financial engine of the dictatorship.

Such is the minefield that the negotiators of Total surveyed. Without realizing it, they were following in the footsteps of Anton Zichka, a specialist in economic questions who was famous in the inter-war period. In 1933, he eruditely explained, "Tobacco, tea, coffee and cotton you may find in Indochina, but there is one thing which is completely lacking and which is lacking in all the French colonial possessions: oil. France could, however, find it close to Indochina. In central Burma, close to the Irrawaddy, are the rich plains of Yenang-Uaung; and all along the border of Tonkin, oil flows in abundance. Burma wants to be detached from England. Burma very much wishes to withdraw itself from English domination. However, it cannot survive on its own. It would have to rely on another power. And there is only France." But he added, a little later, "If Yunnan is French one day, if Burma itself declares its independence and later becomes a French sphere of influence, it will not be the result of machinations or the work of secret agents, neither will it be the result of plans conceived by politicians on a grand scale. It will be a windfall. For France seems to follow Mr. Deutsch de La Meurthe's line of thinking (the big French oilman) who said, "The greatest misfortune that could befall us would be to discover oil reservoirs."

Sixty years later, was it the misfortune of the French gas prospectors to locate promising gas reserves? Considering the multifarious attacks on Total, it is tempting to answer in the affirmative.

A Little Gas in the Oil

Experts regard natural gas as the energy queen of the 21st century. More abundant than oil, its reserves would ensure humanity seven decades of exploitation. It is more widely distributed in the geographical sense, and it is also less polluting. It can be used in various ways. Lastly, people are less afraid of natural gas than of nuclear power. Thus it is an invaluable fluid at a time when ecologist groups have acquired some socio-economic weight.

At the very beginning of the 1990's, natural gas accounted for only 15% of world energy consumption. But by 1995, it had climbed to 20%, and according to forecasters it may reach 26% in the year 2010, and still more in the future. Over the same period, 1990-2010, gas should grow from 7% to 20% of energy production in the European Union.

The covetous parties were well aware of what was at stake. Except for the Anglo-Royal Dutch Shell, second in the world of gas production, Europe hardly had a place on this strategic game board. Just consider the list of the world's largest producers, arranged by size in descending order: Gazprom (Russia), Shell, Exxon (United States), Sonatrach (Algeria), Mobil (United States), Amoco (United States), Aramco (Saudi Arabia), National Iran Oil Company, Rafter (United States), Pemex (Mexico). Their annual production ranges from 560 billion cubic meters for Gazprom to 72 for Shell and 26 for Pemex.

A number of North American companies (or those with North American capital) are on this list, but no French company is. It doesn't take much to explain the energy problems in a country that lost control of the Saharan resources in the 1960's and that harbors within its own borders mighty few oil-bearing or gas-bearing reserves. This estab-lished fact impelled France to take the nuclear power route, the only solution that would allow it to safeguard its energy interests.

The emergence of natural gas as an option changed the playing field. When inertia brings the risk of a new loss of independence, chances must be taken. Total, the sixth largest French company and the twelfth oil company in the world, endorsed this choice. With gas representing almost half of its total production outside the Middle East, the group intended to reinforce its presence in Southeast Asia and increase its operational results from 10-12 to 15-20% in the area from the 1960's to the year 2000.

Exploration in the two contiguous offshore Burmese blocks, M 5 and M 6, on a total surface of 16,250 square miles, gave optimistic signs for the future. The deposits, baptized Yadana, might hold reserves of up to 140 billion cubic meters.

Yadana is located south of the mouths of the Irrawaddy, formerly the stomping ground of General Wingate's "Chindits". To the north-east, the Gulf of Martaban pierces deeply into the lands of the Union of Myanmar. In order to convey the gas toward Thailand, the presumed (desired) terminus, a 220-mile underwater gas pipeline would have to be built. At the exit of this maritime course, the pipeline would follow a land route of an about 40 miles through the Burmese jungle.

The Thai national company PAT-EP (Petroleum Authority of Thailand-Exploitation and Production) appeared to be an essential partner, from the start. Well along on its path toward development, Thailand needed energy. Yadana could increase its capacity by 20%. Under these conditions, a draft agreement soon emerged. While Total would run the pipeline works up to the Thai border, the PAT-EP would build a gas-fueled power station at Rachaburi, west of Bangkok. The same company would, at the same time, extend the gas pipeline some 160 miles over Thai territory. The various construction sites, if the negotiations succeeded, were to be completed by early summer, 1998. The joint exploitation of the Yadana reserves could then run for thirty years. And one could expect considerable profits from them.

Total, In A Hornet's Nest

Total, PAT-EP and MOGE (the Burmese national oil company) were all involved in the negotiations. Like everything that counts in that country, MOGE was in the hands of the military; as for the Anglo-Americans, Shell and Unocal, they were not welcome in the game since eliminating Total from the plan would be their first concern. And the reverse was also true, of course. . . The palace of King Bhumibol Adulyadej in Thailand was presumed to be a significant ally for the French. In fact, it was a princess of the blood who was the principal ally, as she entertained excellent relations with the military circles, who were still very powerful in Bangkok, the capital. The extent of her network of relations led the group to expect a favorable outcome in the long term. All the same, area specialists warned that patience would be required. Charming but inscrutable smiles do not prevent anyone from defending his vested interests, on one side or the other.

In Rangoon, capital of Myanmar, the picture was quite different. "Democratization" was causing a ruckus in a country where the SLORC dictatorship was firmer than ever. To protest against the annulment of the electoral process of 1990, Paris recalled its defense attaché. In his capacity as an officer and thus as a "colleague", this diplomatic civil servant had maintained privileged contacts with the chiefs of the military junta in power. Since his departure, the two sides were no longer talking to each other, despite the efforts of the French ambassador, who had taken up the cause of Total — a leading light of French industry. This situation would not have been too damaging if the French secret service had had a presence in the area. However, such was not the case. In Rangoon, the DGSE* had ceased to exist. Nothing was going on at the diplomatic level, and nothing was going on in the shadows. To make matters worse, Total was not imbued with the "culture of intelligence gathering" specific to Elf, its French competitor, whose savvy in the corridors of influence and in the collection of infor-

*Direction générale de la sécurité extérieure: the French CIA.

mation has for so long rivaled those of the DGSE. For Total, constrained to advance without any cover, in *terra incognita*, the future looked dim. How could they overtake the leaders of Shell, who were so much more at ease in the British ex-colony that is Burma? And how could they outdo Unocal, who benefited from some of the prestige of the powerful America? Better find some unofficial intermediaries.

We will call him Mr. Jean. Formerly a diplomat posted to the embassy of Rangoon, this French businessman familiar with Asia had his small and his large entrées among the Burmese military. Not content with having a personal relationship in the private entourage of the former "Number One", Ne Win, Mr. Jean also hung out with an ex-leader of the local information services. This Frenchman's network of relationships and his field of activities in various companies also extended to Vietnam. Over there, his trade partners belonged to the entourage of Mai Chi Tho, Interior Minister and brother of one of the historical figures of the communist regime, Lê Duc Tho.

Mr. Jean was not only engaged in business, he had a patriotic spirit. Whenever he got a chance, the former diplomat liked to promote French interests in his two countries of adoption. And he didn't mind playing a trick or two on the Anglo-Saxons, whom he scarcely held dear. . . OK: Mr. Jean will see what he can do with his friends at SLORC.

We won't dwell on this character, however colorful he may be. The very evocation of his name makes jaws clench in the La Défense neighborhood of Paris, at Total's headquarters. In Rangoon, his role in the genesis of the Yadana plan seems to be an open secret, but at Total's office tower, in Paris, it remains a state secret. Mr. Jean? We don't know him. Moreover, there have never been even indirect contacts with SLORC. I swear. The only negotiations were those with the MOGE staff.

This is pure fiction, since MOGE's "political" headquarters, the only ones that matter in this national company under army control, are the same as the SLORC headquarters — the apparatus of the dictatorship. SLORC, where the Sergeant-General David O. Abel would follow

19

the developing plans with growing interest. . . Minister for Planning and Finance under the junta, this Anglo-Burmese with gracious manners was convinced of the advantages of a potential agreement with Total and PAT-EP. Not because the man was the slightest bit liberal in his thinking, but because Abel, more realistic than most of his friends, was ready to grasp any straw that might decrease the regime's isolation. His recommendation: development, to be well-fertilized by foreign investment in Myanmar's unexploited assets, i.e. industry and tourism.

If You Dine With The Devil...

A former intelligence agent, Mr. Jean remained a man of secrecy. Did he spell out to his partners at Total the complexity of the Burmese theater of operations? Did he, on the contrary, minimize it in order to retain his position as the obligatory intermediary between the two parties? An additional element must be added to the equation: his French interlocutors' excessive self-confidence. Total had considerable experience in how to proceed with dictatorial régimes, practical experience that the French petroleum company was liable to apply mechanically to Myanmar.

What was their experience, actually? South Africa, first of all. Shortly after apartheid was established, in 1954, the French petroleum company started up its refining and distribution activities there. In the 1970's and 1980's, this earned them the wrath of a certain number of Anglo-Saxon pro-Third World organizations who were looking to expand the boycott of the regime. But convinced that it was acting within its rights, Total refused to give in to their injunctions. The French considered that they were not entertaining any but the strictest economic relations with the white South African authorities. The racist laws that were in force, they felt, were extraneous to their company insofar as Total was not practicing any segregation within its personnel. Total even set out to train indigenous managers, whether black or of mixed races.

In fact, the oil group supposedly was assured of "benevolent neutrality" from the African National Congress (ANC) whose leader, Nelson Mandela, was festering in a cell in the Robben Island prison. This neutrality was supposedly guaranteed in several attestations from the leaders of the nationalist movement. . . documents that unfortunately I was never permitted to see, despite my repeated requests.

For lack of documentary evidences, we are reduced to conjecture. Let us assume that the French petro-company followed the example of other Western firms. To avoid having their installations sabotaged by Umkhonto We Sizwe ("Spearhead of the Nation", the armed branch of the ANC), these far-sighted contractors disbursed donations to the nationalist movement throughout all the years of apartheid. Indirectly, of course. This was a double game that did not fool even the Afrikaander government.

This assumption is categorically contradicted at Total's headquarters. An article by Nelson Mandela was published in April 1997 by *Energies*, Total's international magazine, under the title: "Toward a New Partnership". This is supposed to be absolute proof that the French firm was never compromised with the apartheid regime. This is an argument that cheapens the statesmanship of the former South African president, who was able to "forgive" past mistakes if the country's current interests required it. One element seems proven, in any case: the ANC did not hold any grudge against Total for its activities in South Africa. Such was not the case of a handful of veterans of the antiapartheid organizations, who soon turned up on Burmese territory.

One Dictatorship May Be Hiding Others

Indonesia was a second risk zone. After independence, this country that was so sorely tried by a brutal colonization would undergo the demagogic leadership of its first president, Ahmed Sukarno. His reign was leavened by certain anti-American disinformation operations masterminded by the KGB. In September 1965, a successful military putsch brought General Suharto to power. This was the "Djakarta Coup". The new regime would start out by assassinating at least 300,000 real or supposed sympathizers of the PKI (Partai Kommunis Indonesia). Far higher figures — figures that are not absurd at all — have been suggested; this massive repression (a sense of which is conveyed by the images in Peter Weir's movie, *L'Année de tous les dangers*) may have created a million victims! A tragic anecdote: the inhabitants of some of the islands of the Indonesian archipelago did not dare to eat fish for many months, for fear of discovering human remains in their stomachs.

Murder, torture, imprisonment, terror; that was the new order (Orde Baru) — a dictatorship that lasted three decades. It was this durability that made it a credible partner for companies seeking to carry out long-term plans, those who need that rare commodity — economic and political stability — even more than others do. Commodities that are in very short supply in the Third World.

This obligation to carry out long-term plans is the principal characteristic of the oil companies. Their upfront investments are heavy indeed, and only start to turn a profit decades later. And that explains why "the majors" forge ties, per force, with systems that are not very compatible with Western democratic criteria. Take Saudi Arabia, for example: a strategic ally of the United States ever since the Second World War.

Five years after the 1965 blood bath, the Total group, in association with the Indonesian national company Pertamina, carved out a large gas empire in the east of Borneo: more than 200,000 barrels of gas per day in the early 1990's, with a half-million planned for the year 2000. As the second foreign operator in Indonesia, the French firm established a policy of vocational training for the "locals", analogous to that which had already been tested in South Africa.

Curiously, Total's installation in Borneo hardly disturbed the pro-Third World organizations nor the humanitarian associations, who seem to have been more attached to the "symbol" of apartheid and to the "example" of the case of Burma. At the end of 1996, well before Suharto's fall, how surprised I was to hear a leader of the International Federation of Human Rights respond to me, by telephone, that he considered the fact of investing in Indonesia to be "much less serious" than

22

in Myanmar. This remark leaves me all the more perplexed since, contrary to General Ne Win, a pro-Maoist, the SLORC was precisely inspired in every point by "the Indonesian model".

Here's a fundamental problem. Should the relative horror of various dictatorships be fed into the opinion-shaping campaigns that are programmed by *ad hoc* organizations? Then, it occurred to me that partisans of the boycott of Vietnam's "proletarian dictatorship" (hallowed by its victory over the Americans) were quite rare; and that North Korea's starvation regime under Kim Jong still had its "anti-imperialist" supporters in the West.

There are no "good" dictatorships and all of them raise the same questions. Should Western companies abstain from doing business with oppressive regimes? If the answer is "No", then with which ones do they have the "right" to do business? By what criteria do good hearts require an embargo on Myanmar, while condemning the blockade of Iraq or of Cuba? And what shall we say about China, which everyone denounces in resounding terms but which remains a fabulous customer, as everyone knows?

Unless they are willing to give in to their competitors without a fight, the large international companies — modern equilibrists — strive to deal with these regimes without giving them direct support. This exercise requires a fine knowledge of local realities. Indeed, without good sources of information, one runs the risk of finding oneself in the uncomfortable situation of a hostage.

And therein undoubtedly resides Total's error in Myanmar.

With all its promising technical studies, the petroleum company thought it would be able to skillfully remove its chips from the table as it had done in South Africa and Indonesia. But they were forgetting that in these last two cases, the French firm was confronted with regimes that knew the modern world. Neither the Afrikaanders nor the Indonesian Generals were looking to transform their economic partners into political accomplices. Based on autarky, corrupted by the drug trade, Rangoon's military power was not psychologically wired to divide things that cleanly: businesses on one side, political problems on the other.

Excuse Me, Partner...

At Total, optimism is the rule. To such an extent that in July 1992 the company took the unusual risk of signing a contract to share production with the Burmese, without having formal certainty that the Thai national company PAT-EP would indeed acquire 80% of the Yadana gas.

As for the Burmese, SLORC's requirements had to be met. And not only the under-the-table payments, without which no negotiation is possible in this region. Of course, Total savagely denies that there could have been any "baksheesh", aside from an official "bonus" of $12 million that was given to MOGE to recompense its research costs. The dictatorship believed that the French firm had sought to meet with representatives of the minorities and the democratic opposition led by Aung Sang Suu Kyi; it prohibited any further contact of this type in the future. With this express condition, the works were to begin in 1995, under the vigilant eye of General Abel, who would even go to Paris at the end of this crucial year.

Consistent with its reputation, SLORC intended to "soak" its French partner to the maximum. The $12 million given to MOGE were thus used to "justify" in turn every operation that was carried out with money of dubious provenance — and God knows, those are plentiful in Burma! When honest Polish negotiators worried about the origins of funds intended to finance the Myanmar army's purchase of 24 of their helicopters, the Burmese affirmed, hand on heart: "This money comes from the contract signed with Total; it is in no way related to the drug trade". This litany was repeated with each of the four successive payments of $15 million, opening the door to rumors and attacks against the French partner.

Also compromising was the inauspicious overlap between the gas pipeline works and those of the future Ye-Tavoy railway line. Under

the guidance of a Breton, Hervé Madéo, Total then started the construction of the land portion of the pipeline that would have to cross
Burma over 40 miles of rough terrain. The French firm treated its
workmen correctly, paying them 200 kyats (wages significantly higher
than the Burmese average). In addition, Total developed several agricultural micro-projects for the benefit of the villagers of the zones that
were being crossed. Alas, at that very moment, 50,000 workers, under
military guard, were mobilized by force by the SLORC's men; they
were set to construct the railroad; whole villages were moved, families
dispersed.

To mitigate the state of underdevelopment that they had maintained since 1962, the Burmese generals, really Asian slave traders, used
the knout. As a side effect, their brutality was used to hint at a possible
amalgam between the two building sites in progress. The gas pipeline
and the railway line were to cross in the area of Endayaza — a strategic
point that those who opposed the Yadana plan, ecologists and Third-
Worlders, and oil and gas competitors, would delight in capturing.

And they would not be deprived of the opportunity. The factual
elements relating to Total's construction site were skillfully juxtaposed
with those of the railway, thus confusing the image. TV images accompanied by tendentious commentaries caused a commotion. As we have
already mentioned, these images associated one with the other added
up to a horror movie on TV screens the world over. These anti-Total
audio-visual attacks were psychological missiles that played on the
British imagination of POWs reduced to slavery by the Mikado's troops
for the construction of the Bangkok-Rangoon line. And so, an oil company that had more regard for the dignity of its workers than is usual in
"the majors" found itself tarred with the brush of infamy.

The Ambush

That portion of jungle that was carved up with great effort by the
bulldozers working to build Total's gas pipeline (far to the south of the

Karen guerrillas in their armed struggle against the power of Rangoon)
is not the most dangerous part of the country. Only a handful of irregu-
lars and a few weapons caches were turned up in the rare villages of
sympathizers. The Burmese army hastened to empty these villages of
inhabitants, and the army rank and file threw themselves into plundering under the pretext of cleansing the area in the interests of the industrial security of the French company.

The Burmese maintained five battalions in the zone, small units of
300 men, i.e. five companies of 60 soldiers. Poorly paid, poorly housed,
these troops "lived off" the countryside. The pillaging, plundering,
rape, and damage were such that the local executives of Total, outraged, considered (for a moment) whether to provide for their wages
and their requirements in exchange for guarantees of safety for the civilian populations in the sector in question. The proposal was rejected:
the company management back in Paris feared still more virulent attacks, on the theme of how "*Total a*rms and entertains SLORC troops".

Excessive prudence? Vis-à-vis the pro-Castro Colombian guerrillas who were sabotaging installations and pipelines and kidnapping
personnel for ransom, British Petroleum and Western Petroleum were
at that very moment taking steps toward direct intervention. That way
was strewn with obstacles: in October 1996, British Petroleum was
cited in a European Parliament report (leaked to the press by the La-
bour deputy from South Essex, Richard Howitt). Probably in the hope
of finally making some headway, BP apparently decided to partly finance elite Colombian units including the 16th Brigade, renowned for
its bloody exactions and its intelligence organization, B-2, with their
very thorough techniques of "interrogation". For its part, Occidental
Petroleum was accused of having raised a private army of 4,000 men.

For anyone who is properly on guard, nothing is more difficult
than dealing with the Burmese army. Total had to indicate to the military the precise geographical location of the sites where its men were
working. The Burmese also required that any helicopter flight plan be
registered 48 hours in advance. A good 25% of these plans were refused
without explanation, the men from SLORC preferring to keep any po-

tentially awkward witnesses away from the theater of their dubious exploits.

This constraint by the military authorities — savage guardians of "national sovereignty" — had nightmarish consequences for the French oil and gas company. It gave rise to the legend of "*Total* helicopters transporting Burmese intelligence officers". This was an unexpected example of "complementarity" between SLORC officers (experts in manipulation) and those who profess to fight them, and the rumor was bandied about by a number of NGO's.

Locally, the Karen guerrillas were carrying on the most rudimentary combat. Little groups of five to eight partisans would creep into the zone in the wee hours of the night. They would fire two or three mortar shells, launch a few volleys, then withdraw. In March 1995, a Karen commando set up an ambush near the gas pipeline building site. The rebels placed two mines at the place where Total's vehicles would pass. From the first blast, the subcontractor's personnel (Burmese civilians and Thai engineers who, due to a serious lack of vigilance, were riding in the same pick-up trucks with the SLORC soldiers) jumped to the ground, and scattered — as did the Frenchmen from Total and the representatives of the private firm responsible for security at the building site.

Five men died and eleven were wounded. The rumors immediately took wing, and would be amplified by the Democratic Front (an armed Burmese student opposition movement, with ties to the Karens): three French technicians were victims. The information snowballed and quickly became a sledgehammer argument for the NGO's that were hostile to the Yadana project. According to other versions, the dead men were of either Algerian, or ex-Yugoslavian origin — two countries that had become associated, as if by chance, with the eruption of irrational and unforeseeable violence.

According to my information, none of that is true. But, treating the entire episode with haughty distance, Total's public relations service scored some points against its own camp. At the end of 1996, its leader promised to provide me soon with the identity of the ambush victims. In spite of reiterated requests, I am still waiting for those bits of data.

It should be said in passing that Total's reaction to the 1995 ambush illustrates a familiar defect in French companies. They are skillful when it comes to weaving confidential ties with the press (in some cases, pure and simple complicity), but they are out of their element when a crisis erupts. At that time, I was working (as a journalist) on the Asian economy, and I remember dialing the oil firm's number from memory. Before I could ask my first question, Total's press attaché exclaimed: "There are no Frenchmen among the victims!"

That's an ambiguous remark, at the very least, coming from the mouth of a "PR" specialist. An insincere interlocutor would have been quick to deduce from it that Total, scorning its indigenous employees, was expressing interest only in its French personnel.

In any case, the rumor that Western technicians had been killed accelerated the pace of the anti-Yadana operations. Two months later, the *Bangkok Post* published a series of articles against the Yadana project. While the Karen guerrillas were marking time, the anti-Total attacks entered a more active phase. Why?

Confronting the Anglo-Americans

The testimonies agree: in Rangoon, the French company's plans did not meet with any open hostility from the officials at the British and U.S. embassies. Nonetheless, the reaction of polite indifference did not extend to the American, British and Australian private sector. In these circles, it was seen as open aggression when the French emerged in a market already become impracticable due to the archaic dictatorship. While Total had ended up allowing the American oil company Unocal to take a share in the capitalization of the Yadana project in February 1993, the French were still French. Never mind that the Anglo-Dutch giant, Shell, had not been able to take advantage of the prerogative offered to Unocal.

It is hard to gauge the attitude of the U.S. special services, whose numbers were reinforced in 1995-96 with the stated goal of countering the risk of increased Chinese penetration due to the excellent relations between Beijing and SLORC; they might have been busy on other matters (that is, after all, their vocation). . . In any event, the arrival at the embassy of two representatives of the Drug Enforcement Administration, the federal anti-drug organization, attested to the clearly stated intention of the United States to increase its presence on the ground.

Other "aggravating" circumstances played against Total. When the company changed hands on May 30, 1995, Serge Tchuruk handed over the reins to Thierry Desmarest, and the group took a tougher stance. They sought to invest still more systematically in the Far East: Indonesia, Thailand, Singapore, Malaysia, Hong Kong, the PRC, Taiwan, Vietnam, Japan, South Korea and Myanmar. And of course, simultaneously to explore certain geographical areas that were outside the American influence, Iran in particular. In May 1995, Washington issued an economic embargo on the Islamic Republic, so that the Americans were outraged in mid-July of the same year when Total casually announced that it had signed a contract for $500 million with the National Iran Oil Company (NIOC) for the development of the Sirri oil fields, near the very strategic Straits of Hormuz.

"We hope that the French government will change its opinion on its support for this particular market", declared Nicholas Burnes, State Department spokesman, shortly after. This historical agreement touched off a very long controversy between Paris and Washington, a generalized protest that intentionally mixed the political and the economic. Mr. Burnes knew his dossier inside and out; he was very well aware that since September 1993, the French State's share in the capitalization of Total had gone from 8% to 5%, and that this was a multinational corporation. Its foreign shareholding amounted to 40.4% (including 19.6% English capital and 14.5% American capital). Total

Legally, it was a multinational corporation, but historically speaking it was French (Total inherited the French petroleum company, a para-State entity created after the Great War), and it was French in terms of its management, and French again in its strategic orientation — which, as we have just seen, set them at odds with the Americans, weakening the group when the environment was already hostile.

So much for our friends across the Atlantic. For their part, the Englishmen took a dim view of these "Frenchies" stirring things up in one of their ex-colonies. And finally, it would be a mistake to overlook the special role of the Australians, in this part of Asia. Suffice it to say that Total disturbed many people, the Anglo-Saxons in particular.

Convergent Attacks

In this heavy atmosphere, the French petroleum company was the target of several actions, harsh and of course anonymous. First of all, a half-dozen former soldiers from the French army appeared alongside the Karens, after the March 1995 ambush. Former legionnnaires, commandos returned from ex-Yugoslavia, these mercenaries claimed they were in contact with the American secret services. Just the boasting of soldiers of fortune? Maybe. But one detail is intriguing: they had enormous financial resources. What mysterious hand could have filled their pockets so generously? And with what purpose? Was somebody trying to aggravate the war of nerves by waving the specter of new rebel actions over Total's construction zone?

Texaco, the American owners of another offshore oil and gas deposit at Yetagun, was very far behind in its schedule. To the point that Texaco was planning to connect an additional gas pipeline to Total's. Was that the reason for the intense curiosity about the French building site that Eric Dénécé — a former defense analyst at SGDN, now employed by Total — thought he discerned? A meeting between the two firms' representatives took place in November 1995 in Rangoon. Dick Fritz, head of the American delegation, presented himself as what he was: an old truck driver in the oil business. In Angola (a regime claiming to be Marxist) several Anglo-American companies — initially Ranger Oil, then Gulf Oil and Chevron, hired former commandos from among the elite white South Africans, who had become mercenaries, to protect their wells. A specialist in the security of such installations, Fritz seems to have played an unanticipated role in this reconversion.

Dénécé was astonished by the variety and the precision of the Americans' inquiries. If you added up all the questions they were asking (alerted by his admission of past activities), in his opinion they amounted to a research plan that resembled those of the intelligence services.

Was he right? Interviewing an executive at Total at the end of 1997, I was told that such practices are "normal" between petroleum companies. As a newcomer to the field, perhaps Dénécé tripped over his own feet. This personal aspersion would have had more weight, in my eyes, if it hadn't been followed by this disarming declaration: "Oil is an industry where the game is played straight, and no one wastes his time with foul play".

After he left Rangoon, Dénécé wrote up a technical report on Total's activity in Burma. It earned him the wrath of his former employer. The former SGDN analyst mentioned, among other "anomalies", the disappearance of some equipment that Total had placed underwater in January 1996 in the Heinze River estuary and at sea. These materials, which were part of the necessary technical studies for the underwater portion of the gas pipeline, were never found. Neither were the saboteurs.

At the same time, some strange Australian nationals were turning up at the bars in Rangoon. Under the guise of working for human rights, these commercial travelers of a particular style were trying to tap the personnel of Total and their French subcontractors for information. Other Australians, with ties to their nation's special services (according to Dénécé), were also gleaning information, both on the airlines serving Burma and in the airports.

These scattered episodes should be enough to give us pause, at the very least! They are not, on their own, enough to prove that an anti-Total action plan was in the works, beyond what is normal in the game of competition. But as the naive colonels Wood and Wingate learned, in their time, one has to learn to think beyond appearances. I should mention, for example, that while Shell and Texaco were suspected in Paris of conducting a war dance, an independent American group was in fact orchestrating the hardest underground hits against Total.

They were never seen, and never caught. This independent group — let's call it *Group E*, like the "Group W" in *Largo Winch*, Philippe Francq and Jean van Hamme's adventure comic strip — stayed in the shadows and only furtively came out on a few occasions. In 1997, for instance, after the final failure of the great disinformation campaign against Total. *Group E* discreetly probed one of the most famous French economic intelligence consultancies. Would they agree to write, for an appropriate sum, a confidential study on two of our "independent's" French competitors: Elf, and. . . Total? When the French consultant refused, the American emissaries were careful not to insist. They went off, I'm told, to commission the detailed study from a more "friendly" consulting shop.

To avoid any confusion, I should that *Group E* has nothing to do with Exxon. Were they acting on their own? No, and that is the problem. Their role was tactical, as an avant-garde detachment carrying out the fight on the ground against the French "intruder". Having made the error of teaming up with Total without considering the overall defense of American interests in the region, Unocal had to shoulder the burdens of such a partner alone, and it was in the name of this "higher economic logic" that a constellation of Anglo-Saxon actors from the industrial world, government services (secret or not) and even of the press supported Group E's general offensive. Thus, the fight against Total and Unocal's efforts to gain a foothold in Myanmar was connected to a larger plan of destabilization, carried out *sub rosa*, using the methods of psychological warfare and disinformation.

Human Rights and Natural Gas

"Total has become the most powerful support of the Burmese military system. This is not the moment to invest here", Aung San Suu Kyi (1991 Nobel Peace Prize) declared in July 1996. This statement, coming from such a figurehead, was quickly spread to the four corners of the earth as the quintessence of democratically correct thought concerning Myanmar and the SLORC.

After the South African racist edifice crumbled, the human rights militants looked on the economic boycott as their absolute weapon against dictatorships. It doesn't seem to have crossed their minds that this sudden collapse was mostly the result of the implosion of Communism in the East. The fall of the Berlin Wall removed the strategic threat of Russian penetration of South Africa, and enabled the Americans to eliminate their old Afrikaander allies, now useless, from the game. As for blockades, boycotts and embargoes, experience shows that they harm the populations of the countries in question rather than those who oppress them.

If Aung San Suu Kyi believed the opposite, it is mainly because of the military junta. Isolated for years in her own house, prohibited from travel, cut off from her very much hounded democratic Burmese friends, the young woman with the iron will is not fully cognizant of the complexity of economic realities. The drug-dictatorship of the SLORC made her sick. But whereas her compatriots' standard of living was starting to improve, modestly, the penned up Nobel Laureate thought it was falling vertiginously, driving the people into destitution.

The twenty-odd Anglo-Saxon advisers who support the resistant, and who have access to her villa, had a lot to do with the assessment that the U.S. State Department was buying the day when it did an about-face, double-crossing the SLORC; they were preparing "to guide" the future of Burmese democracy — in the direction of American interests, of course.

This strategy, known as *social learning*, is also at work in Latin America, on the ruins of the military dictatorships that the CIA used to support. And no one expressed the American realism, or cynicism, better than the Secretary of State Madeleine K. Albright herself. Answering a journalist who expressed surprise at the difference between the U.S. treatment of the Burmese and Chinese dictatorships, on April 22, 1997, this woman of character explained succinctly, "We will continue to talk about violations of human rights, whether they take place in China, Burma or Cuba. However, we must have a flexible approach in how we respond, according to our national interests, and we need to understand where our strategic relationships require a different approach on our part."

Some of the Western advisers of the Burmese opposition converted to Buddhism, but even so, not all of them acquired the extreme dignity of Aung San Suu Kyi's husband, Michael Aris. Until his death on March 27, 1999, in London, this lofty-minded English academic bore in mind that to interfere in Burmese affairs would be the worst thing for him to do. Moving in a milieu that was hostile to Total, on principle, other Anglo-Saxons who were far less diplomatic would, on the contrary, entertain with pleasure the attacks against the French firm that were made through the networks of NGO's and human rights groups. And what shall we say about those Australians who seemed not to remember how Melbourne had treated their own indigenous populations, and who in addition harbored a stubborn hostility to France because of the nuclear tests at Mururoa?

An Offensive on the Web

It was open season on the Blue, the White and the Red, those bright colors of Total's logo and the French flag. What better tool for sniping at the irritating company than the Internet? It's practical, inexpensive, and for its most experienced users it offers the attractive quality of anonymity. The Web would serve as an amplifier. This high-speed communications tool generates the widest possible echoes from information posted there.

The first media stirring, the first anti-Total "virtual petitions". . . and the subsequent emergence of a good hundred sites — many of them associated with American, British, Australian and especially Canadian universities — created a global arena in which a huge volume of news items from the Burmese front circulated, strikingly detailed and strikingly prone to citing each other *ad infinitum.*

That was the first stage. In the second, newsgroups emerged to broaden the impact. "Stealth planes" of disinformation, these electronic discussion forums where impassioned and generally sincere interlocutors exchange points of view, remarks and experiences (there are already over 20,000 such groups, covering an impressive range of interests) offer a handful of ill-intentioned protagonists the opportunity to steer the debates, under the convenient mask of anonymity. And the rumors grew:

"Total informs on the Karen guerrillas to the Burmese Army", one claimed.

"Total launders drug money", insinuated another.

"Total used forced labor in Burma", added a third.

"Total is an accessory to the SLORC."

"Total was already an accessory to apartheid."

"Total ignores human rights."

"Total thinks only of money."

"Total is supported by the French government. . ."

Total, always Total. Since 1995-96, the French group was transformed into a symbol of industrial cynicism, nailed permanently to the virtual pillory of the Web. The operation reached its apogee in November-December 1996, gradually lessening as the pipeline construction progressed.

It was during this same 1995-96 that the attacks conducted on the Web would lead to a series of negative articles in the international press. The campaign had reached the level of the "serious media", which is an essential goal since any effort to discredit someone must end up in writing, which has longer-lasting influence than the modern but transitory electronic media.

The New Along with the Old

What was being played via the Internet in this fight against Total is nothing but the very old method of "billiard balls"; the Soviets excelled in it, in their day. A newspaper of uncertain significance in some unspecified Asian or African country publishes a false document that "reveals" such and such scandalous Western plan. Photocopies of the article are immediately circulated to newspaper offices the world over, until one or more of the bigger Western newspapers picks it up. Articles published this way are frequently quoted by the media in the Eastern bloc which, logically enough, ascribes the planted information to authoritative Western sources. The Western communist or progressive press then picks it up again. The TV and radio stations recycle the information and amplify it, so that each echo reverberates back and forth, self-confirming.

Let us cite a few examples of these "manipulations" that have been credited to the special services of the Eastern bloc: we have the "American bacteriological war" in Korea; the fake letter from oil tycoon Nelson Rockefeller to President Eisenhower, outlining a plan for world domination; and the alleged anti-Semitic attacks made by neo-Nazi German terrorist groups with the assistance of the Ku Klux Klan. Less known in Europe are the "letter" from the Chinese nationalist chief Chiang Kai-shek to President Eisenhower, and the counterfeit missive from Rear-Admiral Lawrence Frost, chief of American naval information, to Colonel Kawilarang, an Indonesian rebel hostile to President Sukarno.

Since 1961, 31 cases have been identified; add to that some more recent propaganda coups like the "handbook of subversion" attributed to General Westmoreland (1976); the falsified mail from Secretary of State Cyrus Vance to President Carter, full of insulting comments about King Khaled of Saudi Arabia and the Egyptian leader Anwar Sadat (1977); the fake letter from President Reagan offering to help the King of Spain, Juan Carlos, in "reducing the opposition" (1981); and the counterfeit confidential message from General Haig to the Secretary General of NATO suggesting "measures to shake those reticent people of Europe who are to opposed the deployment of nuclear missiles" (1982).

On October 30, 1985, *Literaturnaya Gazeta* quoted an article published by an Indian newspaper, *The Patriot*. According to the article, the AIDS virus had been spread throughout the world from the Fort Detrick laboratory, in Maryland, where the U.S. Army was conducting genetic and bacteriological research. One year later, in September 1986, a report was distributed to the deputies to the 8th Summit of the non-aligned countries at Harare, "proving" that AIDS is indeed the product of American preparations for bacteriological war. The document was signed by two researchers, anonymous, of course, "from the Pasteur Institute, Paris".

At this juncture, a German biophysicist of Russian origin, Jacob Segal, began to "demonstrate" that the AIDS virus is in fact a synthesis of two natural viruses, Visna and HTL V-1, created at Fort Detrick. On October 26, 1986, this "peaceful retiree" was interviewed by the *Sunday Express* of London. But the following year, an investigator from the *Times of India* finally took the trouble of going right to "the primary source". Only to find out that the article from *The Patriot* that started all this . . . never existed! With *perestroika* in full swing, the Russian services then let their Western homologues understand that their disinformation operations had been terminated; a semi-admission that did not keep the rumor from continuing on its irrational trajectory. In 1990, Segal would be interviewed again by a West German television producer for Channel 4 in England and *Deutsche Rundfunk* in Cologne, against a backdrop of images of the famous Fort Detrick.

How To React?

Total finally called upon a very new French company, Datops, to evaluate the frequency, the intensity, and the impact of the attacks against it in the virtual space of the Web.

Created at the end of 1994 in Nimes by Louis Gay, a former Naval Aviation pilot who hardly wanted to play the bureaucrat, this small high-tech company of a dozen people possessed powerful analytical capability founded on an original mathematical model. Its lead product, Pericles, was comprised of several modules designed to conduct and process individualized data searches. This program combed the Web with a number of key words, searching for every electronic posting that made accusations against Total. Collected and collated, these data were then "charted" on graphs that were plotted over time. Datops thus obtained a virtual "film" of the anti-Yadana attacks.

After the State Department's strategic reversal, choosing to isolate the SLORC after having supported it, these attacks began to give way to praise for Apple, Pepsi-Cola, Levi-Strauss, Hewlett-Packard, Texaco, Heineken and Carlsberg, "democratic companies" that withdrew from Burma under pressure from their shareholders or consumers' associations, unlike the "dreadful" French companies, Total and Accor, the hotel group.

So. In September 1997, Texaco, whose project was less advanced than Total's, gave up. Its place was taken by a consortium formed by the English company Premier (who, through bizarre good fortune, escaped the lightning bolts on the Web) and the Malayan company Petronas. None of the other companies that had been congratulated for withdrawing had invested heavy equipment in Burma. They were more mobile, and all of them were able to return once the junta was gone. That was not really an option in the case of Total and its American partner, Unocal. There is no "middle ground" for gas companies: either they remain in a country, or they leave it. Especially since, unlike oil, gas cannot be stored.

The objective was to make Total leave. Having no real choice, the Frenchmen held on: the Yadana construction project was finished on July 1, 1998. For the infrastructure to function normally, they would have to wait until Thailand, delayed by the Asian financial crisis of which they were the first victims, could bring their power station into service. And ultimately Total, denounced as a slave trader, would have paid a far higher price than it ever imagined.

Could it have been otherwise? The way to profits is neither a rose

garden, nor a long, quiet river. Every time they try to establish themselves outside of the zones traditionally reserved for their country,
whether in African domains or, if need be, in Indochina, the French are
taking a risk. A strange phenomenon that one might call: the hidden
face of globalization.

CHAPTER 2

FROGS, GO HOME!

This time, the officials from the Food and Drug Administration (the organization that looks after the health of both the American citizens and their pharmaceutical industry) didn't bother with gloves. A few minutes is all it took them to kill [the French pharmaceuticals laboratory] Servier's leading product, an "appetite suppressant" named Redux.

In administrative terms, the verdict sounds less severe: "Authorization is immediately rescinded for the marketing in North America of the formula *dexfenfluramine*, a weight-loss drug of the category of growth regulators sold in France under the name of Isoméride and in the USA under the name Redux."[1]

But nobody in the profession is easily fooled. The FDA's decision cut Redux out of the U.S. market, the largest drug market in the world,

1. This drug is basically a formula known to professionals in the health fields under its "international non-proprietary denomination" or generic name. The laboratories distribute this formula not under that universal technical name but under various commercial names according to each country. For convenience of reading, in the three following chapters, the names of the formulas will be printed in italics and the commercial names of the corresponding drugs in normal characters

41

forever. In fact, it was its death sentence.

That was pretty clear. By contrast, at the same time, the Feds were showing remarkable indulgence towards *phentermine*, which made tongues wag. This second growth regulator was popular with obese Americans, and was usually prescribed by U.S. practitioners in association with Redux! Why one and not the other, specialists asked.

They found it hard to follow the FDA'S logic. That the federal administration would prohibit Redux is understandable, since the drug carries risks of primitive pulmonary arterial hypertension, a rare but fatal syndrome characterized by a thickening of the walls of the pulmonary arterioles and small arteries. But what about *phentermine*, a formula that has not been marketed in France for ten years but that can be found in every corner pharmacy in the United States and the United Kingdom? What about the very principle of the various "cocktails" of growth regulators of the "phen-fen" (*phentermine-fenfluramine*) type, which are regarded as dangerous in a number of European countries, including France, and which American researchers are challenging even now?

These are two insidious questions that beg a third one: is pharmaceutical truth relative, depending on which side of the Atlantic you call home?

So it would seem.

Servier and Co.

Let's head for Europe. The Seine meanders back from its mouth up to the Paris vicinity. At Servier's headquarters, the FDA decision hit like a hurricane. The winds of defeat howled through the building in Neuilly. On every floor, people were upset; faces were grim. The end of the great hopes came on Friday, September 12, 1997; and with that, a concomitant threat to the profit figures for this "middle weight" of the French pharmacy industry ($150 million in sales for Redux/Isoméride the previous year, nearly 20% of the laboratory's total turnover) and a serious risk to the survival of the group that Jacques Servier, its founder, had led for over 40 years.

Born in 1922 in Vatan, a small city in Berry, Servier seems to be emblematic of the small world of French pharmacy. His father was an industrialist and his mother, a doctor. From these family origins, he derived an interest in health care, a taste for business, and a feel for the lay of the land.

This fortunate businessman had generated a trail of outstanding statistics. His laboratory was created in 1954 and employed just nine people; today it counts more than 3,000. Servier had had exceptionally good years since 1980. The leading pharmacist in the world, in terms of growth rate (+33.4%), ahead even of the English Glaxo, in 1980 it held 55th place in the world in terms of turnover and had a research budget of $67 million. It was Number 5 in industrial pharmacy in France, neck and neck with the local subsidiaries of the two American giants, Bristol-Myers Squibb (Number 4) and Merck (Number 6). By 1997, Servier held something like 4.5% of the fragmented market in France. At the global level, it was in 27th place for sales of prescription drugs.

Jacques Servier had not spared any effort and even less his grey matter to achieve this result. The pharmacist was also a captain of industry with very broad professional connections. Servier knew the strategies of influence, which, at crucial moments, enabled his group to rely on networks of well-placed friends — friends who were tucked away here and there, in the Ministry for Social Affairs as well as within the Confederation of French Medical Trade Unions (CSMF), an organization that is rather right-leaning, politically.

All these allies — or vassals — would be essential at the hour when a competing union of general practitioners associated with the Socialist Party — MG France — began firing off one poisoned arrow after another against the Neuilly-based group in 1984, with the support of the president of the French national health insurance network, Jean-Pierre Davant.

Isoméride was not reimbursable through the social security system, so Davant and MG France focused their campaign on Servier's "veinotonics". These medications were used to combat heaviness of the leg, pains and poor circulation in the lower limbs; doctors frequently prescribed these tablets of micronized, purified flavonods over long periods. That was good business for the manufacturer but not for Social Security. The veinotonics were reimbursed at 35%, making them far too expensive to the community, according to their detractors — from $1.50 to $3.00 for a box of 30, depending on the strength of the medicine. Conversely, they were very profitable to the laboratories: 7.3% of annual growth in turnover for a market that was 150 times greater in France than in Great Britain! MG France and the French insurance system were thus anxious to have them re-categorized as non-reimbursable "comfort drugs". Or at least, they insistently pleaded, to have the prescriptions limited to a period of fifteen days.

Laboratory Lobby

Servier kept his cool. Of course, he took some precautions. This master lobbyist knew as well as anybody how to watch his back. Why else would he have created the "Hippocrates Club", which held debates and get-togethers to improve the already excellent relations between the laboratory and political figures of every affiliation, elected officials that scandalmongers disparage as "Servier's servants".

According to the monthly magazine *Capital*, the laboratory owner succeeded with a master stroke in spring, 1995.

It was a lunch among friends, in the company of Jacques Barrot. The deputy from La Haute-Loire and General Secretary of the Center of Social Democrats was quite disturbed. He needed a capable person to take on the delicate job of communication, within his office. Why not the group's Director of Communications? OK. Let it be so. Fifteen days later, Barrot was named Minister for Social Affairs. Servier's former employee went with him to the Ministry. She did not leave office until after the Right was defeated in the Legislature in 1997 — whereupon she immediately returned to headquarters, in Neuilly.

Is Servier just an astute lobbyist? No. For, besides his sometimes debatable methods of promoting his own interests, the industrialist also has a flair for risk-taking and the art of the offensive, two qualities that distinguish him from most of his French counterparts. And so he chose the field of obesity to make his attack on the American market.

A Market that Promises "Big" Returns

30% of the U.S. population is obese; that means some 60 million potential patients. This number has gone up more than 40% since the early 1960's. One out of five adult males and one out of four women have a problem. And the situation is getting worse among children, with a 60% increase over the last twenty years; and it is even worse among African Americans.

Troubling? At the very least. But this is not just an American problem. 10% of French youngsters are too big, and 3% by serious proportions. During the last ten years, so-called "moderate obesity" increased by 17% in these children and "severe obesity" by 28%. Significant regional disparities exist: northern France has 30 to 40% more obese people than the national average.

The picture is even grimmer among our European neighbors: 6% in Spain, a country of slender people, 11% in Belgium, 16% in Italy and 21% in Germany. In Great Britain, the obesity rate went from 8% to 15% in ten years. In the 35-64 age group, 15% of men and 20% of women are obese, in the Old Continent as a whole.

But you can always find someone who is even worse off than you are, and this phenomenon is not limited to Western countries alone. The wealthier parts of Asia are affected (+53% for the same ten-year period in Japan, +75% in Singapore), as well as South America (approximately 10% of Brazilians of all ages, 6% for women and 13% for men) and the Arab countries (38% of married women and 15.8% of married men).

As telling as these figures may be, they do not, in themselves, give the full picture. Obesity can only be partly explained by genetic or, possibly, viral factors. Obesity is what is called a multi-factorial disease. To measure how grave a given individual's case is, you have to calculate the Body Mass Index, or BMI. This is a simple calculation: divide the weight, expressed (in France) in kilograms, by the square of the person's height, expressed in meters.

If the ratio W/H^2 ranges between 25 and 29.9 (for example, a weight of 75 kg for a height of 1.64 m), the World Health Organization calls it overweight. Between 30 and 34.9 (a weight of 90 kg for the same height), it is moderate obesity. Between 35 and 39.9 (up to 95, even 100 kg), it becomes severe, and beyond that, very severe. Other standards set the beginning of obesity at a BMI of 28.8 for men and 27.3 for women.

The pharmaceutical groups live off diseases for which they can offer treatments. As industrial companies, the laboratories have no choice but to take an interest in obesity, which is an enormously promising market at the dawn of the 21st century. There are hundreds of millions of potential customers, whom the galloping internationalization of the American way of life — unstructured meals, TV dinners, the refrigerator, fast-foods, doughnuts, milk shakes, hamburgers, pop-corn, cornflakes, ice cream, marshmallows, soft drinks, Coke, soda, chewing-gum, bubble-gum, gummi bears, an exaggerated tendency to consider everything a medical problem or, even more so, excessive reliance on psychiatrists — tends to increase on the five continents.

A proper amount of exercise is essential to "burn" surplus sugars, and especially fats. But that's just it: most of those who emulate the "American lifestyle" only participate in sports by proxy, via the small screen. Specialists call the reduction of physical activity and the contemporaneous changes in eating habits a "stage of malnutrition in transition". The same year as the Redux incident, in 1997, a report from the Surgeon General (the supreme medical authority in the United States) estimated that 60% of Americans were "sedentary", and as many as 25% of them rejected any physical activity at all.

Is this a matter of concern for the Americans alone? Not really, because in exporting their lifestyle they also export the pathologies that derive from it. The first victims are the world's teenagers. Since they have emerged as consumers with increasing purchasing power, teenagers all over the world have become the target of all kinds of solicitations; they are the U.S. industrialists' preferred "marks". Through movies and even more so through TV series, teenagers are swallowing not only a way of life and standard of behavior but also a food culture, with all the diseases that it entails.

Millions of drug consumers multiplying from one generation to another in a kind of perpetual motion — that is a huge harvest of dividends to be cashed in. *Dexfenfluramine, fenfluramine, amfepramone, clorenzorex, phenmétrazine, fenproporex*: in their eagerness to pocket their share of the gold, the pharmaceutical laboratories invest amazing sums in perfecting whole arrays of formulas intended to combat or, at least, to reduce weight gain. While no one has succeeded in inventing a drug that really makes patients lose weight, everyone is trying. In industrial pharmacy (as in the other branches of the world economy), life depends on the hope of profits.

For this reason, the phenomenon of obesity has been transformed into a House of Miracles, alive with rumors, attacks, booby traps — a world of false news and genuine backstabbing. And that is why Redux suffered this terrible reversal on the American market.

Good Health and Prosperity

Across the Atlantic, Wyeth-Ayerst, a subsidiary of American Products Home that had contracted to market Redux in the United States, was able to point a finger at the party that was responsible for all this propaganda. Servier's American associates had conducted an investigation. Information collected in professional circles and at the very center of "Obese" associations implicated an American rival — but without absolute proof. This already very well-established laboratory had a reputation for lacking delicacy in its court cases and for waging virulent attacks in the hyper-competitive world of the pharmaceutical industry.

In the United States, conflicts between corporate groups sometimes exceed the bounds of the acceptable — and very often, those of simple legality. In their production of *Fugitive*, the scenario writers Jeb Stuart and David Twohy, and producer Andrew Davis, drew on this sordid reality.

It's a great moment in educational cinema. Debuting in movie theaters in September 1993, the film opened with the murder of Helen (Sela Ward), wife of Dr. Richard Kimble (Harrison Ford), by an unidentified killer, in fact Frederic Sykes, Security Chief for a powerful pharmaceuticals group, Devlin-MacGregor. But it is Kimble who is suspected by the Chicago police force. Sentenced to death, the surgeon manages to escape. He slips through the Federal Marshall's net.

Defying the Marshall's vigilance and the eagerness of the Chicago police, the fugitive manages to identify who was behind his wife's murder: his colleague and "best friend" Charles Nichols and the Devlin-MacGregror laboratories. Secretly working together to promote a "miracle drug" for the heart, RDU 90 Provasic, the accomplices falsified the clinical trials by substituting healthy livers for the livers of the patients treated by their product.

A seemingly insignificant dialogue informs the viewers of the annual sales figures for Provasic: $7.5 billion! As the only man who could prove the imposture, Kimble was an obstacle. Sykes agreed to have him killed. It was only by chance that Helen had gotten in the way of the killer from Devlin- MacGregor. Disturbing the polite murmurings of a medical conference held in one of Chicago's major hotels, Kimble would arrive, in the final scenes, to confront Nichols and to prove his innocence. Good-bye, Provasic . . .

The Rule of the "Prophylactic Wasteland"

Competition between rival American groups does not stop them from banding together to present a "united front" whenever their common interests seem threatened by a foreigner. The defeat of Servier/Wyeth-Ayerst must be seen as an application of the warlike doctrines adopted by nearly every American drug manufacturer. These doctrines are summarized in a few rules that are unspoken, and unwritten, but are very much in everyone's mind. For convenience, we will only look at the principle of the "prophylactic wasteland". It can be formulated as follows: since nobody has discovered an effective drug against obesity (growth regulators attack it only tangentially), "the national interest" requires that the American market be protected from any attempt at foreign incursion, even the slightest — including the Servier/Wyeth-Ayerst alliance.

Everything is strategic. By killing in the nest any attempts by European mavericks to penetrate the market, an essential opportunity is preserved — the great American pharmaceutical groups' chances in one of the most promising markets of the new century. Tomorrow, Abbott, Bristol-Myers Squibb, Eli Lilly, Johnson & Johnson, Merck and Co., Pfizer, Pharmacia & Upjohn, Schering Plough and Warner-Lambert will launch savage commercial battles, exclusively among compatriots. And all will remain for the best, in the best of all possible competitive worlds, in the shade of the star-spangled banner.

Occasional exceptions in favor of the Brits are allowed, on the basis of a few tactical and cultural considerations having to do with a tradition of "partnership" that is still in force. Such favors should not be expected for the other Europeans. Germans, Swiss, Swedes, Spanish or French, keep out. And the same for the Japanese. We should also note that the principle of the "organized wasteland" is backed up with a very high degree of vigilance. Since 1995, the American industrialists have been watching Servier's successful maneuvers of seduction with great apprehension. The powerful "Obese" associations and the politicians who support them have not failed to take note.

"There was nothing more we could do, *they* maneuvered too well", concluded the Wyeth-Ayerst people, a bit demoralized.

After that conversation, the Servier executive committee went into a huddle in Neuilly. Their agenda: the feverish search for an antidote. Contrary to their American counterparts, who are more businessmen than practitioners, the heads of French pharmaceutical laboratories must have medical degrees. Alas, as the good Masters of the Faculty of Medicine told them during grad school days, there is no miracle cure.

There remains the placebo of modern communication, and the effect of advertising: one can always try sacrificing the dead branch in hopes of saving the tree. They let the whole world know that, "as an extreme precautionary measure", Servier withdrew its formula from the 80 countries where it had been marketed. When the airship is rocked by storm, one should not hesitate to jettison the ballast: for good measure, they simultaneously proceeded to withdraw another of their appetite suppressants, Ponderal.

By Monday, September 15, the vultures were already at work. Modern vultures, they operate via the Web. Several American Internet sites on medical problems posted message after message and, as chance would have it, they all said pretty much the same thing. To the obese patients who had been taking Redux with *phentermine*, they announced this exciting news: "Fear not, those of you who suffer from excessive weight; other drug combinations s are just as effective." And they immediately cited two leading products from an American competitor to Servier/Wyeth-Ayerst. Responding to "general demand", this American laboratory made it a priority to increase the marketable quantities under its own label as soon as possible.

The Redux Story

The history of a drug is first of all a history of calculated risks.

The history of Redux began about fifteen years ago. French scientists at the Ardix laboratories (a unit of the Servier group), discovered and then tested a new formula, *dexfenfluramine*.

According to the Vidal dictionary, the doctors' bible created in 1914 and considered an authority regarding drugs ever since, the formula of *dexfenfluramine* "acts on weight regulation by decreasing the level of adjustment of the ponderostat", the central physiological system that determines and maintains a stable weight in a given individual. It thus has "a specific action on food behaviors liable to induce obesity" (note, carefully, that this definition was then modified by the addition of a warning to practitioners that "observations of severe, often mortal, arterial hypertension, have been reported among patients who were treated with growth regulators").

It was approved for sale in France in 1985 and was marketed as "Isoméride". It is not insurance-reimbursable; a box of 60 capsules sells for a suggested retail price of approximately $30. And it sells in large quantities: several million boxes per year — nearly 5 million at its height.

Success on this scale is not achieved without an intense mobilization. To attain their ends, the Servier people conducted an insistent campaign to charm the "opinion leaders", including medical and university people, celebrities and specialized journalists. And, naturally, doctors.

"Pharmaceutical marketing"? Without going that far, we can take another look at the practice that begins upstream from marketing, in the very choice of the drug to be manufactured. It is not as widespread in France as in the U.S., where marketing is especially active when it comes to OTC (Over the Counter) products.

In France, when a product that is so delicate to handle as a growth regulator is to be launched, older methods are used, tried and true. The aim is to create and then to lodge in everyone's mind a conditioned reflex associating the name of the drug and the benefits that are ascribed to it. The name is selected with the greatest care, by the advertising and marketing departments. That was the case for Isoméride in France and Redux in the United States — these terms sound better than the international non-proprietary name of *dexfenfluramine.*

Medical information remains the most effective means of "launching" a product. A whole panoply of options is available. Newspaper and magazine articles can be initiated, either out of goodwill or for more subtle reasons — especially in the medical press, which is so dependent on advertising insertions from the laboratories. Conferences and congresses financed by the same businesses then serve to amplify the message, as their in-house organs will do, after their own fashion — professional journals that are openly financed by the manufacturers and that convey accurate but biased information.

The second phase of the operation is public relations. This can range from direct contacts to offering training to practitioners. Enough often, you might even hear about "formatting". In the public hospitals, often strapped for resources, the laboratories help out the targeted divisions by donating computer equipment, for example. And let's not forget, finally, the 17,000 medical sales representatives who cultivate relationships in the doctors' private offices, where three quarters of French physicians practice. This activity accounts for 70% of the promotional expenditures for a new drug, a considerable sum since, in all, the pharmaceutical industry spends some $2 billion annually on product launches.

Smaller-scale efforts like supplying free samples and complimentary books, pamphlets and, let's be modern, cassettes or CD's, round out the campaign. In France, direct advertising is limited by the reimbursement system dictated by the existence of Social Security. It applies only to the famous elective drugs and is closely supervised by an ad hoc committee that practices *a priori* control. In 1996, "Social Security" rejected 117 cases out of the 1,342 presented by various manufacturers of nonprescription (and thus non-reimbursable) products: syrups, ointments, pills, vitamins.

To Charm and Persuade

Conceived with the aim of pinpoint-targeting the audience of practitioners, advertising documentation crops up in various forms: hand-outs and flyers, slide shows, pamphlets and brochures, reports from medical conventions. As soon as a new product has obtained authorization to go to market, the laboratory can send doctors all sorts of documentation by mail, even by Internet, or in person via its sales reps — on the condition, of course, of leaving an example of such documentation with the Drug Agency.

Subsequent control is left to the game of reciprocal monitoring between rival laboratories. Only in the event of a formal complaint from a competitor will the documents in question will be pulled out of the Agency's files. If no dispute comes up, the manufacturers' assertions are considered reliable. If a dispute does arise, sanctions can go as far as banning, on the basis of a simple proposal from the Drug Agency. Thus, at regular intervals, the columns of the *Official Journal* are adorned with announcements of bans, with detailed explanations concerning the reason for prohibition: inaccurate allegations, biased interpretations, etc..

There are plenty of ways for the laboratories to lead the doctors in the desired direction. Concerted persuasion campaigns can add up to a virtual siege. Day after day, the 88,000 general practitioners and the 90,000 specialists practicing in France are worked over, with a barrage of missiles hitting their brains. As potential prescribers, they are the essential links between laboratories and patients.

To reach the general public directly, persuasion may use indirect routes. Let's talk about obesity again. According to aesthetic criteria unrelated to medicine, thousands of women wrongly consider themselves overweight. From Kate Moss-the-Emaciated to Twiggy, the starved-looking model from the 1970's, how many top-models with skeletal bodies have taken off, with help from the pharmaceutical companies, and imposed a certain image of feminine beauty? Never mind the 1.2 billion Barbie dolls sold since 1959 around the world — a thread-like ideal, long in torso and setting unattainable goals for little girls and their mothers. As a result, eight out of ten French teenagers are or have been dieting, generally without any medical supervision, and 70% of them are still too round.

Maintaining one's figure at any cost, losing weight no matter what — especially if you are over that "fatal" number of 112 lbs — these are the key words in a false hygiene of life. How many anxious parents think they have to make their children lose weight — without any medical advice — when they are "too well-padded" for their taste? Apparently, it's no longer the fat lady who sings.

The Karate-Chop Growth Regulator

From Servier's point of view, Isoméride was introduced onto the French market under ideal conditions. However, not everyone was satisfied with the new formula. In March 1986, *Prescrire*, the only medical journal that was completely independent of the pharmaceutical industry, published a critical article signed by its editor, Gilles Berdelay, entitled "Growth regulators and food behavior, in connection with the Isoméride effect". Quoting excerpts from the presentation file that Servier had provided to physicians, Dr. Berdelay questioned the scientific value and the general orientation of the laboratory's brochure, saying it was not impartial and that it over-simplified the subject.

This first false note did not deter the Isoméride product launch. It made a stir in medical circles. Not entirely favorably, however. In November 1990, *Prescrire* responded again to a Servier ad and published an article casting doubt on the product: "Media Barrage: the practical conclusions of a test may be far less significant than the noise that accompanies them".

According to the journal, paid inserts in the "general press" were presenting an exaggeratedly rosy picture of the results of an "International test of long-term treatment of obesity by *dexfenfluramine*" under the direction of a celebrity of the profession, Prof. Bernard Guy-Grand, chief of the medicine and nutrition department at the General Hospital. Published the previous year in the very highly regarded British medical journal *The Lancet*, this document had every imprimatur of seriousness. The French edition of *The Lancet*, created in 1989 and distributed to a subscriber base of some 15,000 practitioners, had just republished it.

"Let each one judge for himself", *Prescrire* concluded. "In any case, there is nothing here that merits filling the front pages of newspapers that mean to present quality information and not advertising in disguise."

By condemning not the contents of the study but how it was presented, the journal was responding to the manufacturers' increasingly common practice of highlighting quality scientific works — when they support the laboratories' interests. And the journals' tendency to qualify paid ads that are based on perfectly genuine analyses as "media hype". Prof. Guy-Grand retorted, in November, blaming the journal in turn. "This looks like disinformation, and appears to be part of a media counter-hype, which certainly does not serve the patients' interests."

Disinformation?

Disinformation: the word was out of the bottle, with each side calling the other one the disinformer. A few lances were broken, a few more undercover attacks were launched, but the polemic began to fade and Isoméride achieved its rather spectacular commercial course without a hitch.

The serious troubles only began after 1991, when the vascular and pulmonary disease specialists at the Antoine-Béclère de Clamart hospital fired the first salvo — or cannonball, rather. According to them, Isoméride was liable to cause certain patients to suffer a primitive pulmonary arterial hypertension (HTAP), a grave disorder that can lead to death.

While it considered the charge to be excessive, Servier did not reject it completely. In December 1991, eager to have a clear conscience, the Neuilly laboratory didn't hesitate to take part in financing an epidemiological investigation. It was called the International Primary Pulmonary Hypertension Study and it was to be conducted under the guidance of Prof. Lucien Abenhaïm, Director of the Center of Clinical Epidemiology and Public Health Research at the McGill University in Montreal. The study was carried out in France, the United Kingdom, the Netherlands and in Belgium, and it was supplemented by a national investigation under the Center for Pharmacology Oversight in Besançon.

To be worthwhile, a study of this type requires a long time — in this case, a few years. And the results were hardly encouraging. On May 17, 1995, Didier Tabuteau, director of the French drug agency, decided to restrict the use of Isoméride as well as that of eight other growth regulators including Ponderal, the other Servier product. He prohibited prescribing these growth regulators in conjunction with each other, and decreed that any prescription of the drugs in question would have to be re-examined every three months, maximum.

The folks at Neuilly were stunned. While they affirmed that in general Dr. Abenhaïm's work was excellent, the Drug Agency had interpreted them too radically. And don't forget that the goodwill of the laboratory was indisputable, since it was Servier that contributed part of the financing for this study that was so deadly to two of its drugs. Servier was the honest gardener maliciously squirted by his own hose.

On the contrary, "the conclusions are very clear. The tests show an indisputable association between growth regulators (of whatever type) and the risk of primitive pulmonary hypertension", declared Anne Castot, head of the Pharmacology Oversight department at the Drug Agency, commenting in *Le Monde* on the position taken by her superior, Didier Tabuteau.

In fact, the International Primary Pulmonary Hypertension Study attributed 22 deaths to growth regulators. But it should be noted that these deaths seem to be due to people failing to follow the manufacturers' recommendations, so that the manufacturers were not responsible, strictly speaking.

Servier on the Defensive

They were not responsible, but they took a beating nonetheless. Suspicion settled in. On October 25, 1995, Prof. Jean-Michel Alexandre, director of Drug Evaluation at the French Drug Agency, and Jean-François Girard, Director General of the Health Ministry, cosigned a letter addressed to French doctors, explaining to their colleagues why the prescription of weight-loss treatments, including Isoméride and Pondéral, would be more strictly regulated in the future. Only hospital doctors would be authorized to prescribe them.

Another body blow came in July 1996. The Committee on Medical Products at the European Drug Agency in London came to a similar conclusion, saying that growth regulators present "a rare but serious risk". As a result, they should be prescribed less often, and the length of treatment must be carefully respected (even reduced), meaning that the European countries agreed with the French position.

· The effect on sales was, naturally, deplorable. This looked like a disaster, coming at the very moment when Servier was trying at all costs to penetrate the strategic U.S. market. To do so, the laboratory renamed Isoméride as Redux, which sounds better to the American ear. Taking into account the local market's "traditional" rejection of European medications, Servier took care to line up two solid local allies. The distributor, Servier America (the French laboratory's U.S. subsidiary), had formed an association with Interneutron Pharmaceuticals Inc., which would see to the manufacture of Redux in the United States, while Wyeth-Ayerst would handle the marketing.

Why so many precautions? Nothing could be left to chance when one of the most promising markets in all the pharmaceutical industry was at stake. In the U.S., "obese" associations looked favorably on the advent of Redux. In spite of the traditional mistrust of drugs that were invented outside of the United States (and thus, chemically incorrect), these patients' associations were as active as could be wished in demanding FDA approval of the French appetite suppressant. And their enthusiasm was backed up by that of certain politicians, who were happy to take up the cause of their overweight constituents.

Lobbying, pressure. In vain, initially — the first vote was negative. But in the land of "happy endings", this initial setback was soon followed by a victory. In May 1996, by 6 votes to 5, the FDA authorized the marketing of Redux.

Servier was in Seventh Heaven. Its appetite suppressant looked to be on the way to joining the very closed club of "blockbusters", those pharmaceutical jackpots thought to be successful in treating today's endemic evils: heart trouble, stomach pains, depression, head aches, hypertension. . . and obesity. Their therapeutic qualities and their universal applicability mean that these formulas have a worldwide audience, which means fabulous profits. Losec, the world leader in 1997, had annual sales of $5 billion, Zocor had $3.5 billion, Prozac and Renitec were approximately $2.5 billion each, followed by Azantac and Novasc at around $2.25 billion.

This victory so easily won over a market that is usually less inclined to favor the newcomer was not entirely a surprise. The harbingers of success had arrived at Neuilly-on-Seine a few months earlier, when the American press opened fire against the FDA, which they accused of excessive prudence in delaying the commercialization of the long-awaited growth regulators. Of course, Redux benefited from this powerful campaign, constantly pressed by Overeaters Anonymous and other overweight associations.

Still, the skies were cloudy. Redux's side effects were not fully understood, and famous figures such as Dr. Abenhaïm continued to condemn the drug. But there is a multitude of obese people in North America, who consider themselves vulnerable to other problems as a result of their excessive weight. The prospect of a few complications and possible fatalities was less distressing to the over-sized populace than the wave of deaths directly caused by overweight.

The Medical Press Enters The Fray

A confused episode occurred in summer, 1996. Scandal arrived in the persons of JoAnn Manson, an epidemiologist and endocrinologist, and her colleague Gerald Faich, a pharmaco-epidemiologist. These two experts wrote an article in the *New England Journal of Medicine*, eternal rival of the British *Lancet*. (The *New England Journal* was created in 1812, in Boston, and the *Lancet* in London in 1823. They have been competing fiercely ever since. Manson and Faich entitled their article, "Pharmacotherapy of Obesity — Do the Benefits Exceed the Risks?" In the Anglo-Saxon practice of using debate as a means of delivering serious and balanced information, the document was intended to counterbalance the submission from Drs Abenhaïm, Moride and Brenot, bearing the title "Appetite Suppressing Drugs and the Risk of Primitive Pulmonary Arterial Hypertension".

As you might guess, Drs Abenhaïm, Moride and Brenot's paper was not favorable to Redux in any sense. That of Drs Manson and Faich, on the other hand, was a godsend to Servier's directors.

"*Dexfenfluramine* is a new and important drug in the clinician's arsenal, albeit not without risk. Although the doctors and the patients need to be well-informed, the possible risk of primitive pulmonary arterial hypertension associated with *dexfenfluramine* is slight and seems to be outweighed by the drug's benefits, when it is used appropriately", concluded the two experts. The adjective "appropriately" seems to refer to the different ways it was used in France (where Redux was restricted by official decision to the severely obese, under a very strict control), and in the United States (where doctors, pressured by their patients who demanded fast results, usually prescribed the product together with *phentermine*). The doctors were under less control, and they prescribed these drugs with fewer precautions.

According to Manson and Faich's calculations, Redux would save some 280 human lives per million inhabitants, while presenting a risk to 14 others — a ratio of 1:20 — which, while it did not completely exonerate Servier's product, made it possible to present is as beneficial, overall. All things considered, losing one's appetite thanks to Redux was less dangerous than not doing so.

The debate between those in favor and those against the growth regulators was in full swing. In any case, it was carried out under conditions of perfect transparency. The *New England* editors had a clear conscience. Since 1984, the directors of the medical weekly had asked the four protagonists to fill out a questionnaire establishing all their possible ties with pharmaceutical laboratories, a practice that the Americans call a "declaration of conflicts of interests".

Alas, things took a bad turn. Three days before a launch scheduled for August 29, 1996, the New Englanders received an alarming phone call. One interlocutor stated that Drs Manson and Faich in fact had close ties to both Servier and its two American partners. This initial communication was followed by many others, which suggests either an amazing spontaneity in the warning, or, more likely, close communication between the participants (to put it bluntly, a premeditated campaign).

What to do? Accustomed to reciprocal denunciations between competing laboratories — which constituted the daily bread of their editorial activity, and pressured by the demands of "going to press", the journalists decided against holding things up. Why act as though there was a catastrophe? The readers were not children. The debate would have to be continued in the next issue. Ongoing discussion is the role of a high quality medical publication.

Except that, meanwhile, on September 7 the *Lancet*, pleased to have an opportunity to throw a monkey wrench into the works, published an editorial entitled, "The Policy of Full Disclosure", which lit the bonfire. JoAnn Manson, the journal said, worked "very occasionally" as a consultant at Interneutron Pharmaceuticals between mid-1995 and November of the same year, and worked intermittently for Servier. The FDA had interviewed the researcher in September-October 1995 about Redux. As for Doctor Faich, who had also been questioned by the FDA, served as an part time consultant in pharmaco-epidemiology at Servier between 1994 and 1996 and served as an advisor to the Wyeth-Ayerst laboratory.

The New England Journal of Medicine was annoyed, and had to come up with a fairly arduous clarification. In its October 3 issue, it confirmed the *Lancet*'s assertions. "What we understood only too late is that Drs Manson and Faich had both been paid consultants of companies interested in the sale of the anti-obesity agents in question."

What a way to sow the doubt about the conditions under which *dexfenfluramine* had been permitted access to the American market, and just at the very time when, in its home market in Europe, the diet aide was starting to have so many troubles.

Between a Rock and a Hard Place

On December 9, 1996, the European Commission decided to modify the market authorizations for Isoméride, Ponderal and seven other products that were under dispute in the Community. Ten days later, the Drug Agency published an official statement announcing that it was upholding its ruling to restrict the sale of growth regulators because of the risk of serious side effects.

Caught between a rock and a hard place, one in the United States, the other in Europe, Jacques Servier could not allow this decision to pass without a response. "This type of drug has existed for 34 years and was authorized last May by the very demanding U.S. administration", he declared in *Le Monde*. "There never was a controlled study to prove these allegations, only the impressions of one or another professor, and an impressive but distorted study by Prof. Lucien Abenhaïm of McGill University, Montreal, published in *the New England Journal of Medicine*."

"We are being treated like assassins without any proof", added Servier, with all the emotion of an offended industrialist and doctor. His situation was hardly enviable. There was no more question of turning this into a "blockbuster"; only a vague hope of being able to salvage something from the wreckage.

The Descent into Hell

In fact, this was the beginning of a descent into the abyss. In the United States, anguish moved to the other camp. Whereas just yesterday the associations of the obese had been demanding prescriptions for Redux as loudly as they could, sharply criticizing the FDA for its closed-mindedness, now they did an about face and demanded the product be immediately removed from the market as a health hazard. Fear reigned. "They are trying to kill us", one of them would go so far as to claim — a highly effective argument, even if it is a little bit theatrical.

Catching the blame from all sides, the FDA stood fast and refused to change its position until one association, citing two of the FDA commissioners and threatening to haul them into court, won the battle — under conditions that we have already discussed. Called in by the FDA, the representatives of Wyeth-Ayerst had to witness Redux's withdrawal from sale on September 12, 1997.

On October 14, Prof. Abenhaïm granted an interview to *Le Monde*. Reiterating his criticisms against *dexfenfluramine*, he speculated about the FDA's reliability, "often presented as an infallible American agency, above any suspicion, categorically free of interestedness". Then he denounced the trend of marketing drugs as soon as they have been formulated. "Obviously, we have to take into account the pressure of an extremely powerful industrial lobby. But — and it takes guts to say so — a lobby of patients and associations of patients also exist, sometimes subsidized by the pharmaceutical laboratories."

That poses in clear terms the problems created by the strategies of influence that are used every day in the field of industrial pharmacy, complex operations that aim alternatively or simultaneously at various potential targets, including decision-making organizations to be persuaded, doctors to be incited, patients to be reassured or worried according to the needs of the moment and, finally, competitors to be destabilized in every possible way, with false information as much as with the truth.

Cut to the quick, Servier retorted in a letter published by *Le Monde* on December 27. "We never accused Prof. Abenhaïm of having dis-torted the results of his study. We simply pointed out the importance of the biases in how the studies were interpreted, and in particular the bias of the media." New details appeared in *Le Figaro* on December 31. "Over 35 years, more than 60 million patients have been treated with *fenfluramine*, and more than 10 million with *dexfenfluramine* in the last ten years, in 85 countries, including the leading nations having the most demanding legal authorities, without any neurotoxic effect being found by the pharmaceutical watchdogs."

By mid-January 1998, the French Drug Agency gave a partial an-swer, offering recommendations for monitoring patients who were tak-ing products such as Isoméride or Ponderal. Taking care to be precise, one of its representatives mentioned to journalists at *Prescrire* that there had been a limited number of cases of "left valvar insufficiencies, gener-ally moderate". About 40 cases, it seems.

In the course of the ensuing months, this figure would grow slightly: some fifty people were affected, 30% of them women, as of October 8. On that day, Paul Nahon and Bernard Benyamin, the editors of *Envoyé spécial*, published an explicitly entitled article, "Warning: Drugs", dealing with victims of arterial hypertension, among others. A recognized expert at the Antoine-Béclère hospital, Prof. Gerald Si-moneau did not conceal his feelings in connection with the appetite suppressant: "In 90% of the cases, these drugs were taken by people who were not obese." And he added that other products displaying similar risks, amphetamines in particular, were still on the market.

There's No Miracle Cure

The market, or rather the extension of the market well beyond those patients who would actually constitute the market from a strictly medical point of view, is indeed the most serious aspect of the problem. As a tangible result of a well-conducted promotion campaign, rumors and word of mouth confirmed its reputation as a "miracle drug". These means of "communication" pushed patients to demand more and more useless prescriptions from their attending physicians. Why should the laboratories complain? Many products show a profit only in this gray zone of prescription. And the medication thus takes on a double nature: a blessing, since it helps some, and a menace, since it can make people sick or even kill them.

.   Still, steps would have to be taken to avoid messing up; nothing hurts more than a failure. In lieu of damages, American Home Products had to pay considerable sums in compensation to Redux consumers, an expense that was so burdensome that it contributed in large measure to blocking a planned merger with the British company SmithKline Beecham. To avoid a fiasco similar to Redux's, the Swiss company Roche soft-pedaled the U.S. introduction of their new anti-obesity drug, Xenical, claiming that they preferred to wait until it was proven reliable. Perhaps this prudence was justified: only at the end of April 1999 did the FDA finally authorize the marketing of Xenical, after complementary studies were concluded to investigate a possible risk of breast cancer.

In France as well, Isoméride fell from its status as a godsend for the obese to that of a plague. In its March 28, 1998 edition, *Le Parisien libéré* accused the appetite suppressant of having been "directly responsible for the deaths of about thirty people in recent years". Servier's representatives, in fact Laurent Pernet (Director of Research and Development), certified on the contrary that "Isoméride is an invaluable drug for thousands of obese people and has saved lives".

These are serious divergences of opinion that give a fair measure of the extent of the real problem. What were Isoméride's detractors saying? That taking this medicine can lead to arterial hypertension in certain patients.

This controversy is still ongoing. In May, 1999, pending a full complement of medical expertise, the County Court of Nanterre deferred its judgment on a case filed by a young woman against the Neuilly laboratory and her own attending physician.

Disappointed but not discouraged by its failure on the American market, Servier changed weapons. Noting that "medical needs are enormous; spending on medications represents only $23 per capita in Russia versus $186 in Germany", the head of Servier for Northern Europe and the East, Yves Langourieux, decided to accelerate the group's development in the formerly communist countries.

With five subsidiary companies in Poland, Hungary, Russia, Czech Republic and Slovakia, since 1993-95, Servier decided to invest $33 million in Warsaw. Anpharm, a small laboratory in the suburbs of the capital, became the first foreign laboratory, working in direct connection with the Instytut Farmaceu Tyczny. Its goal was to go from 350 million to 450 million in annual sales by the end of the century.

This was an unusual sign of dynamism within the universe of 300 French laboratories, most of which are more accustomed to demanding frivolous and ineffective neo-protectionist measures from the political leaders (70% of France's market is already in the hands of the great foreign groups) rather than fighting, investing, innovating. French firms came up with 4% of new formulas between 1990 and 1994, as opposed to 15% twenty years earlier; that's no way to earn a place in the sun. Even less by obstinately missing every train: biogenetics, beta-blockers, calcic inhibitors, gastric remedies, antiviral drugs, immuno-suppressants. As a result, the French pharmaceutical industry is always a step behind, while its competitors chalk up record profits: up 23% in 1998 for the American groups.

Chapter 3

The Great Drug War

The North American pharmaceutical industry learned a lesson from the tragic fate of the Indians who were decimated by their forebears: without an inviolable hunting ground, survival is out of the question. Anything goes in the effort to perpetuate a "priority right" to the U.S. market for their sole benefit, and European competitors have to bear the costs of this defensive pugnacity. A few examples will suffice to support these assertions.

The Centeon Episode

Rhône-Poulenc Rorer was born in 1990 when the American company, Rorer, was acquired by an old French chemistry and pharmaceutical "institution", Rhône-Poulenc SA. In the following years, this merger would result in a shock of corporate cultures that led to a process of creeping "Rorerization" of Rhône-Poulenc. Far from holding their own, the French gave way. They even gave in to American management and marketing methods, choosing American or "American-trained" personnel to head up the group's subsidiaries.

In spite of the rampant Americanization of its executive personnel and its operating methods, or perhaps even because of it, Rhône-Poulenc retained its unquestionable spirit of initiative. At the international level, its preferred ally and future associate was Hoechst Marion Roussel (HMR), a German group that had bases in France and in the U.S..

Armour Pharmaceutical Company, one of Rorer's subsidiaries, merged with BehringWerke AG, a subsidiary of Hoechst Marion Roussel to become Centeon. With an army of 4,500 employees and $1 billion in capital, the joint venture based in King of Prussia, Pennsylvania, entered the game as world leader in the manufacture and marketing of plasma proteins. It confidently laid out three simultaneous objectives: to increase its investments in research and development, to improve use of blood plasma resources, and to create significant improvements in the safety and the viral purity of plasma derivatives. This was a judicious choice in economic terms. The American blood derivatives market is the largest in the world, both in size and in promise of financial gain, and holds considerable potential. But one has to expect serious counterattacks, for no U.S. government agency or industry representative will look kindly on the arrival of a French-German subsidiary on the American scene. As the fourth largest pharmaceutical manufacturer in the world, Hoechst Marion Roussel was not welcome on that side of the Atlantic: it had just inflicted a scorching humiliation on the Americans by taking over Marion Merrell Dow, a troubled U.S. firm. And, to make matters worse, France did not have a good record in plasma derivatives since the contaminated blood scandal.

Just before the end of the year, while Centeon was optimistically looking forward to a turnover of some $1 billion, the first signs of trouble emerged in the form of several cases of septicemia among American patients who had been given two Centeon plasma albumin products, Albuminar and Plasma Plex.

While this was unpleasant for the victims, this "incident" did not upset the community since the bacterial contamination did not occur during the manufacturing process but during transportation. As a result of mishandling, several batches fell to the ground and, according to experts from Centeon, the phials must have cracked, infecting the products inside.

What to do? Fuss about and wait for everything to blow over by itself? That would be counter-productive and an inevitable gift to the competition. It's far better to act than to react. And quickly! By mid-October, Centeon announced the recall of batches of Albuminar and Plex Plasma. Its executives considered this a simple precautionary measure. This event had nothing to do with the French blood scandal much less its Southern Ireland equivalent, which was more on the mind of the U.S. public because of the large Irish-American community — they'd been seeing TV images of demonstrations of hemophiliacs who had been contaminated, and their families, organizing a siege around the Dublin residence of the Prime Minister of Eire, Charles Haughey.

Hemophiliacs, whatever their nationality, constitute one of the most significant groups of international public opinion. In the U.S., their associations are far better organized than their French counter-parts. They were among the first to communicate with each other by Internet. When they heard that Centeon had withdrawn batches of Albuminar and Plasma Plex from the market, these associations de-manded that the federal authorities increase their vigilance.

In November, an FDA team presented itself (as it has the right to do) at the blood derivatives plant in Kankakee, Illinois. A thorough inspection of the site led to its being temporarily shut down, a catastro-phe for Centeon since Kankakee was its only production facility on American soil.

The temporary manufacturing halt led to a shortage of Monoclate P, "an anti-hemophilia factor VIII". Centeon immediately proposed to provide its other factor VIII's to the American patients for free. A waste of time and effort: rising up against the Franco-German industri-alist, the patients' associations called for more stringent measures to be taken against it. The *Philadelphia Enquirer* printed demands for the out-right recall of those bottles of Monoclate P still in circulation.

Centeon had no choice but to take the hit, and to stand by while this market segment was reconquered by its competitors, mainly

American. The affair ended in a double reversal, in terms of image as well as financially — to the tune of some $50 million.

A Setback at Roussel

Hoechst Marion Roussel is just one branch of the Hoechst group, which was number one in chemistry worldwide. But HMR is one of the most profitable, with its agrochemical and animal health sectors. This group with multinational goals was formed through a series of complex acquisitions, mergers and takeovers, including that of Marion Merrell Dow, of course, and also that of Roussel-Uclaf.

The sad story began when the energetic Jean-Claude Roussel, looking to strengthen his group without losing control of it, decided to introduce Hoechst into the capital of Roussel-Uclaf. The idea is not bad, but it assumed a certain continuity in execution. Unfortunately, Roussel died in an auto accident in April 1972, before being able to see his plan through. After interminable discussions with the French government, his new German partners obtained authorization to purchase 100% of Roussel-Uclaf's capital.

Roussel-Uclaf's American woes could be used as the lead story in an anthology of French bad luck in exporting, or in a treatise on American inhospitality in the pharmaceuticals industry.

Here are the facts. In 1989, the chemistry division of Roussel-Uclaf acquired a 60% stake in the Italian laboratory Biochimica Opos. The acquisition followed on the heels of a decision by Roussel to get into the "generics" market (officially: "essentially similar specialties"). We all know that these are actually knock-offs of proprietary formulas whose patents have fallen into the public domain, where they are recreated at little cost and thus at lower prices. In Article R–5133-1, the French Public Health Code specifies that, to merit designation as a having "essentially similar properties", the new product must have "the same qualitative and quantitative composition in active ingredients, the same pharmaceutical form" and "if necessary, the bio-equivalence between these two brands [must be] proven by suitable studies". And the

Commission on Competition stated in May 1981 that generic drugs (or "copies", or "imitations") are drugs made by companies other than the inventor of the formulas, whose patents have fallen into the public domain.

These are the "governing principles" that led to Roussel-Uclaf's interest in Biochimica Opos, even before it was bought by Hoechst. Synthesizing these generics just happens to be the specialty of this Italian laboratory. Biochimica Opos manufactures cephalosporines, a class of oral or injectable antibiotics similar to penicillins and whose principal outlet is the U.S..

Biochimica was making "essentially similar specialties" of medications coming from American laboratories such as Eli Lilly (Cefazoline, Cefalotine, Cefaclor, Cefamandole), Upjohn (Clindamycin) and American Home Products (Minocycline), which gave the laboratory a dominant position on the U.S. market. Biochimica sold practically all the North American generics. That's an enviable commercial position: the American system is based on private health insurance plans, so there is savage competition over retail prices (in the U.S. these prices are not set by a Social Security program). Generic drugs, since they are less expensive than the original drugs, are highly prized.

They brought in well over $1 million in net profits in 1992, on annual sales of $70 million. In July 1993, Roussel-Uclaf decided to acquire 40% of the capital, just below the threshold that would have made them, effectively, the sole owner. Everything seemed to be turning out for the best in the best of all possible pharmaceutical worlds. Only a few legal controversies with Eli Lilly over the patent on the synthesis of Cefaclor marred the picture slightly. Manufacturing generics often poses this type of problem and the Eli Lilly Company, founded in 1876 by Colonel Eli Lilly, is known for its pugnacity.

The storm would burst in 1996 in the form of an anonymous denunciation addressed to the Food and Drug Administration. A telephone call from a well-informed source, it was claimed. In the U.S., this is common practice — various federal agencies (starting with the legendary FBI) accord great consideration to information on hostile people or companies, as long as it bears signs of being sufficiently serious.

Was that the case, this time? Apparently so. According to the anonymous caller, Biochimica Opos was manufacturing its generic drugs without heeding all of the pertinent regulations; and to provide some specific details, was apparently conducting industrial espionage operations beyond the Alps.

When the Food and Drug Administration heard this important revelation, it immediately opened a file. The details given by the "informant" were enough to enable it to launch an investigation. And since these pharmaceutical intrigues were supposedly taking place at the Milanese factory of Agrate, a stronghold of Biochimica Opos, the experts would have to make a site visit immediately.

In Italy? This long-distance practice is more widespread than you might think. Given the U.S.'s status as a superpower, the FDA has long arrogated the "right" to inspect foreign firms. This is in order to protect the interests of the consumers in the New World: no product marketed in America can escape its vigilance. In 1991, for example, a surprise inspection by FDA specialists to an English pharmaceutical factory led to the suspension of its authorization to market two drugs in America.

Naturally, the anonymous tip-off was a golden opportunity. The FDA's G-men would have no problem proving that Biochimica was not "adhering to" its list of conditions. The Italians were caught red-handed: they were using an intermediary maufacturer in China, clearly outside of any supervision. Worse yet, the Milanese firm was at best carrying out only the final stages of synthesizing the Céfaclor and Clindamycin generics in its factory.

They were guilty, and they'd have to be sanctioned. When the American medical authorities informed them of these sins, the leaders of Roussel-Uclaf and Hoechst, furious and anxious, decided to take the initiative. They suspended marketing for all the products manufactured by Biochimica Opos! And, in a step worthy of a new entry in the Book of Records: by withdrawing market all the generics containing Céfaclor, Minocycline and Clindamycin, the two Europeans kicked off the largest product recall in all of American pharmaceutical history.

For Roussel-Uclaf, the loss was hard to overcome: $15 to $25 million just in 1997. Invade the U.S. at your own risk.

Sex, Lies and Internet

Sanofi was born in 1973 out of the expressed will of Elf's founder, Pierre Guillaumat, who was eager to diversify the French public group's activities by intelligently re-investing Lacq's oil revenue. This strategic task was entrusted to Jean Fouchier and especially to Rene Sautier, Director of Development at Elf. The two men recruited a young engineer from Lacq, Jean-François Dehecq, to head up the new operation. Meanwhile, the National Petoleum Company of Aquitaine acquired a share of the capital of Labaz-France, the pharmaceutical subsidiary of a Belgian group.

The group was initially called Omnium Financier d'Aquitaine pour l'hygiene et la santé, then Sanofi, and finally Sanofi Winthrop. Growing through acquisitions and taking positions in other holding companies (35% of Institut Pastor Productions, in 1976, in particular), by 1997 it was the second largest French manufacturer — by size: with $6 billion in turnover, a 4.8% share of the national market, and annual growth of approximately 3% — and even more so by its connections. The parent company, Elf Aquitaine, had close ties with the State and with the right-leaning political parties and even, since May-June 1981, those on the left, a delicate posture and hugely embarrassing, as the Elf scandal would soon make clear.

Even leaving aside such questionable interests, Jean-François Dehecq, founder and chairman of Sanofi, had long entertained very good relations with the president of France, Jacques Chirac; it would not be an exaggeration to say that they were personal friends.

Dehecq likes to think of himself as one of the French captains of industry who is most aggressive in foreign markets. They say that he even knocked on doors at the highest levels of the State to seek direct support from the DGSE for the French pharmaceutical industry — albeit without success.

Under the leadership of Dehecq, the combatant, the new company would set out to invest in the American market. It knew what to do. In principle, it is fairly simple: you have to establish a local network of medical offices, buy a local laboratory that is already "licensed", and create a joint venture with it. But the American terrain is mined, and heavily.

So, in 1977, Sanofi created Sanofi Research Co., Inc. to study the possibility of clinical experiments in the U.S.. Five years later, the French pharmacist signed a contract with American Home Products to develop and market in the U.S.A the French parent company's medicational innovations. In 1985, a new agreement was signed between Pasteur Diagnostics, controlled by Sanofi, and Genetic Systems to actively collaborate in developing tests for monitoring AIDS.

Two years later, the planned buyout of the A. H. Robins Company failed at the last minute. It was a good thing, for the company had just been at the center of an incredible fraud and disinformation scandal that led to the death of some fifteen Americans and 14,000 legal complaints were filed: this was the Dalkon Shield birth control device scandal. If the French had bought it, the result would have been the worst possible combination.

In 1988, Sanofi bought a U.S. company that specialized in diagnostics, Kallestad. Six years later came the takeover of the prescription drug branch of Eastman Kodak. In 1996, Elf's subsidiary expanded its activities on the North American continent by acquiring Bock Pharmaceutical Company, a laboratory serving general practitioners. The same year, it launched a new drug, Photofrin, in America.

And they had plans, so many plans. Sanofi had plenty in mind; first of all, it was close to coming out in the U.S. with a homologue of two anti-hypertension medications, Aprovel and Plavix; then a partnership with the Beckman Group, a specialist in marketing automated analysis equipment, would come about as a result of a technology transfer agreement on Access, an immunological analysis apparatus developed by Elf's pharmaceutical subsidiary that should generate partnerships in the field of reagents and instrumentation.

They had great market penetration, and excellent prospects! And best of all, all these promises of continuous expansion did not seem to be kicking off the usual general outcry from the Americans. In fact, there seemed to be enthusiasm. In 1996, anonymous positive messages were circulating on the Internet (a means of communication that pharmaceutical laboratories are using more and more freely, and as are associations of pharmaceutical consumers). Anonymous parties sang the praises of several of Sanofi's products. And what were they saying about the company's neuro-degeneration (Alzheimer's and Parkinson's diseases) drugs in particular? That they were "triggers" that could multiply the consumer's sexual power tenfold!

This spectacular "information", intended to catch the attention of elderly male customers who were prone to nerve degeneration, would bring heavy consequences. One message followed another, inciting people to sexually stimulate themselves by means of drugs intended for a very different use — and, therefore, to run the worst risks in the vain hope of achieving superhuman performance.

This false "praise" of French pharmaceutical products created astonishment and concern at Sanofi. What a catastrophe it would be if an old man should drop dead for having wanted to combine medication and a loving impulse — a drama that could not fail to set off a vigorous media campaign against the French killer-drug. The group's recent establishment in the U.S. would not survive such an event.

A second note: the timing of this unexpected campaign was quite precise. Eager to concentrate on its basic business, oil, Elf was planning to sell a share in the capital of its pharmaceutical subsidiary. But who were these anonymous writers? Jokers? Con artists in lab coats, unscrupulous retailers acting with a purely mercantile aim as they are wont to do everywhere? Or destabilization professionals, looking to cause a serious incident in order to bring down Sanofi's stock value?

To have a clear conscience, the corporate staff set the cyber-detectives on the trail of the "invisible mover". The trail led to two laboratories who retailed pharmaceutical products. The first one was Swiss. The second, domiciled in Manhattan, had a very attractive website: it had everything, even photographs of the employees with their white lab coats and their gracious smiles! Placed under close surveillance, it was not long before it revealed its secrets. The webmasters were using "virtual consultations" to direct the website's visitors only toward drugs marketed by their laboratory! The French cyberdetectives noted that they were, for example, conducting a shameless propaganda campaign in favor of an American psychotropic that had such questionable secondary effects that the British authorities had withdrawn it from the market in 1992, and 15,000 of Her Majesty's subjects had taken the manufacturer to court. . . We will never know whether the New York laboratory was working on its own account or if it was merely the agent of more powerful groups.

A new demonstration of commercial-sexual aggressiveness came near the end of 1998. For three weeks, web surfers looking for information on Sanofi products, mostly pharmaceutical professionals, were systematically "rerouted" to a pornographic site! It was impossible to connect to the site without being confronted at once with vulgar images. The first time, of course, the "joke" made people laugh. But it got old very quickly. As a result, serious customers started logging onto the competitors' sites. This was a new form of "spamming", the technique of blocking Internet sites by flooding them with messages (the Serbs, for example, did some of that during the NATO air offensive in April 1999).

Given this infinite variety of maneuvers, it would be no surprise if, during their sleepless nights, the French pharmaceutical industrialists went as far as to curse the name of Christopher Columbus himself. (And they wouldn't be the only ones to do so.)

Calcium Channel Blockers: a Murky Situation

Many experts in international pharmacological circles believe that the medical controversy over the risks of "calcium channel blockers" is basically a cover for the violent conflict of interests between the American-British chemical community and the German group, Bayer SA.

Calcium channel blockers? That's a rather motley pharmacological class. These products inhibit the influx of calcium ions into cardiac muscle and smooth muscle membranes, relieving angina. This characteristic certainly confers upon them a role in the treatment of arterial hypertension and angina pectoris, two diseases that are so common that they constitute a market segment in their own right.

Our story begins when Bayer decides to market its calcium channel blocker, *nifedipine*, in North America. This formula is effective in the symptomatic treatment of a specific form of *angina pectoris* known by the delicate name of Prinzmetal's Angina, and it was to be distributed in the U.S. by a rising star among American laboratories, Pfizer, which had a calcium channel blocker formula of its own, *amlodipine*. The two partners had the imposing market of 50 million hypertensive Americans in their sights. To market *nifedipine* in the U.S., they chose the more appealing name of Procardia.

This partnership did not seem to be anything out of the ordinary — except that, following the example of the Servier/Wyeth-Ayerst alliance, the Bayer/Pfizer agreement was counter to the interests of several American pharmaceutical groups who, since the 1960s, had committed themselves to another approach to treating hypertension and coronary diseases. They were betting on a different class of drugs, the "beta-blockers" (or ß-blockers), which slow down the heartbeat and reduce blood pressure.

With their strategic interests threatened by the intrusion of Bayer and its *nifedipine*, the American beta-blocker manufacturers did not hide their concern, and neither did certain scientists, even if their concern was of a different nature. In March 1995, Drs Curt Furberg of Winston-Salem, North Carolina, and Bruce Psaty of Seattle, Washington, presented the results of a "control study" conducted by Psaty and his team, comparing the experience of 623 Medicare patients who had had myocardial infarcts with that of 2,032 patients taking anti-hypertension medication but without infarction. The study suggested an increased risk (1.6% as opposed to 1%) of cardiac incident among patients treated with "short-term action" calcium channel blockers: *nifedipine, verapamil* and *diltiazem.*

This was a hard blow. Bayer and its American partner resigned themselves to facing this misfortune with a stout heart. Unfortunately, this was not the end of their woes: fifteen days later, the debate was already resounding among the 2,500 doctors from all over the world who had come to attend the 44th scientific session of the American College of Cardiology (the AHC). While admitting the gravity of the problem that might arise from short-term action, the AHC and American Medical Association kept their distances, noting that "control studies" are a relatively inconclusive form of scientific investigation". These two prestigious associations agreed that there was a pressing need for longer-term studies before deciding the issue.

The International Society of Hypertension (ISHIB) was more radical in defending the use of inhibitors; it declared that "it would be a real catastrophe if a small case study had the effect of leading the 5.3 million Americans currently taking these inhibitors to give up their medicine". But the National Institutes of Health (NIS), on the contrary, repeated its recommendation of two years before: that doctors must give priority to beta-blockers and diuretics, drugs they considered to be more certain and in any case less expensive.

Then things began to snowball. In August, Psaty and his friends S. R. Heckbert and T. D. Koepsell published the text of their study: "The Risk of Myocardial Infraction Associated with Antihypertensive Drug Therapies" in the *Journal of the Medical American Association*, the famous *JAMA*. The same month, in the company of another specialist, J. V. Meyers, these two experts co-signed a report on a meta-analysis under the direction of Furberg, in *Circulation*: "Nifedipine. Dose-Related Increase in Mortality in Patients with Coronary Heart Diseases".

Their argument against calcium channel blockers made waves. The American Heart Association, an organization that defends the interests of heart disease patients, feared that scientific information abuot the safety of the inhibitors was being distorted. Nothing would be more prejudicial than a biased (or worse) debate: it would set off an irrational panic. The AHA therefore attempted to calm the turmoil. "Don't decide to stop your medication on your own; consult your doctor", it advised patients via the press, direct telephone contact, and postal and electronic mail.

And still the polemics went on. An American hypertension specialist sharply criticized the articles by Furberg, Psaty and their colleagues, and he was soon suspected in the *Lancet* of being linked to Bayer. The covert attacks were even more vicious. After the congress of the European Society of Cardiology, held that August in Amsterdam, an anonymous letter was circulated among French general practitioners and cardiologists. This unsigned indictment attacked the work of the American doctors who were against calcium channel blockers.

In November 1995, tempers were still rising. Dr. Sidney Wolfe, one of the leaders of Public Citizen, the consumer defense group founded by Ralph Nader, asked the federal administration to strengthen the warning statements that went with the notes of calcium channel blockers. Contrary to the National Heart, Lung and Blood Institute, a subsidiary of the NIS, Public Citizen made no distinction between those calcium channel blockers with a "short term effect" condemned by Furberg, Psaty and their peers, and the "long term relief" ones that nobody was criticizing. That made Bayer and Pfizer howl with rage: the two partners were in the process of testing long-acting, time-release *nifedipine* and *amlodipine* formulas.

A verbal confrontation between Dr. Furberg and his colleague Franz Messerli, of New Orleans (an ardent supporter of the calcic inhibitors), did not improve the environment. Their duel took place during an official session of the American College of Cardiology. Quite enraged, Messerli compared Furberg's two articles to a "bad stew". "Most patients die in their beds, but it is not their beds that kill them", he said. To which Furberg's associate immediately replied, "You can believe in God but for everything else, you have to show evidence."

Beta- vs. Calcium Channel Blockers: the Ongoing Controversy

The controversy took a new turn in March 1996, with a study by Prof. Lars Werkö, President of Satens Beredning för Medicinsk Utvärdering, the Swedish State Committee for Medical Evaluation. Even though he questioned whether the laboratories might be seeking to manipulate the cardiologists, this former research director at Astra, the Scandinavian pharmaceutical group, sided with Furberg. As an example of tendentious information, he cited the panel that was assembled for a press conference held during the famous congress of Amsterdam. According to him, Bayer influenced the selection of panelists.

In August, *The Lancet* opened its columns with a new Italian-American study that was very critical of the calcium channel blockers. This research was an extension of previously published studies, and it associated the use of the inhibitors with an increased risk of cancer. Naturally, this "paper" caused a ruckus; and certain people took pains to amplify its effects. Even before it was published, the American Department of Health started exhorting patients not to stop their medication. By way of "reassurance", it emphasized in the press that the study in the *Lancet* incriminated short-term calcic inhibitors specifically and did not relate to the "time-release" variants.

While it was justified, from the public health standpoint, this message nevertheless induced rather serious side effects. Without helping to quiet the debate, it called the patients' attention to a matter that few of them would have chanced upon in the *Lancet*. So it was an all-out war on Procardia and the two other drugs in question.

Poor communication? A flawed media plan? Not in the opinion of Dr. Roger Sachs. "We are under heavy fire, under what seems to be a campaign purposely orchestrated against one of the greatest classes of cardiovascular drugs in the history of medicine", commented the Vice President of Pfizer for medical affairs. And he sourly denounced "the small group of authors who keep mining the same data to find new means of attacking these great drugs". "This is frightening the patients, and it is deplorable", Sachs concluded. Did he have in mind only the article in the *Lancet*? Or was he talking more generally about the Health Department's initiatives? And the rumors that they were fueling and which were already spreading so rapidly? It's hard to say. As a savvy manager, the Pfizer VP was careful not to overstep certain bounds in the interest of his profession.

This prudence did not stop the questions from flowing. Was this or was it not a case of disinformation? If so, in which direction? Was it coming from those in favor of calcium inhibitors? Their adversaries? Or from both at the same time? In an attempt to clarify the matter, *The New England Journal of Medicine* (a competitor of the *Lancet*), launched a statistical study of 86 physician-authors who had written articles related to the controversy. Without any financial support from the laboratories, the journal, like its English rival, is proud of its independence.

This work was based on individual questionnaires, and although it was inevitably limited by the reduced size of the sample, it enabled *New England* to establish that 96% of the authors "favorable" to the inhibitors admitted having financial ties to the manufacturers of these products, compared to 60% of the "neutral" authors and 37% of the "critical" authors. Conversely, 88% of those who were pro-calcium channel blockers admitted having such ties with the producers of competing anti-hypertension drugs such as beta-blockers or inhibitors of conversion enzymes, compared to 53% of the "neutrals" and 37% of the "anti-". Lastly, all of the "favorable" authors admitted to links with at least one pharmaceutical laboratory, while 67% of the "neutrals" and 43% of the "criticals" acknowledged having such relations.

The least we can say is that these statistics opened a wide avenue to those who opposed the calcium channel blockers. Still, Bayer managed to maintain its position, and even to improve it. Despite the NIS's repeated recommendations in favor of beta-blockers and diuretics, the calcic inhibitors continued to keep up with their competitors on the American market (which was estimated at $24 billion). Advertising and marketing were the principal architects of this favorable balance of forces. In a presentation to the American College of Cardiology in March 1998, Drs Thomas Wang and Randall Stafford (from the Massachusetts General Hospital) noted that calcium channel blockers were the most-advertised drugs in. . . the *New England Journal of Medicine*.

With their backs covered, the American industrial groups had the time and resources to devote to the conquest of foreign outlets, starting with the flourishing French psychotropic drugs market.

Sad Psychotropics

"The worldwide dissemination of North American psychiatric diagnosis criteria has generally supported the development of lobbying by osmosis. These criteria come from works by the American Psychiatry Association (APA), which is in a very large measure financed by the pharmaceutical industry", affirms Prof. Edouard Zarifian in *Le Prix du bien-etre, psychotropes et sociétés* [*The Price of Feeling Good — Psychotropics and Societies*], a journalistic version of his report on the consumption of psychotropics that was commissioned by Simone Veil and Philippe Douste-Blazy and presented to the French Minister for Social Affairs and Health, Jacques Barrot, in March 1996.

Zarifian, a professor of psychiatry and medical psychology at the University of Caen, spoke out strongly, and it was the *Diagnosis and Statistical Manual for Mental Disorders*, the DSM, that he had in mind. Since its first edition of 1952, this handbook has been one of the most frightful weapons in the psychotropic war — it delimits the battlefield in advance, at the same time that it enacts the laws that govern it.

This severe criticism was not driven by envy or hard feelings. Prof. Zarifian had nothing to prove: he was an authority in his field. This added weight to the warning that he was proclaiming, denouncing the excessive increase in consumption of medications in France. And the expert added this very telling description: "Simplistic equations are taking the place of advertising slogans and are getting everybody used to the idea of automatic prescriptions. Sadness = depression = serotonin = IRS[*]. A pseudo-scientific apparatus is used, with borrowings from

---

[*] The class of antidepressants known as serotonin reuptake inhibitors. (Author.)

neurobiology, and academic-sounding discourse is added as a guarantee to reassure the prescribing doctor."

In more ordinary terms, you could call it a case of "commercial brainwashing" under a scientific umbrella. It is hard to disagree with Prof. Zarifian when he says, "The way that the link between suicide and depression is shown provides a good example of disinformation that leads to the prescribing of more and more antidepressants. Opinion leaders have affirmed in a peremptory tone that "treatment for depression prevents suicide." Did they simply forget to add, "for those who are depressed"?

As he points out, the consumption of antidepressants has increased over the years, even as the number of suicide attempts continues to rise. Doesn't that seem to indicate that this is another example of a market for drugs being extended wrongfully beyond its "natural" limits? By linking depression and suicide, prevention of suicide and the prescription of psychotropic medications, a number of French doctors fall right in line with the conclusions suggested by the pharmaceutical laboratories! Everything they say is right: systematically blaming government authorities, journalists and even their lab-coated colleagues for "mortal negligence" if they balk at giving in to the therapeutic ukase. Here once again, we touch the special nature of the pharmacy market. When advertising executives incite us to consume more and more cars, household appliances, televisions, computers or airplane tickets, they are only hurting the citizens' wallets. When the drug industry turns its ploys of psychological influence to persuading doctors, friends, and the media that psychotropics alone are capable of relieving the pain of real life, of resolving family dramas or professional anguish, it goes beyond its field of competence and effectiveness. It is selling mirages at the expense of the health insurance system.

"Maybe not all our drugs are quite as useful as we claim", they concede in private, "but they guarantee the good economic health of the pharmaceutical industry, which is a factor of progress and contributes to continually extending human longevity." This is a contradictory argument that contains both truth and fiction. It is true that only a strong, i.e., profitable, industry can conduct ongoing research. But it is not true that artificially extending the market in the name of profitability extends human longevity; it has led to abuses that threaten the health of the very patients they claim to be helping.

All's fair in the war to offer new outlets to the manufacturers of psychotropic medications. Between the first and the fourth edition of the *Diagnosis and Statistical Manual for Mental Disorders*, the list of 180 psychopathological entities has grown to more than 300. Some of them are highly contestable: the 1995 edition of the DSM classified "menstrual syndromes" as a category of "psychiatric disorders", and only the prompt reaction of feminist groups forced its editors to beat a hasty retreat of fear of being denounced as "male chauvinist pigs"! How many successful attempts have there been, to counterbalance a few such tactical setbacks? Turning everything into a psychiatric matter is just one more demonstration of the American propensity to export its own lifestyle — a tendency that goes as far as "shaping" the criteria by which diseases are assessed to suit the interests of the pharmaceutical laboratories, strongly resembling the strategies of influence that we have already discussed in the arena of obesity.

Jules Romains must be rolling over in his grave. It's the Americans, and not the Frenchmen, who have come up with a real-life application of prophetic *Knock, or the Triumph of Medicine*: "Everybody who is in good health is sick but just doesn't realize it."

Suffer the Little Customers to Come to Us

Sick or not, the French consume massive quantities, passionately and even insanely: more than 200 million boxes of tranquilizers, hypnotics, stress remedies, nerve sedatives and antidepressants (at a cost of some $450 million) per year.

The anxiolytics, or tranquilizers, which are supposed to treat behavioral disorders, are the most widely used: 60% of the prescriptions for a wide range of products including Témesta (Wyeth laboratory) and Lexomil (Roche), leaders in this class. In 1995, these drugs were, respectively, third and fifth place in drugs most often prescribed by French doctors, all categories combined.

Hypnotics are intended to treat sleep disorders. These sleeping pills or sedatives generally belong to the benzoidiazepine family. In 1995 again, three French products shared first place in France: Imovane (Rhône-Poulenc Rorer) — another medicine that would suffer some underhanded attacks on the American market — Rohypnol (Beaufour), and Stilnox (from Synthélabo).

Nerve sedatives (also called anti-psychotics) are for treating various kinds of nervous disorders, and are frequently used in hospitals. The most common were Haldol (Janssen-Cilag SA), Dogmatil and Solian, both from Synthélabo.

Last but not least, antidepressants make up a category that is currently in full expansion. The French Number 1 — more than 40% of sales — is Prozac.

"The Prozac Revolution"

Prozac. The word is as famous as "Frigidaire". Daring commercial techniques implanted the name permanently in the minds of the general public, making this antidepressant the king of its class. Sales inevitably followed. In 1998, the tenth year of development, $2.8 billion in turnover made Prozac the third biggest drug in the world (according to this criterion).

Across the Atlantic, marketing was in full swing. "Prozac books", like *Listening to Prozac* (a *New York Times* bestseller for 23 weeks straight), *Talking Back to Prozac* and *Prozac Nation*, were joined by "Prozac cartoons" and even "Prozac movies". A troop of Canadian comedians, The Kids, produced *Brain Candy* — the moving odyssey of a pharmaceutical company saved from bankruptcy when it discovered an anti-depression pill,

Gleemonex, which any well-informed viewer would immediately identify with the "happy pill".

In *Disclosure*, Barry Levinson's 1994 suspense film based on Michael Crichton's novel by the same name, Tom Sanders (Michael Douglas), a top executive at Digicom, learns that contrary to expectations he will not be named Vice President of the high-tech company. His job seems to be in jeopardy, and Sanders suspects someone is out to get him.

— "Are you OK, Tom? You want a Prozac?" his false friend Phil Blackburn suggests to him, in the most natural tone.

Prozac daily-life? The drug was introduced in France only in 1989, after it had beaten all records in the U.S., Canada, Great Britain, and Germany. The dosage recommended there is lower than elsewhere: 20 Mg per day of *fluoxétine*, the name of the formula, compared to 40 to 80 Mg. The insurance programs reimburse it at a rate of 65% to 70% and the price of a box of 14 capsules fell from $20 to $15. But the laboratory managed to influence a body of "Prozac professionals" — the teachers; "Prozac reference groups" — hip people of every kind, golden boys, groupies of both sexes, artists and mainstream folk, intellectuals, advertising or "creative" executives; and, of course, "Prozac doctors". A handful of "Prozac journalists" can also be identified — psychotropic scouts always ready to praise this potion at length in their columns. On the one hand, Prozac helps people, as a solution for "major depressive episodes, i.e. emotional and "obsessive-compulsive" disorders; on the other hand, murmur the initiates, it makes you "high", and it increases sexual prowess ten times over.

To manage a simple pharmaceutical product, however delicate it may be, so that it becomes a phenomenon throughout society cannot have been an easy task. And even less left to chance, the anxiolytic drug *Lexomil* was blessed by having its name cited explicitly by François Cluzet in an excellent film by Daniele Dubroux, *L'Examen de minuit*.

The launching of a new drug is based on an art that is sometimes forgotten in France: the art of psychological warfare. It is important to choose the right moment, when the public's mind is ripe and thus in phase with the evolution of morals and conduct. While the public is said to have a short memory, the industrialists still remember the American troubles suffered by Valium. This anxiolytic that was literally "planted" in the U.S. in the 1960s; it came too early into a world that was not yet receptive enough. Clashing with the mindset of the day, it was perceived as a kind of "strait jacket imposed on the American people". Valium was warmly appreciated in Europe, but it could not fully penetrate the other side of the Atlantic.

Since then, the U.S. has lived through its "Cultural Revolution", and the Old Continent gradually fell into alignment with the themes imported from America. The result was not long in coming. Rowdy or scatterbrained kids were locked, for years, in the ADD category ("Attention Disorder Deficit"), and executives haunted by the prospect of dismissal boosted their productivity by taking amphetamines, hormones, and so-called "enriched" food, cocktails of super-vitamins and even anabolic steroids. A considerable proportion of the population exemplified and became victim of this phenomenon of medical over-consumption. And, above all, old or young, people "clung" to the anxiolytic, especially women.

"It is mostly misused", warned Dr. Patrice Boyer of the National Institute of Health and Medical Research (Inserm), during the Bichat Interviews in 1995. "Only 30% of the patients taking anxiolytics show major anxiety disorders." But apparently, not everyone shared this opinion. The practice of treating psychic difficulties with medication gained some friends among prestigious advocates including Prof. Frederic Rouillon, a psychiatrist at the hospital Louis-Mourier de Colombes, who declared: "All this talk by the detractors of drugs for the central nervous system has always been based on a moral concept: that it is bad to resort to chemical relief for one's emotional suffering."

Without wishing to draw any conclusion as to the philosophical bases of such arguments, let us note how they play into the interests of the laboratories. If drugs can cure everything — from overweight to heartache on a lonely evening, from the exhaustion of the corporate manager on the brink of a nervous breakdown to the stress of the computer programmer tied to his seat by foolish production schedules — then they become the supreme guardian of the evils of the society. So much the better for those who are marketing them, and so much the worse for the insurance and welfare systems.

More drugs, less drugs? The question was on everyone's mind during the famous Bichat Talks in 1995.

"Today, it is politically and economically correct to denounce such abuse, but epidemiology shows clearly in France, as well as in other countries, that one third of the population is handicapped by a mental disorder that could be cured or reduced by suitable treatment. Mental suffering exists and medicine is the simplest way to cure it", declared Prof. Marc Bourgeois, from Bordeaux.

One third of the population? That means a market of 20 million consumers! It is easy to understand why Eli Lilly, the Indianapolis laboratory that manufactures Prozac, considered it necessary to pour all its assets into the French game.

A "Tiger" in the Pharmaceutical Jungle

Eli Lilly, at that time America's fourth-largest manufacturer, is regarded as dynamic and inventive, but very aggressive commercially. People in the know readily classify it as one of the "tigers". A 100% unofficial label, this characterization applies to manufacturers who thrive in the pharmaceutical jungle by using the same cunning as a big cat. A different image is used to indicate the biggest companies of the sector, who can crush the competition through sheer mass, without needing to resort to techniques as offensive as those of their challengers: they are called the "elephants".

So Eli Lilly was known as a "Tiger". And it attacked like one. In 1996, under the headline, "Lilly Pays Alcoholics to Test New Drugs", the *Wall Street Journal* affirmed that Eli Lilly's clinical research center had used an abnormal quantity of homeless people, alcoholics, for its Phase

I pharmaceutical tests. These subjects were supposedly paid $85 dollars per day, which is less than what the competition was paying. To support its allegation, the newspaper lined up declarations from SDF, and directors of homeless shelters. And it quoted the disillusioned Vaughn Bryson, chairman of the Indianapolis firm who was dismissed in 1993; he admitted that his former company's use of alcoholic homeless people "is no secret".

In Phase I of the tests, the effects of the formula are observed in a small number of healthy subjects; does the drug produce the same effects in man as in animals? The subjects are all volunteers and are well-informed of the risks that they are running. It would seem the newspaper's accusations were on target. But the "Tiger" knows how to stand up to such charges. Eli Lilly responded promptly. Rejecting the *Wall Street Journal*'s charges, the company stated that before signing up for the tests, the volunteers had had to sign a declaration certifying that they had not abused alcohol in the last six months. With the credibility of a world-renowned manufacturer at stake, all the group's foreign subsidiaries were mobilized. Dr. Jean-Claude Salord, Public Relations officer of Lilly France, proclaimed his certainty. "All the participants are given complete medical examinations before starting the tests. In short, it is wrong to think that the pharmaceutical company could work covertly, using irregular medical practices, without that being known at once."

Another direct attack against Eli Lilly took place in the summer of 1997. A report from New York City Advocate, a consumers' association, stated that people in Indianapolis had supported "Project Prozac" in 1994. This trivial code name camouflaged a very special lobbying operation: they were trying to have Zoloft, an antidepressant competing with Prozac, removed from PCS Health System's list of "recommended products". According to the same source, 30 million messages to doctors were to be sent.

Zoloft is marketed by American Pfizer, Number 8 in the sector; a few days later, Pfizer estimated that "Project Prozac" had increased its rival's sales by some $171 million. Was the project actually implemented? Or was it nothing more than a battle plan on paper? PCS (which was taken over by Eli Lilly in 1995, subsequent to these charges being made), defended itself, claiming that the strategy was never applied. After all, during the acquisition, Eli Lilly and the Federal Trade Commission had signed an agreement prohibiting any interference between the two entities. A company spokesman said, "We think that all our actions and those of PCS are legal, are appropriate, and are in conformity with the agreement." And he stressed that the acquisition of PCS was not a great deal, financially, since it obliged Eli Lilly to seek more capital. Furthermore, New York City Advocate, anxious to show that it had nothing against Eli Lilly in particular, pointed out that the two laboratories which had already bought other Pharmaceutical Benefit Managers (PBM, the same type of company as PCS) had not been obliged by the Federal Trade Commission to sign an agreement like the one it imposed on the group from Indianapolis.

Anti-Competitive Practices?

A natural-born warrior, the Tiger attacks even better than it defends itself. Here is another story, quite French this time. On March 5, 1996, the Council on Competition publicized (under number 96-D12) a historic decision, related to the anti-competitive practices of Lilly France in the sector of proprietary medical products for hospital use. A proprietary medical product, prepared in advance under particular circumstances, bearing a particular name and sold in more than one pharmacy, "does not benefit from a special regime derogatory to common patent law. In particular, patents confer upon their holders an exclusive right with respect to third parties for twenty years" (in practice, ten years on average, after taking into account the time required for experimentation and then for receiving government approvals).

For this reason, Lilly France in all legality held the monopoly on sales in France of its Vancocine (generic name: *vancomycine*.) This is a powdered medication that can be suspended in liquid for drinking, or can be injected. Three dosage levels (125, 250 and 500 Mg) are intended for treating diseases caused by various staphilococca, streptococca pneumococci, lactobacilla and actinomycia, and are used almost exclusively by physicians in the hospital environment. But with the patent "falling" into the public domain, two competing laboratories decided to offer the hospitals their own generic equivalents of Vancocine 500 Mg: Vancomycine Lederlé, in 1988, then Vancomycine Dakota Pharm in 1989.

The Lederlé laboratories are a subsidiary of Cyanamid France, itself a subsidiary of American Cyanamid. Dakota Pharm is a subsidiary of the Swiss company Siegfried AG. Their debut in this market segment had the immediate effect of weakening Lilly France's market share: from 100% in 1987, to 89.7% in 1988, 79.9% in 1989, 69% in 1990 and 67.3% in 1991. That year, the respective shares of Dakota Pharm and Lederlé were, respectively, 23.5% and 9.1%.

In theory, Lilly France certainly should have accepted this established fact, which may be unpleasant but is in conformity with the law and the logic of the market. However, investigations by the Council on Competition tended to indicate otherwise. Starting in the second six-month period of 1988, the date when Vancomycine Lederlé appeared, Lilly France began an illegal practice: in its sales presentations to the buyers at various public and sometimes private hospitals, it started including "supplementary advantages", tying discounts on another of its drugs, Dobutrex, to purchases of Vancocine.

However, as the Council on Competition notes: "The Lilly France corporation is the only laboratory in France to manufacture and market Dobutrex, because of the product's patent protection." Since there were no equivalents to Dobutrex, it had a monopoly for all intents and purposes. The Council considered that "linking purchases of Dobutrex to purchases of Vancocine" had the goal of dissuading hospital pharmacies from turning to either Lederlé or Dakota Pharm for *vancomycine*.

Offering discounts on Dobutrex on the condition of Vancocine purchases was a discriminatory artifice. In short, Lilly France was guilty of competitive practices that are prohibited by Article 8 of the ordinance of December 1, 1986.

In the first instance, the company was assessed a penalty of $5 million and was compelled to publish the entire text of the Council's decision in the doctors' periodical, *Le Quotidien de Médecin* and *Le Moniteur des pharmacies et laboratoires.*

This penalty for "abuse of a dominant position" would not be good for business. "We dispute the basis of the Council on Competition's decision", Lilly's executives declared in *Le Monde*. "Indeed, our firm never occupied a dominant position on these markets because there are several drugs available that can be substituted for our antibiotic and our cardio-stimulant."

Maintaining that the decision was based on inaccurate market research and that substitutes for Dobutrex do exist, and therefore that there could have been no abuse of a dominant position, Lilly France immediately lodged an appeal with the court system. Lilly demanded a reduction of the fine and requested the cancellation of the obligatory press notices.

On May 6, 1997, the economic and financial chamber of the Paris Court of Appeals rejected Lilly's claims concerning the fine, but decided that the decision to require publication of the decision in the press was insufficiently justified. On May 22, the laboratory filed an appeal in cassation; it was rejected two years later, on June 15, 1999.

Lilly France was not placing so much importance on this case because of the $5 million (which only represents 1.66% of its turnover). Rather, their emphasis on successfully canceling the press notices indicates that its principal objective was to protect Lilly's public image as an irreproachable manufacturer and, beyond that, to protect the image of Prozac: the best-selling product that brought in such high revenues. The 20 Mg "happy pill", taken by some 25 million patients worldwide (almost a half-million in France, alone) may have looked like an ivory and green capsule but really it was golden.

Under these conditions, it was important to keep the myth alive about this miracle antidepressant. Press articles piled up. "America Has Fallen in Love with a Pill", read the headlines in *Santé* magazine, April 1990. Five years later, several hundred similar "papers" had been printed, while innumerable rumors made Prozac into a kind of legal drug that could be taken in broad daylight. Sometimes it was called a "tranquilizer", sometimes a "high", a sexual stimulant, an "aphrodisiac". Alerted by all the clamor, certain customers began to demand that their doctors order this specific antidepressant from Eli Lilly. Sales took off; Prozac. . . it's great.

A paradoxical initiative cropped up within this context of generalized fervor. To suppress the rumors, Lilly France hired a public relations agency and immediately let the public know that it had done so, via a passionate article in *Capital* magazine. Did its executives know that contradicting inaccurate information so openly generally ends up making people believe it more? And did they also realize that a manufacturer who is savvy enough, by its own admission, to dissuade the media from saying "anything" against its products, reveals at the same time its ability to influence the media in the opposite direction so that they say "good" things about it?

The Best Defense Is a Strong Offense

In any event, Lilly France intensified its self-defense campaign for Prozac. "Citing information published in the British journal *New Scientist*, several members of the French media have recently echoed the alleged effects of an antidepressant drug from Eli Lilly", stated *Le Généraliste* on October 3. And they added, at the request of Lilly, "Certain publications seem to believe they can talk about orgasms resulting from nothing but a yawn, after someone takes this drug. This 'information' is unfounded and is seriously misleading. . . . It is neither serious nor responsible to claim that this drug has 'orgasmic properties'. Lilly Laboratories reminds everyone that pharmaceutical enterprises are prohibited [in France] from communicating about their products in media that are not targeted to health professionals. We are, however, constrained to remind everyone that the drug in question is prescribed only to fight depression and obsessive compulsive disorders, diseases that should not be treated with derision. It is unacceptable to suggest that such a product might be diverted from its proper use and that Lilly laboratories might be, in any way, the instigator of or an accessory to this situation."

The British-American rumor mill was already endowing the "Happy Pill" with new qualities. In May 1986, the *Wall Street Journal* ran an article with the fabulous title: "If You are at Risk of Depression Due to Your Obesity, A New Drug May Solve Both Your Problems at the Same Time". Who hasn't dreamed of losing weight in complete happiness? The rumor swept through France.

This offensive marketing style is, above all, wild marketing. As a good "feline", Eli Lilly has demonstrated its aggressiveness through, among other incidents, the U.S. campaign against Dr. Peter Breggin. Director of a Center of Psychiatry and Psychology Studies, Dr. Breggin testified as an expert witness in the high-profile criminal trial of Joseph Wesbecker. Was Wesbecker acting under the influence of Prozac when he assassinated one of his former colleagues? Yes, according to his lawyers and Dr. Breggin. No, according to the jury — who said he was responsible for his actions at the moment of the murder. The fact remains that Eli Lilly's antidepressant suffered a loss of reputation due to the hearings, and that Breggin "aggravated" the situation by publishing, one after the other, two successful works on the serious side effects of mind-altering drugs, Prozac in particular.

How could they get rid of him? First, the rebel psychiatrist was accused of being a member of the Church of Scientology and of having sold his soul. The rumor certainly was destructive: the pseudo-scientific cult founded by L. Ron Hubbard is anathema, and rightly so.

Later, rumors were also circulated in Paris accusing a woman magistrate in charge of sensitive legal matters of having ties with Scientology.

What is important in these matters is to render the adversary forever suspect. As this "suggestion" was not enough to completely discredit him, Breggin became victim of a second campaign of rumors supported by many articles in the "friendly press". This time, he was portrayed not only as a follower of Scientology but as a marginal member of the medical profession, without supporters. Start to sound familiar? Similar calumnies were circulating shortly thereafter in connection with an anti-Prozac Belgian, Dr. Robert Bourguignon.

That's harsh! "A New York radio station even received a letter from Lilly, cordially inviting it not to give any air time to this "highly dubious" author", according to *Marianne*, in September 1997. The weekly magazine went on to explain how, in a later incident, "the lawyers of the pharmaceutical firm learned that the defense was going to bring in some awkward witnesses; Lilly preferred to buy the plaintiffs' silence, inducing them to withdraw their complaint at the last minute". The article was never contested.

The Dalkon Shield is a prototype of the great American scandals of medical disinformation. This birth-control device was responsible for the deaths of at least five women in the U.S.. Since 1969-1972, this episode has illustrated how important it is for American laboratories to marginalize those who dare to "complain" about their products. Sometimes they go as far as to conclude "financial" arrangements with them that may be in conformity with the letter of the American law but that are in no case compatible with the European outlook. Here, we have another demonstration of aggressiveness, this time against a judge. An executive from Eli Lilly's leaders expressed to journalists "the most express reservations over the mental health of this unstable judge" — in fact, the honorable John Potter, a magistrate from Louisville who was accusing the Indianapolis firm of having made secret agreements with the victims' families!

Let each one judge for himself. But from seductive maneuvers to concerted counter-attacks, from psychological inundation to under-handed maneuvers, Eli Lilly serves as a good introduction to the forms of combat used by the American pharmaceutical industry.

CHAPTER 4

UNCLE SAM'S PHARMACISTS

Merck, Sharp & Dohme (Number 2 or 3 in pharmaceuticals, worldwide) are prime examples of the "elephants" category. Founded in New Jersey in 1927, this company holds, or jointly holds, the two biggest "blockbuster" drugs in the world, and is very well-endowed: it has financial clout, experience, technical capability, and an innovation "pipeline" loaded with the formulas of tomorrow, the best marketing networks, advertising know-how, and an ear in Washington — friends in the House of Representatives, the Senate and the White House. All of these assets the "tiger" Eli Lilly possesses in considerably smaller quantities — not that we can consider Lilly to be a pathetic little creature.

A tiger versus an elephant — now, there is an image that would have delighted the late Vietnamese communist leader Ho Chi Minh, who was so fond of battle-related metaphors. The powerful pachyderm, he explained, would crush the cat if she had the imprudence to allow herself to be caught. But the tiger is not simple-minded: she keeps moving. Marauding around her enormous adversary, she weakens it through a series of scratches. The elephant slowly bleeds, and weakens. As the fight goes on, the elephant will be worn down and finally killed.

A Marxist-Leninist trained by years of militant and clandestine activity, Uncle Ho made the tiger the mascot of the popular guerrillas; Western imperialism was identified with the elephant. Ho foresaw everything — except the demise of the USSR, which was to make the United States, elephant and tiger at the same time, the only global super power after God.

And it is a super power that plays with the combined virtues of the concerted, planned and multifarious offensive. Whether they draw their distinctive features from the pachyderm or from the cat, the American-English laboratories also borrowed from Greek legends the tactic of the Trojan Horse. Why not take advantage of the fact that a fascination with the American way of life (and the consubstantial linguistic advantages relating to it) had traced a magical trail into the unconscious of their future consumers?

Do You Speak "Pharmenglish"?

With grammar and spelling rules imposed by Bill Gates, the language of Shakespeare reigns in the globalized universe, especially in the universe of the pharmaceutical industries. It is hardly an exaggeration to coin the term "pharmenglish".

In practice, this curt term shows up as a concrete reality: a battle for influence, already half-won. Publishing articles in *Nature*, *The Lancet*, *New England*, *The British Medical Journal*, *JAMA*, *Pediatrics*, the *Journal of Clinical Epidemiology*, the *Journal of the National Institute Cancer* and the many American-British journals specializing in medical questions is always more worthwhile than publishing locally (the Germans have long understood this, and they invest in this sector massively). It is also more productive to let one's discoveries be known and accepted in "pharmenglish" on the scientific sites on the Internet, which are essential. And it is even better to be recognized by one's "colleagues" across the Atlantic, who are considered to be unquestionably super-competent, unquestionably "hyper-advanced". And to justify this attention, one has only to look at the drugs they produce, which are inevitably more innovative.

This phenomenon dates back to the 1960's. It expanded during the 1970's, despite the anti-Americanism inspired by the ambient Leftism. It was a miracle of gradual familiarization: first, the Americans hired young European doctors to conduct specific research projects, then offered them support to conduct their own research. And finally, U.S. channels appeared as the preferred path toward any individual promotion. An invitation to work at a laboratory in the United States was the supreme recognition, an act of allegiance transfigured into a dubbing ceremony.

We can call the result of this process of psychological subservience "American-dependence". It may lack elegance, but the expression has the merit of reminding us that we are not talking about philosophy but about the pharmaco-industry, with its profit margins and cumulative profits. There were plenty of young French researchers; in all their "innocence", they were flattered to be finally given some consideration, happy to find their own writings in the columns of the American-British scientific press, relieved to take their revenge on the highly stratified French teaching hospital hierarchy with all its entrenched interests.

Everyone looked to New York and San Francisco as the fatherlands of innovation, dynamism and inexhaustible wealth for the most intelligent. In Europe, we had the claustrophobia of tight budgets, the confined atmosphere of feuding clans; over there, in the West, there was pure air, broad horizons, and the lyrical illusion of a radiant professional future. The future's so bright. . .

New "Fellow-Travellers"

Has anyone outside the medical world ever heard of the "Merck Fellows"? This reservoir, for a long time, fed one of the most effective pipelines for diffusing "American-dependence". Starting one's career as a "Merck Fellow" meant that you already had been distinguished in the U.S., that you already had some clout.

While the terms of such an arrangement were only implicit, they were nonetheless perfectly clear: we can help you to become a celebrity and, in exchange, you will help us to introduce our drugs into your country's teaching hospitals. How many great figures in French medicine accepted that approach — a Director of Public Health, for one (as strategic a post as there may be) and one of France's most famous "medical consciences". How many of today's decision-makers sitting on the commissions that authorize new market introductions are former "Fellows"? You think we have independence?

Something here recalls a past that is not as distant as we may think. From the 1930's to the 1980's, the Soviets strove to recruit an army of "fellow-travellers". Coming from the twin molds of antifascism and anti-imperialism, this phalanx of "useful idiots" was engaged in conditioning minds to accept the prospect of the inescapable world revolution. Involuntary accomplices of the totalitarian system, they worked side by side with proven auxiliaries, "organizers", ideologues, agents of influence, manipulators of every stripe. That is how things were in the era of "progressive thought" that went far beyond the bounds of cocktails and dinner parties.

There is no sign of a comparable Machiavellism on the part of the American pharmaceuticals business; at least, that is the opinion of the professionals whom I interviewed. And they all note that the practice of naming "Fellows" has come to a standstill, as the French begin to wake up. But maybe it's more complicated than that. For example, let's look at the corporate-university connection. In the United States, this is extremely well developed, where "eggheads" readily mix with businessmen. This gives rise to the assumption that, protected by the oceans from Soviet subversion, the Americans had the entire cold war period to try out the disinformation techniques used by their adversaries. Not being on the front line, they had time, leisure and space. Moreover, exiled by Fascism or Nazism, familiar with Communist dialectics and happy to have found an American refuge, the survivors of the European intelligentsia could be used as machines for producing concepts.

Did the "Yankees" learn theoretical lessons from these efforts? We can't rule that out. And more utilitarian lessons? They weren't born yesterday. The Soviets benefited from people's fascination with an idealized picture of the world they were developing: the USSR, "the workers' fatherland". America only had to adapt this method on a different register, using an attraction that was not so much ideological as frankly material, founded on a blend of profit-sharing and admiration. And this, among other things, led to their effectiveness in penetrating the hierarchies of the French teaching hospitals in the 1970's-1990's.

Intelligent Cowboys

One French pharmaceutical professional who has been socializing for a long time with the leaders of the American mastodons of this sector, basically considers them to be "intelligent cow-boys".

Intelligent — even if some imbeciles imbued with their own sense of self-sufficiency persist in taking them for idiots! And cowboys, at the same time, it is true; and as such, aggressive, enterprising, liable to shoot on sight. For the last two decades the American laboratories, flanked by their British allies, have been carrying out a masterful policy of systematically buying, absorbing or allying with small, advanced, biogenetics companies and university laboratories. They make tender offers on "start-ups", young firms on the point of takeoff, and they match that with tender offers on the brains involved. This thorough campaign had catastrophic effects on French, even European, pharmacy, sucking its blood like a vampire.

But that was only one of the tactics in the American offensive. The "wild horde" of the U.S. pharmaceutical industry has many arrows in its quiver. It imposes on the rest of the medical world a continual lowering of the "thresholds" at which normal conditions become pathologies. Thus the number of subjects "at risk" — or better yet, subjects who have been self-persuaded that they are at risk — goes up every day. The ultimate stage of this hypochondriacal process would be to consider the whole of the social body as a medical problem! We are not there yet, but we are well on the way. By adopting criteria of evaluation that are more and more Draconian, we only broaden the potential field of customers for the pharmaceutical "majors".

We have already seen how this tendency works in the field of mental discomfort and illness but, to tell the truth, every highly profitable sector has been targeted. The rate of glycemia that distinguishes healthy individuals from diabetics has, for example, come down substantially. And so has the threshold for hypertension, and for anticholesterol, according to Prof. Marian Apfelbaum, president of the French Society of Nutrition and Dietetics. "By lowering the alarm rate from three grams to two grams — as was done with a great brouhaha in the United States and as was recently tried here in France — more than half of the adult population would become their prey." ("They" being the U.S. pharmaceutical industries.)

Finding Allies

As they went further into this strategy, the pharmaceutical giants secured the support of the large agro-alimentary firms and, beyond that, the implicit or explicit support of the professional associations. Until 1992, recalls the same Prof. Apfelbaum, the American Cardiological Association granted (with the help of comfortable royalties) manufacturers of food products a label that said "Good for the heart". The leaders of this market were "cholesterol free" and "reduced fat" foods. This publicity with a medical alibi also related to various "anti-obesity" foods. All the same, this was finally prohibited.

In France, the development of the "health food" market presents contradictory aspects. The agro-alimentary industry uses the health argument, as can be read in this excerpt from a booklet published in 1997 by the Astra-Calvé company (a subsidiary of the Unilever group which markets, *inter alia*, many oil-based products). We read:

"Information from the agro-alimentary industry centered on cardiovascular diseases is principally concerned with today's food supply as a primary means of prevention. The Unilever Group should be recognized for its work in several European countries (Fruit d'Or Recherche in France, Flora Project in Great Britain, Becel in the Netherlands). . . the essence of a hygieno-dietetics approach to prevention of cardiovascular disease is to look for a better balance between the various categories of lipids, the distribution of which directly influences the risk of atherosclerosis."

Medically irreproachable and commercially effective! And further reinforcing the link between food and health: "it has been noted, for example, that increases in the consumption of sunflower oil appear to be closely related to decreases in deaths from cardiovascular problems. . . Could this be one of the explanations of the famous French paradox?"

The convergence between agro-alimentary groups and pharmaceutical groups is not complete, since they have somewhat different interests; however, by placing it squarely in the center of the public's concern, this convergence contributes to unifying the disease-health duet. And, at the same time, it influences "favorably" the consumption of medical or ancillary medical products.

And, finally, there remains the weapon of disinformation. In the pharmaceutical field, it is used either to cast discredit upon a drug through lies and insinuations or, conversely, to praise its merits through hyperbole and rumor. Highly sensitized to any matter that may touch upon its health, traumatized by the irresponsibility shown by the medical and government authorities in the contaminated blood scandal, the public has become more wary and, at the same time, easier to manipulate — wary, because it doubts the apparent truth; easy to manipulate because, weakened by this loss of confidence, they are easier to "incite" against a pharmaceutical product.

A game in which the Americans and the British excel.

Disinformation Habits and Customs in Pharmacy

In attacking a drug, two golden rules apply — the same as in fencing: surprise, and speed of execution. As in the noble art of swordplay, anticipation is the mother of victory. Striking in anticipation, i.e. while the unfavorable product is still only in its experimental phase, is the surest means of action. Competing drugs are most surely killed when their credibility is sapped while they are still in their infancy. At the least, a few well-conceived maneuvers will delay their arrival on the market. And if these undercover ploys should fail, one is still free to try a direct frontal attack (more dangerous and more expensive, needless to say).

The techniques are many. Nothing forbids you, for example, from conducting comparative studies on the competitor's formula in your own laboratories, with your own technicians. This is a good means of proving what you want to prove: it is not hard to demonstrate that a new drug has negative effects, since that is almost always the case.

The second method is sponsorship. If an astute scientist detects one or two doubtful elements in the drug's effects, his fortune is made. The rival laboratory, transformed into a patron, will then finance any research work for the deserving researcher on his way to glory.

And that is how it goes, in the discrete Eden of pharmacy: muddling along. By sending a steady supply of experts' reports to the national and international drug agencies, by keeping the courts, the doctors' guilds, and the patients' associations supplied with discreet and well-directed "information", such and such precise charge can gradually be imposed as truth. The goal is to make the adversary waste precious time. The fastest route is via the pharmaceutical oversight agencies in the target country. The rival product, your in-house experts can say, is suspected of being carcinogenic. Out of prudence or legal-judicial timidity, the national public health authorities will require the laboratory to conduct a new series of tests. This takes two years, on average, creating a serious delay in getting the product to market.

The Chemical Steamroller

If you want to win at this game, you'd better be American. The strategy of the Anglo-Saxons is based on one fundamental asset: power. Aside from the Swiss, the Europeans are far from having a comparable deterrent force. In 1996, just five pharmaceutical groups accounted for the lion's share of financial clout: Novartis (Swiss, $23 billion), Roche (Swiss, $18 billion), Merck & Co. (United States, $12 billion), Bristol-Myers Squibb (United States, $8 billion) and Pfizer (United States, $6 billion). And by 2001, the Club of Five showed every evidence of increasing these sums respectively to $53 billion for Novartis, $25 for Roche, $30 for Merck, $20 for Bristol-Myers Squibb and $20 for Pfizer. This is a global potential of more than $150 billion.

Even though the creation of the euro might shore up the positions of manufacturers in the European Union by extracting some of the British from the "big one" (the United States), it is hard to avoid the steamroller. Things being what they are, the financial capacity of the American-British allied laboratories enables them to impose on the rest of the world manufacturing and research criteria that are in their own interests. This is a magic wand that they have no intention of losing.

To delay the introduction of generic versions of a foreign product in the United States and on the world market, the Americans exploit the timeframe by constantly increasing the parameters of the studies required to win approval for the product. It takes ten to twelve years, now, to produce a knock-off of a new formula — that is to say, a minimum cost of $330 million (up to $600 million by the end, if you consider the research expenses lost on drugs that will never be marketed because they turn out to be dangerous or not very effective).

So it is understood: money is the second frame of the diptych. When they make up their minds to penetrate a given foreign market, U. S. manufacturers pull out of their bags colossal studies based on an astronomical quantity of patients: 10,000 patients, for example, including

5,000 on placebo and 5,000 taking the drug in question, when their European rivals can only line up a few hundred of them. Such impressive figures cannot help but influence the local pharmacological authorities, and associations of patients and consumers, who are inevitably very demanding when it comes to the safety of medications.

Finally, let's consider the targets of the disinformation. They range from the government agencies to doctors, pharmacists, care-providers in the hospitals, the entire hierarchy of the public health and welfare agencies, insurance networks, patients' associations and, finally, the general public itself. The spectacular expansion of pharmaceutical marketing must also be taken into account.

We have seen the conditions under which the media can be used as an ideal means of disseminating disinformation, either in the "positive" sense, in order to promote a product among medical professionals, or in the "negative" sense, to attack a competing drug, in the general public's perception, using general newspapers, magazines and popular TV programs — all of which prefer spectacular denunciations and dramatic scoops over happy, uneventful approvals that will not boost ratings nor subscription bases.

Letters to the Editor

Other, subtler techniques are no less effective. Letters to the Editor in the popular newspapers and especially the medical publications can, on occasion, serve as mail bombs. No law prevents Dr. Smith from seeking to inform the public or his colleagues about the progress of his experiments. The honorable physician has all the leisure in the world to remember one of his patients experiencing a certain rare symptom and to wonder, in all his ethical responsibility, about how and why this happened.

Opportunely, Dr. Smith may recall that his patient had taken drug X; could there be any relationship between this and the health disorders that the patient then suffered? Moved by the insatiable curiosity of the conscientious professional, our honest doctor would like to correspond with colleagues who may have had similar experiences, or even with patients who have observed the same problem.

Let us imagine that the good Dr. Smith acted under some influence, that a "friendly laboratory" had suggested this to him — the same laboratory that subsidizes his research or gives him needed support in another form, since direct corruption is fairly rare. There is nothing random in the physician's conduct: before he sits down to draft the letter, the engineering departments of the attacking laboratory will have done their homework and selected a rare symptom that could be caused by the competing product.

British doctors like to correspond between colleagues, in the same way, and the English public is quick to make its reflections known by writing to the newspapers. Anyone who thinks he has had a comparable experience may pop up. Dr. Smith's letter will have a good chance of instigating others. Never mind the animal-lovers who object to vivisection and animal testing, and therefore to pharmaceutical laboratories in general, and the innumerable hordes of good souls who, a little bit confused about everything, are quick to take any perch from which to express their views on the whole world.

Dr. Smith's letter spawns others, and the campaign becomes self-sustaining through a spectrum of contradictory answers that mix everything up, at the expense of the accused drug. Where there is smoke, there is fire: a product is being blamed, so it must be guilty of something. The mail starts to pile up, the accusations grow and multiply, the rumors come and go, creating a current of negative "information" that, with all the "clarifications" in the world (and through pressure on the newspaper editors), the laboratory in question may not be able to suppress. Can you counterattack, legally speaking? It's difficult, for in England, letters to the Editor are a sanctuary, a holy zone of "free expression".

Are such practices also found in France? Rarely, for the moment. But as the bulk mail and computerized database industries gear up, the possibilities are increasing exponentially. The number of general practitioners and specialists who are connected to the Web is growing, and concurrently, so is their ability to diffuse quasi-news or "professional questions" like those of Dr. Smith.

The Internet is another channel for the Anglo-Saxon pharmaceutical offensive. Until now, we have been speaking about the American-British couple as a homogeneous and functional community. But in industrial pharmacy, the English aim much higher than the role of a brilliant second (which they have accepted almost everywhere else, since the end of the Second World War). The long conflict in anti-ulcer drugs is a case in point.

The Battle of England

London, January-February 1996. The Royal Pharmaceutical Society opened an investigation into the advertising techniques used by Tagamet 100, the new form of the best-known anti-ulcer drug in the world, generally recognized under its generic name of *cimetidine*.

The Society took this step in the aftermath of the publication of an outraged letter from Nicola Gray, a pharmacist in Manchester, who had just revealed in the columns of the very respected *Pharmaceutical Journal* that the American-British company, SmithKline Beecham (manufacturer of Tagamet and the world's ninth largest pharmaceutical group), was bombarding some 250,000 subjects of Her Gracious Majesty with semi-informative and semi-advertising documents.

"The most cynical among us might think that the purpose of this information is to prepare the consumers to get around any question likely to dissuade a pharmacist from selling them Tagamet", said Nicola Gray, whose understatement is a perfect instance of the technique so familiar to her compatriots. Translation: in polite terms, the physician was accusing SmithKline Beecham of influencing British patients. Such a campaign seemed to be all the more suspicious as a case of brainwashing, according to her, since any normal mind would rightly wonder by what miracle the drug industrialist could have managed to gain access to such a precise database! Gray's second revelation was no less interesting: none of the 250,000 recipients of the SmithKline Beecham documents was selected randomly. These subjects of the Queen all suffered from indigestion, and thus constituted an ideal target for Tagamet advertising.

This is not a horror story, and there has been neither malice nor mystery, countered Allan Chandler, SmithKline Beecham's spokesman. He told the Royal Pharmaceutical Society that the names of these 250,000 people had come straight from a study of consumer habits conducted by Shoppers National on a sample of million people. Among the various questions they had been asked, was: "Do you suffer from indigestion?" SmithKline Beecham thus had only to draw up a list of those who had answered affirmatively (a quarter of them), to establish the database in question — a database whose existence Chandler confirmed, in passing. He willingly admitted that the 250,000 mailings contained details on the questions that the recipients' pharmacists were likely to ask. Without any intention of short-circuiting the latter, of course! Who could think such a thing, in the kingdom of fair play?

"We do not think that it is shocking", concludes Chandler. "It is just a new way of using of the media. Is it really any different from advertisements for "over the counter " drugs that are not reimbursed by insurance and that address themselves directly to consumers via television?"

Enemy-Brothers

Such is the atmosphere, these days: a merciless war between ulcer remedies, Tagamet against Azantac, SmithKline Beecham against Glaxo Wellcome.

Tagamet is just twenty years old. It was in 1976 that the American laboratory of SmithKline & French (about to merge with the British firm, Beecham, to form the American-British group SmithKline Beecham), launched the ulcer medicine that was qualified by the Food and Drug Administration as a "considerable therapeutic progress".

Such a good report is extremely rare. Five years later, Tagamet, leader in drug sales worldwide, was bringing in 60% of the American-British group's profits.

But there is something Darwinian about the hyper-competitive world of the pharmaceutical industry and a new drug always seems to come up to supplant its predecessor. This was proven once again in 1981 when Glaxo, then 100% British, decided to take up the ambitious challenge of dethroning Tagamet.

Glaxo pinned its hopes on Azantac, to wipe out this rival. This antihistamine's chances of success were, however, miniscule, since it differed from Tagamet neither in its composition nor in its means of combating ulcers. What physician could be induced to take his chances on a formula that had not yet been proven reliable, when a powerful and confirmed drug was already available on the market?

Seemingly, the "Glaxo challenge" looked like a foolish gamble, although the managers of this laboratory (which was founded early in the 20th century to market dried milk for babies) included some of the most dynamic in the pharmaceutical world. The group is considered to be very "innovative", since it dedicates nearly 20% of its manpower to research and development. In addition, Glaxo is not afraid to fight, betting on both tactical intelligence and the most daring promotional methods. One third research, two-thirds PR — that is the recipe for a successful drug, according to Glaxo's leaders.

Azantac, the Blockbuster

The first stage was the organization of an international conference on gastroenterology, focusing on Azantac. Attracted by the promise of enthralling debates, pleased by the "young" tone of the documents prepared by Glaxo, many specialists traveled to the conference. They were treated royally, and did not regret their trip.

This project led to an "industrial" quantity of articles in the press, echoing nearly verbatim the prose of the sales brochures. Long live

Azantac, a "simple, fast and reliable" product that, even better, cost 20% less than Tagamet. In the United States, the media effect was prolonged by a direct advertising campaign on various TV channels. Twelve million people were reached. According to later evaluations, the campaign generated nearly 600,000 visits to doctors.

On the strength of these early results, Glaxo very quickly climbed the spiral of success. A triumph! In 1986, world sales of Azantac exceeded those of its rival, reaching the $20 billion mark. And then came the wrath of the Food and Drug Administration. In spring 1986, the federal organization warned the directors of Glaxo by mail (I should point out that this is purely British, whereas SmithKline Beecham is mixed American-British) that its promotional methods exceeded the usual limits for this field.

The FDA disputed various assertions made by Glaxo, three in particular. According to the FDA, Tagamet did not take any longer than Azantac to produce its effect, but an almost equivalent lapse of time: four weeks in both cases. And, as the representatives of the British group kept insisting, certain ulcerous conditions did indeed respond better to the drug marketed by Glaxo — but the reverse was also true. In addition, the subsequent expenses for laboratory monitoring with Tagamet were no higher than those called for by its competitor.

"No substantial and appropriate data has been communicated to us that would make it possible to show that Azantac is better than Tagamet", summarized an FDA official in the professional newsletter, *Scrip*.

Until 1994, Glaxo's blockbuster drug would occupy first place in the world hit-parade, in front of Renitec, the conversion enzyme inhibitor from Merck, which was also marketed in a way that was scarcely appreciated by the French authorities. Minister Claude Evin denounced it on April 27, 1989, in front the cameras, saying, "This famous laboratory which sends 2,500 cardiologists to China over three years — I'mtalking about Merck laboratories and I'm talking about their product Renitec, which is a hypertensor."

The Men from Glaxo

1986-1994: eight years of unequaled happiness that generated impressive profits for Glaxo, led toward new challenges by the firm hand of its chairman Paul Girolami. They enjoyed internal growth, first of all, with the arrival in the "pipeline" of a group of new drugs and the maximization of profit rates, and external growth through several ambitious acquisition plans.

Girolami and, even more, his right arm Ernest Mario (ex-CEO of Squibb, the American laboratory based in Princeton) were certain of one thing. Glaxo could make it to the leading group of the great pharmaceutical companies of the world. And if Glaxo can, Glaxo must! There was no hint of the timid management style with humanitarian overtones that prevailed at Wellcome (another British laboratory that its new leader, John Robb, a consummate businessman with unrivaled experience in pharmacy, was hopelessly trying to bring into the modern age of marketing). Offense, energy, boldness, profit, cash flow, and combat management became the watchwords of the manufacturers of Azantac, as they set out on the road to win the place that was their due.

Management has to do with products, but also with personnel, and Glaxo selected them with the greatest of care. Richard Sykes came in as a researcher in the antibiotics division in 1972, and in 1984 returned to home base after a sojourn at Squibb, where he had acquired solid skills in marketing. Nurtured by Ernest Mario, who had noticed him at Princeton, this great beanpole of an Englishman with his fine gold-rimmed glasses and quiet suits joined the board of directors in 1987. In reserve, already, "Glaxo" Republic.

Edwin Nathan didn't ask anything more than to follow him in the upper echelons of the company. A go-get 'em type, and courageous, this social psychologist by education liked to quote Sun-Tzu, the Chinese theorist of *The Art of War*. Having been a sales representative and then a consultant and student at the London Business School, Nathan was appointed marketing director of Glaxo France in 1984 by the chairman,

Christopher Adam. In five years, this tandem quadrupled the subsidiary's turnover, taking it from roughly $50 million to over $200 million. In 1989, Glaxo France became the eighth largest French laboratory with a 60% market share in anti-asthmatics and 50% of the market for anti-ulcer medications.

To get there, nothing was spared: especially not staff training and motivation through a war-like regime including marketing seminars, and strategic seminars for managers and, for the others, training courses that were called "boot camps" or "weapons camps". Nathan did not hide what he was up to. The pharmaceutical industry is business, and business is war. "Demand faster results, to save time vis-à-vis the competition (the enemy to be killed), and know how to take risks. Be more concerned with results than with men, for if you take care of results, you will inevitably take care of the men since without them, no result is valid for long. Create a climate of winners and don't accept any excuses. Always seek innovation and destabilization. Think differently from the rest of the profession. Lastly, put the executives under stress by creating a siege mentality to repel attacks from all challengers."

Ernest Mario, Number 2 of the international group, used similar martial language. According to him, it was thanks to its "sales force" of 9,500 people that Glaxo was able to respond to the demands of a global pharmacy market where, equipped with a new drug, the company must "gain its share of the market as quickly as possible before the rival firms can bring competing brands to market". And Glaxo leapt from success to success, until the day when. . .

Why Have You Come, Losec?

Known in France as Mopral and in the United States as Losec (which we will use from now on, for convenience), *omeprazole* seemed to be a formula with many anti-ulcer properties. Among other things, it permits the treatment of evolutionary duodenal ulcers, evolutionary gastric ulcers and oesophagitis from reflux. This drug hunted on the same grounds as Azantac; its inventor, the Swedish company Astra, made an alliance with a "heavy-weight" in the sector, the American "elephant" Merck, Sharp & Dohme.

Astra, created in 1913 at the initiative of 424 doctors and pharmacists, was eighteenth largest manufacturer in the world and the second largest Scandinavian laboratory. It was a very innovative firm, devoting 16% of its turnover to research, which was conducted at five decentralized units (four in Sweden and one in Great Britain). In 1979, the group selected Losec, among 500 other substances, to be tested on human subjects. Three years later, the results of the phase I, phase II and phase III studies caught the attention of the international conference on gastroenterology in Stockholm, filling Losec's "fathers" (Ivan Ölstholm, Sven Erik Sjöstrand and Enar Carlsson) with pride.

Losec was launched in 1988, with resounding success. By 1990, it was third in the world, behind its rivals Tagamet and Azantac, with approximately 20% of the market share in France (the first foreign country to have granted it market authorization on April 15, 1987), the Netherlands, Switzerland, and Belgium. In 1991, it was a drug leader in Sweden, and was being marketed in 60 countries. In 1992, it had a spectacular début on the American market.

Glaxo's leaders were already aware of the danger. The new formula was a direct threat to Azantac, which they had had such difficulty in making the most- consumed drug in the world (at the expense of Tagamet). A vigorous reaction was required; and the time factor would be decisive.

The first phase of the counter-attack developed in July 1989 with an insert in a special supplement of the *Internal Medicine World Review*. This supplement enjoyed an "educational grant" from Glaxo. Ostensibly dealing with recent advances in gastroenterology, the promotional document went into great detail about a meeting of the FDA's GI Drug Advisory Committee on March 15. In fact, the article was mostly about Losec, mentioning the possible risks of mutagenicity that appeared in experiments dosing rats with elevated amounts of the medication. This was the first blow to the Swedes.

The FDA does not like polemics. In the autumn, it let Glaxo know that the magazine supplement "was lacking in equity and presented in an inappropriate way the deliberations of the GI Drug Advisory Committee. It exaggerated the possible risks associated with prescribing Losec and, at the same time, ignored the fact that the potential benefits of Losec exceeded those that might be expected from a prescription of Azantac in similar cases".

Dotting their "I's" and crossing their "T's", the feds went on to state that they viewed this initiative as "an apparent effort by [your] firm to discredit Losec unfairly, via scientific/educational activities preliminary to its being replicated as a generic drug". Glaxo defended itself, declaring that no member of its staff had delivered information nor influenced the technical contents of the supplement to the *Internal Medicine World Review* before it was published.

There could be no question of giving up, even so. The second round began in 1990 in the columns of the *Lancet*. On January 27, two letters from physicians named Losec as a possible cause of gastric inflammations. On February 17, the pressure was accentuated. The *Lancet* published two contradictory articles under the general title "Studies of genotoxicity of drugs that inhibit gastric acids". The first was the fruit of works by Drs Burlinson, Moriss, Gatehouse and Tweats, who proclaim their affiliation with Glaxo Group Research Ltd, the research unit of the British laboratory. The second was the work of Drs Ekman and Bolcspoldi, of Astra, and their colleagues MacDonald and Nicols, Research Department of Merck, Sharp & Dohme, which had allied, as you may recall, with the Swedish group in the marketing of Losec. An editorial entitled "*Omeprazole* and genotoxicity" preceded the two texts.

Tumor alert! According to Glaxo Group Research, Losec appeared to be carcinogenic. Scalpel well in hand, Burlinson, Moriss, Gatehouse and Tweats went straight for the jugular: "A primary carcinoma was observed in the stomach of a rat after completion of a study of carcinogenicity associated with Losec, whereas no tumor had been noted beforehand in this rat's forebears." Further, they refined their point, saying that: "The critical difference between *loxtidine* and Losec may be the latter's capacity to act as an incitator agent (through its genotoxic properties) and as an instigator (through its effects on cellular proliferation), allowing the expansion by cloning of initiated cells, which is the basis of the progressive stages of carcinogenicity."

One suspects that the Astra-Merck team would hold the opposite opinion, since Drs Ekman, Bolcspoldi, MacDonald and Nicols conclude: "Long term studies in which Losec was administered to a rat for more than two years, to a mouse for over eighteen months and a dog for over a year did not produce any proof of carcinogenicity potential, in the stomach or elsewhere."

The Postman Always Rings Too Loudly

The debate might have remained at the scientific level, but Glaxo was spoiling for a fight. It was far too tempting to use these results in its public relations communications. The British laboratory started by writing to Astra and to the *Lancet*, "officially" warning them of the dangers that Losec represented. Then came an assertion by Richard Sykes, Director of Research and Development at Glaxo, to *The Financial Times*. "This test cannot be rejected as 'a marketing trick'. The results raise important questions that must be taken into account and lead to an independent evaluation by the international scientific and medical community."

Astra, a medium-sized manufacturer in global terms, was not used to using such virulent methods of competition. Disconcerted, the Swedish firm responded as best it could, questioning its accusers' scientific methodology. Shortly thereafter, in May 1990, Astra produced its own study on Azantac, before launching an advertising campaign centered on the slogan "With Astra, ulcers are a thing of the past" — on the British market, its rival's stronghold. This, in turn, drew a harsh response from Glaxo: 1. Ulcers are a recurrent disease, therefore nothing can rid you of them forever, not even Losec; 2. We developed a formula similar to that of Astra, and we chose not to put it on the market because of its potential dangers.

Far from leaving it at that, the British group then intensified its attacks at the international level. In December 1989, Astra's sales representatives in France anxiously advised their bosses that an article entitled "Controversy over treating hypersecretion disorders with *omeprazole*" had been just distributed to hospital doctors and private gastroenterologists. A speedy inquiry revealed the truth: the flyer was none other than a French translation of the litigious document from the *Internal Medicine World Review*! Simultaneously, the results of a controlled "survey" appeared in the waiting rooms of many doctors' offices (the question asked was: "If you learned that a drug causes carcinogenic tumors in animals, would you accept having it prescribed for you?"). And naturally, Losec came out badly in this rather specific "general questionnaire".

Rumors were spread simultaneously: Astra, now beginning to question its quality, was supposedly on the verge of halting the marketing of its leading product. This was perfectly false, but that kind of noise is likely to dissuade doctors from prescribing Losec.

Was that the desired effect? And if so, who was wielding so skillfully the deadly pen of disinformation? The magazine *Challenges* set out to find out, under cover of anonymity. It managed to get one of the leaders of Glaxo France to provide only this frankly paradoxical explanation: "And who says that it is not some guys from Astra putting out this rumor themselves, in order to try to discredit Glaxo, eh?"

Elementary, my dear Glaxo. But hadn't SunTzu laid it all out precisely: "When you are on difficult terrain, move quickly; when you are surrounded, invent stratagems; when you are in mortal circumstances, fight"? The heads of Astra France, conforming to the precepts of the Chinese master strategist, sued their assailant in the commercial court of Paris. Considering that distributing the *Internal Medicine World Review* article constituted slander and an act of unfair competition, they asked the courts to prohibit the distribution of any document, leaflet or brochure liable to tarnish Losec's reputation, with a penalty of $20,000 for any infringement.

The matter seemed to have been settled. Before the judge, on February 21, Glaxo made a commitment to "cease the distribution of selected excerpts" from the *Internal Medicine World Review*. But fifteen days later, the company made an abrupt about-face. Asserting that there was a very significant scientific controversy as to whether Losec was harmless, it solicited the Paris Court of Appeals to annul the submitted ordinance. But the court established by injunction on April 26, 1990 that "the first judge considered, with good reason, that distributing the article in question constituted an obviously illicit act, characterized by an unfair competition", confirming the decision and sentencing Glaxo to cover the trial expenses.

Ernest Mario, General Manager of Glaxo International, admitted to journalists from *The Economist* in April 1991 that the pharmaceutical market had changed greatly in recent years; very often under his company's initiative, he added.

Every time they developed a new drug, their laboratory organized expensive symposiums. Does that count as psychological manipulation? No, answered Mario, companies simply use these events to assess a product's market potential. The team from *The Economist* then turned to another problem: "under cover" promotion of medical products — denounced by Dr. Bill Inman, of the Drug Safety Research Unit, a humanitarian organization based in Southampton. According to him, when a new product was launched, Glaxo and certain other companies set up small-scale studies in order to evaluate their drug's performances. However, the "subjects" of these studies were recruited from within the normal population and not from panels selected according to any medical criteria suitable for clinical trials. Theoretically, this was in order to keep an eye out for any undesirable effects, but the doctors who conduct these studies are remunerated, so that one has to doubt the objectivity of the test scheme. This argument was not in the least disturbing to Mr. Mario, who does not think that post-marketing studies are unethical.

Blue as Hades

So everything was going well. . . except for Glaxo Group Research. Its conclusions were being criticized more and more. As were the parallel conclusions revealed by the Japanese doctor Furihata before the European Society of Mutagenesis in 1990.

It doesn't take a brain surgeon to figure out the reason for this growing skepticism. As Losec's sales exploded, throughout the world (and particularly in the United States where they had tripled since 1991), exceeding $300 million, the doctors' fears had waned. The genetic damage that had been forecast with such great clamor had still not appeared, whereas the number of patients treated by Astra and Merck's anti-ulcer formula had grown substantially.

If Glaxo's and Dr. Furihata's remarks had been well-founded, examples of the harmful effects would certainly have come to light. But such was not the case. In early 1991, Glaxo's research group even made an attempt at back-pedaling in the journal *Mutagenesis*.

A letter expressing the opinion of Dr. Rory McCloy, of the Royal Manchester Infirmary, was published on October 5. In addition to this startling text, on the same day, the *British Medical Journal* brought to its readers' attention the contributions of two eminent experts. Drs Goodlad and Wright, of the Royal Postgraduate Medical School of London, were speculating as to which conclusions should be drawn from what they themselves called a "curious affair".

"We will probably never know the reasons that led to such a premature publication [the initial text from Glaxo Group Research]. But it poses the problem of quality control over dubious data and its implications in the test programs of the internal research groups of certain pharmaceutical companies", they wrote. The third letter came from some doctors at the South Carolina School of Medicine. They did not see any tangible proof, over the course of time, of genotoxicity associated with Losec. Rather, "At present, the clinical experiments now extend to more than 15 million patients under treatment." In other words, the real numbers categorically contradict Glaxo's assertions.

How should they respond to this barrage? At first, the British firm pretended to stick to its guns, supporting Dr. Furihata's study. But that position was not tenable. A few days later, Glaxo took a more realistic approach and gave it up, acknowledging in the *Pharmaceutical Business News* that its researchers' study in connection with Losec's potential carcinogenic effects might indeed have been biased. This was the beginning of a strategic retreat that turned into a commercial failure: Astra and Merck had gained the upper hand.

Did Glaxo's defeat contribute to the spoiling the atmosphere at the great English firm's headquarters? In 1993, a conflict erupted between Ernest Mario, who favored growth through strategic acquisitions, and Paul Girolami, who prefered to develop new drugs. Mario was dismissed. He would be replaced by Richard Sykes, who had masterminded Glaxo's absorption of Wellcome two years later, then the aborted plan to wed Glaxo Wellcome and SmithKline Beecham, a $70 billion transaction that would have made of a American-British behemoth Number One in the world of industrial pharmacy — if it had not fallen apart in February 1998 for certain fundamental reasons. People, especially.

Meanwhile, the prospects were growing dim for the respective ulcer medications of the two weakened companies. Tagamet was coming to the end of the road. Azantac, which "lost" its patent in the United States on July 26, 1997, also began to mark time. When ten generic versions hit the American market in 1997, its turnover fell by 22%, dropping to 13 billion pounds.

Losec's "carcinogenic effects" never materialized. Nobody filed any complaint. Instead, the Swedish ulcer medication developed a solid reputation for effectiveness and reliability over its nine years on the market. This product was the most prescribed in the world, in 1997, generating gross revenues of $4.5 billion, double those of Azantac; this was largely due to the pugnacity of its manufacturer.

By energetically repelling Glaxo's successive attacks, Astra and its American partner Merck managed to extend their market share: the best counterattack imaginable. In spite of their unequal sizes, these two friends of sixteen years had found a compromise that enabled them to share equitably the splendid profits from Losec, before separating for reasons of incompatibility.

Glaxo, by contrast, was still suffering from complications.

The Sumatriptan "Headache"

Initially known under the code number GR 43173, this migraine formula (from the family of serotonin agonists) was designed to take the place of Azantac, financially speaking, whose patent was due to expire in the year 2002. In the form of a subcutaneous injection, it was very expensive: approximately $30 per injection in 1991. Even in the form of a tablet to be taken in the event of crisis, it was still expensive: $12 per dosage. Understanding that these prohibitive prices were a major obstacle to Sumatriptan's widespread adoption, Glaxo's international staff decided on a two-fold strategy.

The first consisted in creating a need. To achieve this goal, they would have to create receptivity in the minds of all the "useful" targets: the medical press and the general press, doctors, associations and patients. The second phase of the operation called for intensive lobbying of the state authorities. Taking advantage of the climate of a "general demand" for this migraine medication, Sumatriptan was generously reimbursed by the public and private insurance programs.

In France, the affair was once again conducted by the masterful hand of Edwin Nathan. While increasing the pressure on the Public Health agencies, Glaxo generated a slew of eulogistic articles praising the drug's amazing effectiveness. This point was disputed, at the pharmacological level, in spite of the optimistic conclusions of the 8th Migraine Trust International Symposium of September 1990, when several studies opportunely happened to demonstrate remarkable results for Sumatriptan.

There were many articles, perhaps too many. More and more conferences were held, and journalists from all over the world were more and more freely invited to attend; the topic of "migraines, the curse of our era" began to appear with great frequency. A climate was created that encouraged enthusiasm (conditioning) in both the practitioners and the general public, always attracted by miracle cures. A climate, we might note in passing, that could only have a positive influence on the negotiations with the Health Ministry.

Alas for the British manufacturer and its French subsidiary: the hour had come for economies and the instructions were firm: to avoid excessive expenditure as long as "the black hole" of public health coverage seemed to be one of France's biggest problems. On March 16, 1992, Jean-Louis Bianco, Minister for Social Affairs, entrusted the mission of gathering information on the migraine treatment to law professor and former member of the Ethics Committee Catherine Labrusse, and François-Claude Hugues, a therapy instructor at the Laennec hospital of Paris.

This was a discreet warning that Edwin Nathan should have understood. But listening only with his fighter's temperament, a style that was suited to British manufacturing but not to the French health profession, the chairman of Glaxo France decided to force the issue. He made an offer, in the public domain, that smelled like blackmail: Glaxo was ready to invest one billion francs in constructing a factory or research center in France, provided that Paris approved its migraine medication. But headquarters considered these strong-arm tactics to be dangerous, and two weeks after these spectacular declarations, Nathan was let go. Christopher Adam took command, temporarily, and then Michel Zurmhule.

There was a change of command at the French Social Affairs agency, as well: Réné Teulade replaced Bianco. It was Teulade who would receive the Labrusse-Hugues report at the end of September 1992. In the meantime, the pressure had increased: no fewer than 18 countries had given Sumatriptan approval to advertise — including France, since market authorization had been granted. However, France had imposed considerable limitations that were not at all to Glaxo's liking: the Health Ministry was persuaded that only 50,000 to 100,000 "real migraine sufferers" could benefit from the new product, and they had no intention of opening the door to the entire French market. "Migraine: On Probation" was the title of an article in Le Quotidien du médecin — an apt summary of the conditions under which France accepted the migraine medication, which would be reimbursed only for specific pathologies.

To tell the truth, the conclusions of the Labrusse-Hugues report were far worse for the English laboratory. Its authors questioned, if they didn't condemn, Glaxo's promotional methods, stating that even the media campaign concerning Sumatriptan could be described as "advertising". These heaps of articles in the press "incited" the public to eagerly anticipate the market arrival of this anti-migraine medicine that was being portrayed as a godsend.

The campaign was centered on a dubious insistence on the drug's supposed effectiveness. "This data serves as an almost automatic preamble to every article that has been printed on this subject", wrote Catherine Labrusse and François-Claude Hugues. They criticized the success of Glaxo's "media plan" in these terms: "By now, no migraine sufferer could be unaware of this drug."

Their conclusion was equally caustic. They recommended possible legal sanctions, and they also called upon the Higher Council on Audio-Visual Supervision, the National Committee of Ethics, the National Council of the Order of Physicians, and the National Council of the Order of Pharmacists to take action, "regarding the contents, the methods and the sanctions of ethical information regarding health, and the influencing of health professions via the press, in particular when . addressed to the non-professional public".

There is no need to add anything to this vitriolic condemnation: the entire mechanism of Glaxo's promotional campaign was indicted. But the project had achieved one of its goals: to create demand. A black market in Sumatriptan was created, and the medication was being brought in from bordering countries where it was officially authorized. The President of the National Council of the Order of Pharmacists, Jean Parrot, denounced the network in *Le Monde*: "This illegal market has its roots in foreign drug stores and many other places. I have even heard of a network of taxis that has been set up to re-sell this medication."

In August 1994, the Social Affairs Ministry established a two-level prescription plan. Imigrane SC, a form of Sumatriptan recommended for "the treatment of migraine crises, when other treatments for migraine crisis have not been effective during preceding crises", would not be reimbursable. Imiject, another form of the drug, for adults only (over 15 years and under 65) who suffer from crises of vascular pain in the face, a terribly painful disorder that affects 10,000 to 15,000 people in France, would be reimbursable.

Despite its approval in a good forty countries, Sumatriptan did not achieve its goal in France: proof that the most aggressive methods of promotion are not always the most effective.

No Miracle for Viagra

But you don't have to play that rough. Following American Pfizer's example, certain groups have endeavored to play other cards, for example, that of paid persuasion. A big scandal came out when France's public television station, FR3, scheduled a promotion of *sertraline*, an antidepressant from Pfizer. Five thousand experts were the intended viewers. But the TV unions exposed the plan, and the outrage lingered on for months. In March 1997, FR3 filed a complaint for "fraud, theft and concealment".

The $50 billion "blockbuster", the *sildenafil* formula (in other words, Viagra), had an even more spectacular media launch. Even before crossing the Atlantic, this treatment for male impotence was preceded by a flattering reputation as a "winning formula from the Pfizer group". Building on the effusions of the already seduced U.S. press — which went as far as to call this "a new era in lifestyle drugs" — certain French commentators heralded the drug as a "revolution" in our way of life.

Seduced, did you say? Viagra caught the attention of the French media, and enjoyed an outpouring of free publicity. This was a rare, an extremely rare level of fanfare: all the conditions of success seemed to be coming together.

The commercial miracle did indeed occur in the United States, with 2,700,000 prescriptions written between March 26, 1998 (the date it arrived on the market) and the year's end, giving Pfizer a historical $3.35 billion net profit. But it was not replicated in France. Only 100,000 patients received Viagra prescriptions between its official début on October 15, 1998 and January 15, 1999. It is true that a grey market had developed via Internet. Pharmaceutical retailers were offering the drug at a discount, without a prescription — a practice that did not help Pfizer's business any more than it did Sanofi, whose products had been praised (wrongly) as "sexual stimulants". Obviously, the new commercial phenomenon that appeared on the Web, that of parallel sales, brought with it its own share of disinformation.

Viagra's semi-failure in the French market shows, in any case, that just because something is good for the American pharmaceutical industry, that doesn't mean that it inevitably can be imposed on the rest of the world. There is no reason to think that Europeans, by defending their own way of life, cannot at the same time encourage their own economic interests, following the example their competitors in America.

The Europeans do not always doggedly defend their interests.

However, it pays to fight. While the European pharmaceutical industry, badgered by its American rival, staggered and almost fell, Airbus
did not yield — in spite of competitors' attacks that were every bit as
underhanded.

CHAPTER 5

LOW BLOWS AT HIGH ALTITUDE

Every month in the mid-1960's, the salons of La Truite Saint-Honoré in Paris played host to a rather special group of guests. There were twelve of them; like the apostles. Twelve men who, between the aperitifs, the pears and cheese, spoke freely about the past, the present and the future.

It was a happy time. How warm it was, there, so close to the palace of the Elysée, two steps away from the President. For these monthly reunions were sanctioned by the de Gaulle regime. Our twelve apostles of La Truite Saint-Honoré, veterans of either the free French Air Forces (such as General Fourquet), or of the domestic Resistance in the image of Jean Sainteny, were Gaullists through-and-through, with unshakable convictions; nonetheless, they did cultivate their own secret gardens. They may have baptized this little abstract society the "Charles Club", but it was not in honor of the man who brought us the 18th of June (when De Gaulle rallied the French to overthrow the Fascists) but in remembrance of another Charles. This World War I ace, now deceased, had been the pilot-instructor of several of them in Great Britain; his surname had slipped their minds. Only their memories and comradeship remained.

Thin as a reed in his no-nonsense three-piece suit, hair slicked back, glasses thick as a Coke bottle, speaking abruptly with a cigarette clamped in the corner of his mouth, the youngest and newest member of the club stood out amidst his elders. Jacques Chirac completed his studies at the ENA*, not on the airfields. He saw neither the Battle of England, nor those of the Liberation. The echoes of his victories can be heard only within the small world of the Ministerial offices and the higher realms of public administration.

Even so, Prime Minister Georges Pompidou's representative could pride himself on having some elementary knowledge of aeronautical matters. By family tradition: before the War, his father Abel had been general manager of the Potez factories. As a child, young Jacques met all the major airframe manufacturers of the time, and even sat on the lap of the legendary Marcel Dassault. In 1962 he met "Cloclo" — Pierre Clostermann — the Free French ace fighter pilot with 33 confirmed air victories, a writer, Gaullist deputy, and deputy manager of the Rheims-Aviation Aeronautical Company. The two men hit it off, in spite of the age difference, and the aviator had the ENA alumnus admitted as a junior member of the Charles Club on an exceptional basis.

Little Aeronautical Plots between Friends

In addition to the pleasure of finding oneself among friends around a good meal, the monthly meetings at La Truite were occasions to invite guests of honor. The man of the hour was Henri Ziegler, CEO of the Louis Bréguet Aviation Workshops.

In Gaullist circles, this central figure of the French aircraft industry was known as "Zig". An innovator and a man of action, he was born in 1906 in Limoges. He was an engineer and an alumnus of the École Polytéchnique, a test pilot, and deputy manager of an Air Force aviation test center. Ziegler did not weep for one moment over his beautiful lost professional future when, in 1941, he jumped with both feet to join the

---

*The École nationale d'administration, the principal graduate school for future public officials in France.

clandestine resistance movement before making it to London. "Colonel Vernon" of the Free French Air Force, in 1944 he molted into a chief of staff of the FFI under the command of the future marshal Koenig.

Zig took full advantage of these varied experiences. His stay in London during the war enabled him to become familiar with the arcana of the British aircraft industry. Another foreign visit, to the United States this time, gave this committed observer the opportunity to size up America's industrial power. This led him to produce an official report in August 1945 when, after a clear-sighted analysis of the causes of "the forfeiture of a country that had long held the lead in world aviation", Ziegler put to paper these daring lines: "The future of our aircraft industry rests on European cooperation", the only means of counterbalancing the giants on the other side of the Atlantic — Douglas, Lockheed and Boeing.

These were giants who, in spite of their size, had no qualms about delivering one low blow after another. Ziegler knew it. He had seen it when, as head of Air France, he had supported against all the winds and tides the plan for the SE-210 Caravelle, France's best chance of returning to "the greats" of civil aeronautical engineering.

The Caravelle in a Trap

The Caravelle: a jewel. On May 27, 1955, this "jet" with the fine silhouette, its two engines placed on the tail — an innovation — took its first (quite successful) flight. And on May 15, 1959, only seven months after the Boeing B-707 went into production for commercial use with Pan Am, the French apparatus was simultaneously making its début at Air France and SAS, the Danish-Swedish-Norwegian company.

Surprise: it was a success! A technological success, since it turned out to be of excellent quality; and a psychological success as well, with thousands of enthusiastic young Frenchmen decorating their rooms with models, miniatures, and photographs of the new plane. General de Gaulle, who had returned to business, spoke lyrically about "the beautiful, the fair, the sweet Caravelle". Still, they had to market and sell this symbol of aeronautical pride somewhere beyond the hexagon of France and a handful of European companies. In the United States, for example...

Just such an opportunity seemed to be taking shape. In February and September 1959, the Electra four-engine turboprop jet had two successive accidents, making trouble for Lockheed, its American manufacturer. In spring 1960, the federal authorities grounded this potentially defective aircraft.

An even less enviable fate awaited the British middle-distance craft, the Vickers Vanguard, which was suspected of hidden flaws. Rumors, not all of them spontaneous, lumped together the fourteen accidents involving its little brother the Vickers Viscount and the much less serious propulsion problems of the Vanguard. Soon, it was all over: a victim of the secret economic war between Europe and the United States, this promising aircraft fell through the trap door.

Was this Opportunity knocking? Certainly, the Caravelle was relatively small for the needs for the American aviation companies, its speed a little "conservative", its operating range limited. But necessity makes the laws. And that is what impelled the American airlines to violate the fundamental rule of buying "all-American", whereby in the United States one prefers to buy only machines that are made in the U.S.A. William Patterson, head of United Airlines (number one in civil aviation), was first to cross the line. Under a hail of criticism, he announced his intention to order 20 Caravelle VI-R's, an improved version of the basic model.

Here come the French! This cry of alarm could not go unheeded in Seattle, Washington, Boeing's stronghold. But decisions are made quickly in Seattle. The proof: a team of prospectors was already packing its suitcases to go to Toulouse.

Naturally, Sud Aviation welcomed these *missi dominici* with open arms. Without a local partner, nobody ever made it into the American market. Boeing's initiative might offer the French manufacturer a widow to this so greatly anticipated opportunity. The Seattle giant talked about building the Caravelle under license in the United States, the only means of marketing the French short-distance-carrier there with any chance of success.

Georges Héreil, an old friend of Zig and head of the French national airline, could hardly disguise his skepticism. Behind Boeing's proposal, he had a presentiment of some astute duplicitous maneuvering. Boeing's most probable objective was to nail the French rival to the floor while it found a way to produce a 100% American, even 100% Seattle, replacement.

Double Cross

No risk, no gain. Rather than retreating to its home base and waving French flags, Héreil decided to go size things up on the spot. There being no direct flights between Paris and Seattle, the head of Sud Aviation made a stopover in New York. Walking along a corridor, he stumbled into Donald Douglas Jr., a true father's son, who was also in transit. And as aeronautics is a small world where everyone knows everyone else, are our two travelers greeted each other with good cheer. This demonstration of mutual cordiality was reported word by word in an astonishing dialogue in Lew Bogdan's book *L'Epopée du ciel clair* [*The Epic of the Clear Sky*]:

— Georges! Georges, where are you off to?

— My dear Donald, I am on my way to see your enemies at Boeing. Know why?

— Ha, ha, ha. . . You're wasting your time with Boeing?

— Yes, I think I am. . .

That's was a significant quasi-admission. Douglas Jr., all his teeth bared against Boeing (whose 707 had overtaken the DC-8), smelled an opportunity. As a good descendant of the Scots, he knew how to turn adversity to his advantage:

— Better come with me. . . It's better at Long Beach.

Long Beach, the California stronghold of Douglas Aircraft Co., no less! What a day for surprises. And Héreil, tacking back and forth, decided to yield to this diversion by the airframe manufacturer. On February 10, 1960, there were smiles, handshakes, a model of the Caravelle and the flash bulbs of photographers. The two manufacturers initialed the contract of cooperation that would now link their two companies. Douglas thus acquired the right to build the Caravelle under license in the United States, a "deal" that Boeing had so coveted. The Long Beach firm became its partner's sales representative in Great Britain, Japan, Australia, Anglophone Africa, the Middle East, India, Pakistan, and various other Asian countries. In short, all the zones where Sud Aviation lacked a sales infrastructure.

Three days later, the first French atomic bomb exploded in the Sahara. On the strength of technological and industrial successes inherited from the 4th Republic, General de Gaulle wanted at all costs to signal his independence from the United States. This startling demonstration of sovereignty could only reinforce the U.S. manufacturers' aversion for the Caravelle, symbol of French aeronautical renaissance.

More down-to-earth reasons were also at play. The people at Long Beach were only thinking of preserving the market of their DC-8, which had gotten off to such a difficult start, and that of the future DC-9·that was very close to the Caravelle in design. . . the French twin-jet aircraft might take a slice out of both pies. So there could be no question of treating this enemy as an ally.

Sun Tzu explained two centuries ago: to neutralize an adversary, one can use either confrontation, or ruse; preferably the second. Douglas shared this analysis. By signing with Long Beach the contract that he was afraid to sign with Boeing, Héreil was trapped. The proof came when it turned out that Douglas folks never sold one of the Sud Aviation twin-jet aircrafts governed by this still-born agreement. Not one. The opposite, rather, was more true: Jackson McGowen, dynamic sales manager for the American manufacturer, sent his sales shock troops off to tout the new Caravelle as a "bad plane", "dangerous", and "poorly designed".

Anything was fair game in disparaging Sud Aviation's twin-jet, and underhanded attacks were frequent. Drawing their attention to the unreliable Caravelle's two-seat cockpit, which would eliminate the job of the third pilot, the sales team swayed the pilots' unions. (This pretense of defending the personal interests of the flight personnel was a technique of disinformation that would later be applied at the expense of Airbus.)

Every effort was made to tarnish the Caravelle's reputation, to gain time to market the DC-9 — the French twin-jet's hardly more mature "big brother", which actually conducted its first flight only in 1963. Psychological maneuvers, financial stratagems, intrigues of every kind, the whole panoply of indirect hits would be implemented to weaken this irremediably trustful partner. McGowen's men managed to pick up SAS, one of the Caravelle's two "early adopters", and Swissair, which had for a long time dedicated itself to becoming a European stronghold for Douglas, as British Airways is a stronghold of Boeing.

The attack was not limited to the Continent. The "Yankees" did not believe the South American continent had real commercial prospects. But when Sud Aviation landed its first contract with Brazil, they abruptly changed their minds. In Bolivia, Chile, and Paraguay, the airlines bosses and the local politicians were suddenly subjected to a barrage of "gringo" verbal abuse for the Caravelle, by salesmen, lobbyists, members of Congress and, why not, masters of corruption.

The French learned a bitter lesson. The Douglas "window of opportunity" was only a cheap tromp l'oeil. The window had hardly opened, and it was slammed shut. The manufacturer suffocated. Despite its technological success, the Caravelle was transformed into a commercial failure. By March 15, 1973, the date the last model was delivered, only 278 specimens were sold — enough to satisfy the national self-respect but far too little to make any money.

De Gaulle versus de Gaulle

This reality irked Henri Ziegler more than anyone. A man of the tarmac and runways, an aviation man through and through, Zig spoke his mind. He was quick to tell his twelve buddies at La Truite that the planned Concorde — that new whim of the technocrats and politicians — would go down in flames. And before this friendly audience, he honed with pleasure the already sharp edges of the uncompromising report that he was about to present to his own boss.

The Concorde adventure was a bit of de Gaulle versus de Gaulle. He always had a specific idea of European cooperation. It would be controlled by Paris (which didn't owe anything to anybody, least of all the Americans), and the French-German linkage was to involve primarily the nations of the Old Continent, under the doubtful eye of London. It was much later that the Brits would join in, when things were so far advanced that they would be constrained to leave the "Big One" and to relinquish some of their special ties with the United States. This was an approach that the General, fascinated by the futuristic aspect of the plan for a French-British supersonic jet, a transatlantic stone thrown into Washington's garden, neglected for once.

Out of anti-Americanism? Maybe so, but the reverse is also true, if not more so. Fear of being overtaken by the French-British consortium pushed Washington to launch an alternative program, 100% American, for the SST (Supersonic Transport) and to make it a national priority. And in this case, as in most, the American logic prevails: presenting a unified front against the foreigner but, inside, giving free rein to the battle for advantage between American firms. The Federal Aviation Administration, the Pentagon, NASA, the Department of Transportation, the Civil Aviation Board all set to work at top speed to ensure the supersonic's success. As did the big manufacturers, Boeing, McDonnell-Douglas and Lockheed, who also waged a brutal war in the hopes of winning this "contract of the century"!

As a federal program, the SST was of interest to the entire American "intelligence community". The secret services set out down the economic warpath. To coordinate the government departments' and federal agencies' anti-Concorde activities, a committee of presidential advisers on supersonic transport was set up under the aegis of Robert

McNamara, the Secretary of Defense and a former director of Ford, the shining star of American industry.

They had all sorts of tricks up their sleeves. On May 21, 1964, CIA Director John McCone promised to Joseph Califano, McNamara's assistant and First Executive Secretary of the Committee, a detailed report on "the Concorde's progress and its operational calendar; along with the British engineer's opinion on some of the problems and questions raised in the memorandum addressed to the President". He didn't specify, obviously, the name of the Agency's British "mole" within the Concorde program. . . One week later, a State Department analyst, lieutenant-colonel Robert Pursley, provided Califano with a copy of an annotated internal report from the Sud Aviation-British Aircraft Corporation.

Nothing was left out: technological, industrial and even political signals, with a marked predilection for the least harbinger of a break-up between the Brits and the French. Regular reports were sent to the President. The systematic "monitoring" would intensify in the years to come, but at this point it was already verging on the intolerable.

The line was almost crossed at the beginning of 1965, when the U. S. Treasury Department proposed to try the following deception: to make the French and British believe that due to a series of technological advances, the Americans would be able to launch the SST in 1970, seven or eight years earlier than original estimates. This operation, devised by Daniel Edwards, one of the Treasury "egg heads", would break the back of the European supersonic. "Under such pressure", he suggested, "the originators of Concorde might accelerate their program and end up building a very uneconomical aircraft".

The Washington analysts hesitated for weeks before rejecting this idea, which they described as too dangerous. That tells us how much the French-British partnership disturbed and worried the Americans. They were not dealing with a trivial adversary: even if de Gaulle was unaware of all the Treasury Department's plans, he must have been tickled by such a show of aggression with regard to the Concorde. But, by leaving aside for once his own vision of Europe, the French President committed a double error — a political one, in that no rift was created in the Anglo-Saxon tribe, and an industrial and commercial error, since the project's financial failure exceeded the most malicious forecasts: of the minimum production forecast of 200 aircraft, 16 Concordes were sold during the first years to British Airways and to Air France. And that was all. They had sketched out the plans for a true technological wonder without worrying about its potential market. The Americans, acting more prudently, halted the SST program in March 1971.

Ziegler, a fan but not a blind follower of de Gaulle, was one of the few experts to deplore this mistake. His job was not only to manufacture planes, but also to sell them. Without making any explicit reference to traditional de Gaullian views of European matters, he chose to defend a different plan, one that was better thought out, better constructed. In short, a plan that was conceived to succeed. To test the idea, what better audience than our twelve accomplices from La Truite?

"There is an alternative to the Concorde," Zig interjected.

And he pulled out from under the table a tube of paper, which he unrolled in silence.

"What we have to do is this. It is called the Aerobus."

No one was calling it "Airbus" yet, but this was already the plan for the A-300, which would be the first-born product of the European consortium. The members of the Charles Club, captivated, listened as their friend spelled out the broad outlines of the vision, with persuasive ardor and precision. They sat until 4:00 listening to their youngest member, Jacques Chirac.

"Mr. Ziegler, your plan is not . . . I will speak to the Prime Minister about it."

Did the future French president suspect that this adventure would turn into a merciless brawl with the United States?

Becoming a Legend

It was during an Alaska fishing party in the same year, 1965, that Juan Trippe, head of Pan Am and friend of American presidents (and their collaborators and secret services) and his old buddy William Allen (who succeeded Bill Boeing in Seattle in April 1945) decided to launch together a long-distance civilian passenger aircraft of unimaginable size, the Boeing B-747 "Jumbo-Jet".

The two businessmen and their wives had chartered John Wayne's private yacht, the Wild Goose. In a series of private conversations, Trippe and Allen talked about the C-5 A Galaxy, the official designation of the giant troop transport that the chiefs of the U.S. Army were envisaging. The Pentagon had launched an invitation to tender bids and, without waiting to be asked twice, the American eternal "enemy-sisters", Lockheed, Douglas and Boeing, all dove in, hoping to make off with the juicy contract.

Based on the experience it had garnered in the construction of the giant B-52 bomber, which had been flying without a hitch for a good decade, Boeing thought it was best-positioned. Its contacts at the Pentagon confirmed that from the technical standpoint, the Seattle plan was the best. Too bad, it was also the most expensive! $2.3 billion for only 115 airplanes. Once again, Robert McNamara had raised his eyebrows. The Defense Secretary was calling for a systematic policy of "minimum costs". Nothing horrified this top-flight technocrat more than exaggerated expenditure. Nothing pleased him more than costs being cut to a minimum.

His acute sense of economics worried Allen. Did the man from Seattle have a presentiment that at the last moment Lockheed, clever as it was, would get below the fateful bar of $2 million per unit and take over the market? The fact was that, during this party in Alaska in the heart of summer, he was thinking of only one thing: to capture the civilian market for his scheme for very large passenger aircrafts.

This idea seems to have come from Juan Trippe, a character straight out of an American saga. His first name did not much suit this great-grandson of a Cuban businessman and grandson of a bank robber and a barmaid. He was largely of Irish descent — so he was endowed with a taste for impossible challenges. A Yale graduate and friend of the oil tycoon William Rockefeller, Trippe did not speak a word of Spanish. He did not need to, in fact, since aeronautical jargon was his real native language.

Tripe was hard on his competitors, and even harder on his employees. Trippe only liked people with a daring temperament. During the pre-war period, with the assistance of his right arm man Charles Lindbergh, the champion of the Atlantic, he put together Pan American Airways, the first truly global passenger flight system. And he was convinced that Pan Am, indeed, needed a very large passenger aircraft.

A civilian version of the C-5 A, perhaps?

"That's an interesting idea", answered Allen, his heart racing.

A lawyer who had been a member of Boeing's board of directors since 1930, Allen knew that the future of the Seattle firm rested on two plans that depending on the goodwill of the American authorities. It was a question of life or of death for the company: they needed to win with their version of the C-5 A, over the SST, the Concorde's American rival. But if Trippe's offer was serious, a third door was opening.

The head of Pan Am was a calculating man, and a man of bold action. His company was expected to bring in $50 million in profits by the end of the current year. That was a lot of money that would have to be reinvested advantageously. Why not in something gigantic, something new? Something never seen in civil aviation.

"If you can build that plane, Bill, do it; I'll buy it."

Coming from such an empire builder, those were not empty words.

"How many do you want?"

"Let's say 25, half of the money up front and the other half on delivery. I can't do any more than that; I'm already taking a colossal risk."

At $20 million per jet, the expected price in the long run, that makes $500 million. Feeling giddy, Bill Allen racked up one expense after another. Unlike the Galaxy or the SST, Boeing would have to commit just about all its own capital — $750 million — to the "Jumbo-Jet" adventure, without least guarantee from the government.

But how could he pass up such an exceptional opportunity with such an exceptional partner as Trippe? The two gamblers shook hands. The deal was done. Onboard John Wayne's yacht, they had placed their adventure under the most promising auspices. The rewards would soon follow. Their billionaires' wager was indeed to lead to an unprecedented commercial success.

Three decades later, the B-747 remains the largest and most expensive passenger jet on the planet. More than 1,300 units have been sold, and they fly all around the world. Air Force One, the personal jet of the president of the United States, is a member of this glorious phalanx of sky ships. And Boeing joined Coke, McDonald's, Walt Disney, Nike, Levi's and even Microsoft as one of the trademarks of global prestige that are the embodiment of the American conquest.

The Club of Defunct Airplane Manufacturers

This kind of victory doesn't come along every day. In the aircraft industry, every kind of surprise is possible. . . especially the worst, as Europeans know very well. In 1952, the English company De Havilland was the first in the world to bring a commercial jet into service: the Comet. It sold three of them to Juan Trippe. Alas, this pioneering success would be demolished by a series of fatal accidents: May 2, 1953 near Calcutta; January 10, 1954 in the Tyrrhenian Sea; April 8, 1954 in the Mediterranean.

There were no survivors. All it took to convert this revolutionary equipment into a "flying coffin" was a tiny defect, undetectable in an era when the science of measuring metal fatigue was in its infancy. One morning in June 1954, a test was conducted on the Comet, simulating the effects of wear and tear at 36 times the normal rate. The pathetic secret was revealed: a small but growing tear at the corner of the cabin window.

Exit De Havilland. And exit, soon thereafter, the American Convair, which became a humble subcontractor for is former competitors. Boeing was the third largest U.S. manufacturer, after Douglas and Lockheed; and it benefited most from the cataclysm that befell the British aeronautics industry. In July 1954, five years after the Comet's first flight, Boeing's first four-jet B-367-80's appeared (a prototype of the B-707 that would become so profitable for Seattle): 960 units sold, compared to 164 Comets, 278 Caravelles and 556 twin-jet DC-8 from Douglas. This remarkable success was followed by an even more remarkable performance by the B-727, of which 1,860 have been delivered.

The whole playing field had changed. It is not technological innovation that distinguishes the Americans from the Europeans — on the contrary, most aeronautical innovations have come from designers on the Continent. Rather, it is the aptitude for mass production and the sense of business: manufacturing to sell, and selling everything you manufacture.

Still, the two approaches should be blended judiciously. And it is the folks in Seattle who showed themselves best at that. Their fellow-American rivals were getting nowhere. It was the Hesitation Waltz at Lockheed (Burbank, California), where they can never decide for sure whether to concentrate all their energy on military planes or keep one foot in civil aviation. And it was St. Vitus's Dance at Douglas, where commercial and financial errors were piling up and, in January 1967, left it helpless vis-à-vis McDonnell, the St. Louis-based military aviation company, which took it over and formed McDonnell-Douglas.

Douglas was dead, long live MDD! Alas, it was still rough sledding. The Douglas DC-9, which launched after the Boeing 727, suffered from the assembly lines' inability to adapt to varying sales rates, and that opened a clear "runway" for the new Boeing 737. Errors were also made in the pioneering field of "jumbo jets".

A Fight to the Death between Brothers

And the circus goes on! The DC-10 and its enemy brother, the Lockheed 1011 "TriStar", were both launched in the spring of 1968; and both frantically threw themselves into a winner-takes-all competition. Clearly, the market opportunity was not big enough for two quite similar wide-body jets; and the first to market would win. Each of them moved as fast as it could, without sparing any expense. Long Beach was first to move, racking up an order for 35 DC-10's for American Airlines, one of the most coveted clients in the world.

Lockheed was badly hurt by this new turn of events. In 1972, annual sales of the DC-10 reached their historical height, while those of the TriStar were dropping off. The Douglas sales force launched an all-out assault against Lockheed, in the hopes of finishing it off. Anonymous memoranda, biased comparative data, dramatic quasi-confidential warnings and reports magically appeared on the desks of every U.S. decision-maker in the aeronautics field: airlines executives, federal agencies, and politicians from both parties. Like the Caravelle ten years earlier, it was sometimes hinted that the TriStar was an airborne coffin, sometimes a funding sinkhole. This pernicious campaign was eventually curtailed by Jackson McGowen, who was concerned not to let it go too far and jeopardize the whole industry, causing irreparable damage.

The fear of being wiped out entirely infused the underdog with a renewed will to succeed. Far from buckling under the hail of disinformation, Lockheed threw itself into the fight. The Long Beach-Burbank confrontation turned into one long sprint, each of the two adversaries exhausting itself as the people in Seattle attentively looked on. Lockheed finally gave up only in 1982, having neither won nor been defeated. 700 aircraft had been delivered: the rivals "killed each other", threatening the financial stability of both manufacturers. In an industry like civil aeronautics, where the return on investment is particularly slow, "missing a plane" is almost equivalent to signing one's own death sentence.

Let's not exaggerate: MacDonald Douglas was still alive, even if it was in serious trouble. But Long Beach kept racking up errors, and kept going back to ideas for launching different versions of its DC-10 (as a twin-jet, or with a longer fuselage) and to the idea of a technological alliance with the Dutch firm Fokker. The MD-100 never got past the prototype stage; and there was no end to the bad news. They suffered financial losses and a loss of credibility, and were unable to develop a harmonious and complete range of planes.

The Crash

Still, they had the DC-10 — a real wonder, according to the pilots. But in their game of catch-up with Lockheed, the Long Beach airframe manufacturers neglected one detail. Since their prize account, American Airlines, had a marked preference for electric control systems (as popularized by the Concorde), MDD thought they had better stick with that approach. Engineers from Convair, the subcontractor that was making the compartment doors, would have preferred to install a hydraulic lock system; they were not heeded. Moreover, the Applegate memorandum criticizing electric door operation systems was suppressed at the subcontractor's, to avoid upsetting MDD.

A drama was brewing, preceded by a series of incidents. The DC-10's compartment door was not reliable. Logically, the Federal Aviation Administration (FAA) should have forced MDD to change it, as suggested by the National Transport Safety Board (NTSB), the official organization in charge of the investigation.

Only, to some extent the FAA serves two purposes. This federal agency is tasked with defending the interests of the American manufacturers and with ensuring, with equal vigor, the safety of every plane that lands or takes off from U.S. airports. The aeronautical equivalent of the FDA, it coexists on a somewhat unfriendly basis with the NTSB. As a result, due to economic realism (and due to personal ties with the industry), economic considerations often prevail over safety considerations. As evidence whereof, the FAA prodded MDD but did not actually force it to immediately re-do the DC-10 compartment doors.

The biggest air crash to date was the product of this dreadful chain of events. MDD's deference to American Airlines, Convair's deference to MDD, the FAA's deference to MDD. And let's add the nervousness of the salesmen, who were so anxious to sell their DC-10.

Destiny was closing in. On Sunday, March 3, 1974, Turkish Airlines flight THY 981 smashed to pieces in the forest of Ermenonville right after its takeoff from Orly (Paris), killing 346 passengers from twenty different countries. In the aftermath, one of the principal faults of MDD in particular and of the Americans in general was revealed: their inability to acknowledge any inadequacy in the aircraft they build.

Could they graciously admit that the series of DC-10 accidents was probably caused by the defective compartment door locking system? The firm denied it. Our DC-10 is perfect, they protested — in spite of the accumulating evidence and the growing international emotion. They lost precious time that could never be recuperated in terms of public relations. For them and for Convair, the costs of the Ermenonville drama were mounting: $80 million in compensation to the victims' families after 300 lawsuits, plus $40 million to — finally — make the engineering changes that had been necessary from Day One.

As an immediate consequence of this terrible reversal, Douglas lost an important sale to Air Egypt, and Airbus picked it up. While DC-10 sales fell, sales of the TriStar were going up, and reached their highest level since it was launched. In Burbank, there was gloating. That was a serious mistake: one year later, a storm came from Asia to shake Lockheed and then the entire American aviation engineering industry.

Rokkiedo Jiken, the "Japanese Watergate"

"And what is most disturbing of all, we will prove that for years Lockheed made an agent of an eminent leader of the right wing militarist faction in Japan and gave him millions of dollars in fees and commissions. The U.S. government's foreign policy is vigorously opposed to this conduct and to Lockheed's foreign policy, which helped it to stay alive through subsidies that were paid to support the company's sales programs in Japan."

Thus spoke Frank Church, on February 4, 1976, one and a half years after Richard Nixon's forced resignation. A democratic senator from Idaho and president of the Senate Board of Inquiry on corruption, he chose this occasion to drive the stiletto home. The character whom he thus depicted for the public had a dark past. A top-flight spy and former Minister of Finance for the special services of the Mikado in Shanghai, Kodama Yushio had been interned by the Americans in 1946 as a war criminal, then released without trial.

This shadowy man needed only a decade to grow into the key go-between in a hub of relations between the Nipponese underworld, the famous Yakusas, the far Right and the Democratic Liberal party (PLD) that was in power in Tokyo. In 1958, Lockheed recruited him as a salaried agent of influence. That was a judicious — if not moral — choice, since Kodama managed to force the Japanese Air Force to buy Starfighter combat jets, the Burbank firm's superstar product.

Without ever having met him, Carl Kotchian (Lockheed's Chairman), was already calling this extraordinarily valuable intermediary his "Minister for Foreign Affairs" in Japan. In 1969, Kodama was assigned another Herculean task. By contract, Lockheed was to pay him $4 million for the first six TriStars sold to a Japanese airline, then $120,000 apiece up to the fifteenth unit and $60,000 apiece thereafter. Under these conditions, it is understandable that the former imperial spy did not hesitate to turn to his friends the Yakusas to initiate a series of stock exchange rumors to destabilize the president of All Nipponese Airways, Tetsuo Oba, who was guilty of preferring the DC-10 to the TriStar.

In 1971, Carl Kotchian arrived in Tokyo. Escorted by Kodama, whom he was finally meeting for the first time, Lockheed's chief placed $3.5 million on the table in his hotel room. It didn't take anything more than that to convince the various representatives of All Nipponese Air-

ways and other airlines to cancel their orders for the DC-10 and to replace them with the TriStar.

Thus began the Rokkiedo Jiken ("the Lockheed incident)", which
eventually would lead to the resignation of Prime Minister Tanaka Ka-
kuei, the Minister of Transport and Industry, and the General Secretary
of the LDP, all convicted of corruption.

In the post-Watergate context, the American public and the media were firmly decided not to tolerate any evasion of the federal laws.
An investigation was opened under Frank Church's leadership. Under
so much pressure, Burbank soon admitted its wrongdoing, starting
with Kotchian himself.

The corruption discovered the Church commission, was not limited to Japan. In all, $22 million were spent on bribes in Germany,
Spain, and the Netherlands, to extract civil and military contracts. A
major contributor to the building of Lockheed's power, Dan Haughton,
resigned immediately after the Commission's meetings, and so did
Kotchian.

The scandal implicated other American manufacturers as well.
The Commission accused MDD of having paid $21 million in bribes to
"support" its sales abroad, and MDD had to accede to one of those financial arrangements that American law authorizes.

Boeing was suspected of having made payments of as much as $54
million. After denying everything at the top of its lungs, and after several grinding legal battles, Boeing conceded to having made "dubious
payments" amounting to $7 million in Spain, Lebanon, Honduras, and
the Dominican Republic. But Boeing's talent for responding to events,
and the profits eventually derived from the "Jumbo-Jet", consolidated
its position as Number One worldwide. In 1960, the Seattle-based
manufacturer had held only 35% of the world market for civil aircraft,
while Douglas had 39%, Lockheed 11% and Convair 14%. From this
point forward, "Big Daddy" Boeing held 70% of the market versus a little more than 20% for MDD and Lockheed combined. The Europeans

had to settle for the remainder, that is to say 7.5%, all told. And nobody planned to make them a gift of any larger share. Indeed, the first shots were already being fired at the Airbus, which was preparing to come in for its first landing in the United States.

Open Season on the A 300

The Airbus is toxic, the Airbus pollutes, the Airbus gives people rashes. At first, it was hard to believe all this. Then we had to admit the obvious. Was there any doubt? It was there in black and white, in all the newspapers, it was shown on TV, and confirmed by the neighbors. Day after day, the hairdressers and the taxi drivers discussed it with their clients. The local radios in good old Florida could talk of nothing else, and even the FAA was wondering.

That is what happens when you try to break the rules! *America first*: an American transportation company cannot and must not trust any but American technology. But Eastern Airlines dared to deal with those devils from Europe, and brought the Airbus A 300 into service on its Miami-Montreal route. And now, the stewardesses were paying the price for this irresponsibility. The poor young ladies' faces were disfigured, and the unfortunate women suffered from eczema, cutaneous eruptions and itching. According to the medical center, their case seemed desperate. There is never smoke without a fire, agreed the doctors, and of course, no rash without a cause.

The problem came from the A 300. This flying dustbin was assembled in . . . how do you say that. . . Too-loose? To-lose? Ah yes, Toulouse. . . one of those French villages with the unpronounceable names that nobody can ever find on a map. The most well-informed say it must be somewhere south of the Eiffel Tower. What difference does that make, anyway? What counts is what the media says. They had all the details, even photographs. The A 300's pressurization system took too long to start, and that was supposed to give rise to these dramatic skin problems that were plaguing Eastern's stewardesses. And strangely enough, no one bothered to ask why their colleagues, the male stewards, were not affected by this new and sexist disease, neither among the flight personnel nor the passengers.

A Dialogue among the "Pros"

If Frank Borman (Chairman of Eastern Airlines) hadn't had nerves of steel, he would have been losing sleep. Fortunately, the former cosmonaut was trained in the school of hard knocks. He was a decisive man. An emblematic figure — if not a national hero — Borman had been commander of the Apollo VIII mission around the moon in December 1968. He knew he was the only head of an airline who could negotiate with the Europeans without being immediately labeled a "traitor". And he counted on that.

The space veteran had a reliable memory. He remembered his discussions with Roger Béteille, General Manager of Airbus Industries in March 1977, in Miami. The two men had spoken quietly, like poker players — calm, resolute, serene. A dialogue of professionals:

"Since the oil crisis, fuel prices have gone out of sight," said the American. "My TriStars are costing me too much. I like your equipment, but at 200 passengers, they are a little large for our needs. 170 seats would be ideal. But we should be able to work something out. Here is what I propose: for every used TriStar that you buy from me, I will take a new A300."

The prospect of such a swap was not very appealing to Béteille. It would never work: in an era when fuel efficiency was a priority, Airbus Industries would never manage to resell the "TriStar", which were far too thirsty. On the other hand, wouldn't that give the French an invaluable opportunity to wiggle their way into the inaccessible hunting preserve of North American civil aviation? By the back door, if need be...

"I have a better idea. Take our A 300 on a trial basis. Pay us for 170 seats. If you use more, you will only have to pay us the difference."

Not a muscle moved on Borman's face. He looked impassive, but he was keenly aware of the value of this double sign of confidence: in the A 300, and in his own personal honesty. He's a beauty, a real player, this Béteille! Nothing like those bureaucrats with a rule-book for a brain that one tends to imagine at the head of France's nationalized companies. But business is business. The chief of Eastern Airlines was obsessed with his "TriStar" problem, superstars whose appetites were too big in these difficult days of high fuel costs. All over the world, airlines were pulling in their horns, a justified prudence which was not good at all for the manufacturers.

Béteille would have liked to send them all to hell, these cursed "TriStars". An engineer by training, he was an obstinate man. Mulling over the problem from every angle, he finally hit upon a solution:

"Let's try something else, Frank. If I leased you some of our A 300's, say four, for six months, that would allow you to carry out a reasonable test. With no commitment. Afterwards, we can take stock together. And do a deal, I am certain. . ."

The magic words. How could you not feel confident in this daring and highly unconventional interlocutor? Borman agreed. The two men shook hands, a simple gesture of mutual obligation.

In early May, the NASA veteran landed in Toulouse. With Bernard Lathière, head of Airbus Industries, he signed a major contract, committing to the purchase of thirty A 300's, provided the tests were conclusive. And what tests! The European plane would be tested on the Miami-Montreal route, the worst route in the Eastern Airlines network. Before leaving Toulouse, the rose-colored Mediterranean city, Borman secured some further substantial reductions. When you have taken so much trouble to get your first-born off the ground, you don't let details stand in the way. Airbus made sure nothing spoiled the mood.

A 300, a Bluebird of Unhappiness?

That was yesterday. But now, in 1977, the newspapers were piling up on the astronaut-CEO's desk. And they were full of accusations. The A 300 appeared to be both polluted and a pollutant, it was poisonous, maybe carcinogenic. Doctors were speculating, ecologists were alarmed, the pilots' unions made no effort to hide their mistrust. And the feminists, of course, took sides with the poor flight attendants.

Borman did not know which way to turn. What could be more disconcerting than this avalanche of negative articles? It was more dizzying than a space walk. There must be a scientific explanation for these skin eruptions, but what? The doctors from the federal health service, like their colleagues at Eastern, could not understand this new phenomenon at all. And meanwhile, the passengers were fearful, the competitors were laughing, and the cancellations were pouring in.

Should they break up with Airbus? Send the A 300's straight back to Europe? Borman wouldn't even think of it. That would give the competition the sticks to beat him with, and worse, would call into question his own word. Still, the cost was beginning to seem very high. There is nothing more sacred in America than hygiene. The women are afraid of getting blemishes; husbands do not want to find their wives' faces sprinkled with reddish spots. And with no reassuring medical conclusion in hand, Eastern Airlines sat right on the runway.

Béteille was no less concerned than his first (and only) American customer. The general manager of Airbus Industries was also ready to go all the way. If this rumor of eczema persisted for too long, it could mean the end of the European consortium. The A 300, the first and only model to come off their assembly lines, had only come to market three years ago, and sales were poor. As a result, white elephants, unsold units, were cluttering the Toulouse runways.

They were on the brink of financial asphyxiation. If they did not achieve the American dream, it would mean good-bye to the grand plan to produce a complete range of passenger aircraft to compete with the American giants. Unlike the Concorde, the builders of the Airbus did not see it as a single weapon; they were dreaming of a whole "family" of equipment ranging from the smallest aircraft to the largest, a war machine against the aeronautical supremacy of the United States in general and that of Boeing in particular.

Something would have to be done to save their precious child and keep it from joining so many of its litter mates in those gigantic airplane cemeteries where, emptied of their fluids, relieved of their essential accessories, these unfortunate birds sit and age under the dry sun that delays, a little, the oxidation of their metal parts.

No Orchids for Mister Airbus

Béteille remembered well the many pitfalls that accompanied the arrival of the A 300, which was guilty of impinging on the health of the American industry. There was an embarrassment of riches, when he considered the variety of ploys that had been used to hamper sales.

In 1972, Harry and Ci-ke Cho, the brothers who owned the powerful South Korean *chaebol* Hanjin that had controlled Korean Airlines for three years, started to negotiate the purchase of A 300's to expand their regional air routes. Enormous pressures were exerted to force them to change their minds in favor of a more "reasonable" solution, i.e. to purchase American equipment. Ci-ke, the junior, was kidnapped and threatened. They stuck needles under his fingernails, but the man was tough, and he did not give in. In October 1974, the Cho brothers signed with Airbus Industries. As the ultimate slap in the face to Ci-ke's torturers, they ordered five more A 300's.

In 1974, Iberia was on the verge of signing on with Airbus, and the champagne was already on ice. But one summer day, señor Insausti, head of Iberia, touched down in Toulouse in a whirlwind. To sign the contract? No, sir, to cancel it, in the wake of a barrage of "comparative tables" which are — as we will see shortly — one of Boeing's favorite commercial weapons. The heads of the Spanish national company caved in; they backed out of the deal. The hell with "continental" loyalty, Iberia would buy 727's and 747's. And several thousands guests took part in the gigantic victory party organized by Boeing in Madrid's most fashionable suburbs.

In 1977, the *Wall Street Journal* had a scoop. Negotiations were underway between Western Airlines and Airbus Industries. "Western has chosen the European Airbus", they proclaimed, apparently on the strength of some opportune "leaks" from Asia. They were false: nothing had been decided, nothing had been signed. But what does the truth matter? What matters is the scandal that followed this "revelation". Western contradicted the rumor — in vain; nobody believed them. To prove its "innocence", a company that could stoop to doing business with the French (the press had already reduced Airbus to its French component, playing on the vivid American imagination of what may be implied by state control of an enterprise) has to give better guarantees than words alone.

To top it all off, Paris had just released the Palestinian terrorist Abou Daoud, one of the organizers of the slaughter at the Olympic Games in Munich in 1972 (he had been captured on January 7 by the DST). The United States is — as we know — Israel's closest ally, and the French government's political decision went over very badly with the Americans. As badly as the pro-Arabic declarations of Mexican president Lopez Portillo, which had just cost Western Airlines thousands of cancellations for American tourists to Acapulco. Western lost 50% of its sales in fifteen days, giving the company managers plenty to think about in connection with the economic risks of competition.

In such agitated circumstances, whatever was bad for Airbus was good for Boeing. At the height of the tumult, the manufacturer suggested to its competitor, McDonnell-Douglas — very discreetly, since they take a dim view of such commercial agreements in the United States — a temporary alliance against the "European usurper".

"This is a case of absolute necessity. Let's bury the hatchet for awhile. Why don't you offer the DC-10 to Western. And we'll offer them 727's. We'll see about the rest, when the time comes.

That is an astute way of getting around the antitrust laws, which are no less applicable in the U.S. than in Europe. Under fire from all sides, Western had to give in. "Gentlemen, it's been great fight. . . but it has been lost", explained Mr. Kinsay, Western's second in command, to his partners from Airbus. Translation: "To bad for you, buddies, but your goose is cooked."

And there was a chicken in every pot, at Boeing and MDD.

Surprising Discoveries

Fortress-Eastern Airlines was the only one that was still standing up to the increasingly violent attacks and, as had happened in the early days of the Concorde, "technical problems" kept cropping up. "Borman, old man, your Airbuses are too big. The taxiways at La Guardia Airport (New York) cannot support that much weight. Landing is prohibited until further notice."

The A 300's American rivals, the DC-10 and the TriStar, are even heavier, but the astronaut got the message. La Guardia was closed to his four Airbuses, which would have to land far away, at Newark Airport, in New Jersey. That created terrible complications for Eastern Airlines.

The dice were loaded, in any event; there was no truth in the quibbling articles that filled the press, taking issue with the shape of the Airbus's landing gear — its architecture, its spacing, its wheels, its tires. Borman knew it was all bogus. Except, perhaps, the bundle of good old dollar bills that eventually (December 1978), contributed to getting the landing prohibition lifted. To save face, the Americans then forced Airbus to implement a simple change in the spacing of the components of the undercarriage.

But that was not the end of the story. For the time being, the eczema problem still had to be resolved. Far away in France, Béteille was working on it.

"Frank, there is something funny here. The problem of these rashes only comes up in the United States. Everywhere else, our A 300 is flying without the least incident. Do you mind if I send a few doctors to round out your medical team? I have three specialists from the Paris hospitals, a dermatologist, an allergist and a toxicologist; if you like, I can have them in Miami in two or three days."

Borman, who trusted his partner, did not need to formalize this initiative. As soon as they arrived, the Parisian doctors conducted tests. They went over and over not only the gestures made by passengers but also those of the crew. This meticulousness paid off: when the team's dermatologist went as far as mimicking the hostesses, conscientiously miming their "ballet" to demonstrate the use of the life jackets, he realized that the red coating on the safety equipment was coming off, especially upon contact with face cream and make-up.

And that is how the scarlet spots were getting on the hostesses' faces; that was the A 300 "disease" that spared only the members of the so-called stronger sex! The big headlines and the consumers' fantasies had done the rest, and almost "killed" the Airbus in its cradle.

Destiny decided otherwise. The 100% American-made life jackets were returned to the manufacturer. The FAA closed the file. But the U.S.-European aviation war is not over, even so.

Chapter 6

DUEL OF THE GIANTS IN THE SKY

What a slap in the face for Boeing, those photographs taken on August 25, 1998 in Toulouse. British Prime Minister Tony Blair, Noël Forgeard, the head of Airbus, and Bob Ayling, Chairman and CEO of British Airways, are congratulating each other, relaxed and laughing. Forgeard and Ayling have just signed a historical contract: a firm order for 59 planes from the A 320 family for British Airways, plus a series of options on 129 more.

Even though BA had allowed itself the luxury of offering Boeing an order for 32 B-777 long-haul carriers (including only 16 firm) as a "consolation prize", it is understandable that the men from Seattle were not happy. The equanimity and the courtesy of their London interlocutors from Heathrow had only been a cover for some an anti-American underhanded trick. They had thought they were among allies, friends of thirty years' standing, and all the while British Airways was quietly negotiating with the Europeans from Airbus.

Thus came the none-too-gentle break-up of a love affair that had been exclusive for too long. How far away those happy years now seemed, when a frustrated rival once declared that BOAC, an ancestor of British Airways, was "almost entirely in the pocket of Boeing"! How long ago, the blessed era when "Boeing-Boeing" was the title of a light-hearted comedy; when Robert Charlebois sang throughout the French-speaking lands that he would return to Montreal "in a big Boeing, blue as the sea". Gone was the age of happiness when "Nobody was ever fired from an airline for having bought a Boeing. . ." (implying that the same could not be said for Airbus) was a proverb and had the same force as a fundamental law. Faithful as Penelope to the American alliance, the leadership of British Airways made all its purchases across the Atlantic. But a sudden swell troubled the calm waters. Sensing a sea change in favor of Airbus, the Lady of Heathrow suddenly decided she was 200% European.

What could be a more wonderful posthumous homage to Henri Ziegler? "Zig" had died one month earlier, on July 24, at the very moment when British Airways' sudden shift definitively validated the "more Gaullists than de Gaulle" themes that he had been expounding 35 years earlier to his comrades at La Truite. The French pioneer of Airbus was right, all the way down the line. When victory was imminent, the Brits jumped to join the team. Soon, they would start holding out for a bigger slice of the pie. Betraying their loyalty to their former colonies, even occasionally, was a gesture that would cost dearly. Such, at least, was the opinion of the money-men from The City . . . and of their colleagues at British Airways.

Boeing's failure, coming just a week before the opening of the Farnborough Air Show that was attended by aircraft manufacturers and airlines from all over the world, came as a sharp warning to the Seattle executive office. In the wake of Airbus's success in the American wide-bodies market, where it won orders from U.S. Airways, this new setback put Boeing in an unprecedented situation. The absorption of its old American rival McDonnell-Douglas, officialized in July 1997 after much arm-twisting with the Commission, didn't even help. Ten or fifteen years before, "Big Daddy" had flattered itself that it controlled 70% of the world's construction of civilian aircraft with 100 or more seats; today, the giant in Seattle "only" has a little over half, and has to compete neck and neck with Airbus.

The European challenger was just a quarter century old and already pretending to the crown! Dreadful. Was there something rotten in the kingdom of aeronautics? Seattle was mad. "They're not playing by the rules. Producing at a loss is not an option for us, nor for our shareholders", was the curt comment from Boeing. In other words, Airbus owed its successes only to unfair practices like dumping.

Boeing Discovers Competition

More irascible than usual — and that's saying something — Ronald Woodard strode through the corridors of the head office in Seattle. At the age of 55, the head of the sales group did not consider himself a finished man. But Boeing's profits had fallen: $1.8 billion for the first six-months of 1998 versus $6 billion for the last six months of 1997, and the share price was tumbling. The board of directors was anxious; they were calling for heads to roll. Philip Condit, Chairman of the Boeing Company, was not about to put his own head on the block. He already had his scapegoat lined up; it would be Woodard-the-Aggressive.

A few days later, on August 31, the mass was sung. Exit Woodard, replaced by Alan Mulally. A brilliant choice: at 52, this computer whiz had already built an impressive resume. Father of the B-777 (together with Condit), one of the group's biggest successes, he had then headed up the military and space branch — which generates the most profits.

Woodard had hardly latched his suitcase when they were already missing him. . . in Toulouse. This outspoken man had always decried Airbus, giving it unexpected but very much appreciated publicity. Coke constantly enhanced its challenger's reputation by talking about Pepsi, and Woodard did the same for Airbus! Now, Toulouse paradoxically feared a more moderate tone from the new sales team from Seattle; indeed, regarding Airbus's plan for a very large transport aircraft, the A 3XX, they restrained themselves to the very mild comment: "If Airbus thinks that's a good idea, let them try it."

Back in the days of Woodard-the-Aggressive, they would have been saying that this super-giant, with its three bridges and 600+ seats, would fly the Europeans straight into oblivion. They would have been protesting that the A 3XX was going to end up under the Obituaries. They would have been harping that it would not live up to its promises; that it would fly poorly; that it would cost too much; that it would use too much fuel. Airlines executives would have delivered themselves of a few heart-felt sermons concerning the Jumbo-Jet, the best plane in the world, and specialized journalists would have given the world new lessons in aeronautics.

But the tone had changed — a mini-revolution whose meaning was clear to all. Boeing had just learned a new term: direct competition. The aviation giant had dubbed itself world leader in perpetuity, and all at once, this about-face from British Airways tore that pretty fantasy to tatters. From now on, the Europeans could also vie for the title of Number One. To hold onto its leadership position, Boeing knew that it would have to fight every step of the way, re-examining its internal organization and adapting its sales points to the new economic situation: the market.

In a word, Boeing would have to demonstrate a modesty the very notion of which it had forgotten, a modesty to which Airbus had had to yield in its darkest hours.

Drama at Habsheim

"Go around track!" the copilot exclaimed, but his shout was drowned out by the deafening howl of the engines.

"Shit!" spat Michel Asseline, the commander; and Airbus A 320 number 003 (brought into service just two days earlier) smashed into the trees at full speed.

Losing equilibrium at low altitude under a grey sky, the plane blasted through the Alsatian beech forest near the Habsheim flying-club, close to Mulhouse. The right wing broke off, and fuel was thrown forward. The A 320 ground to a halt in a pool of petroleum, and in a moment the fuselage and the interior of the cabin were a ball of fire.

The squealing of the trees scraped by the sides of the plane, the shock of the impact, passengers' screams and thick smoke filled the fuselage. Fighting against panic, the flight attendants organized the evacuation of the 136 people on board. The spectacle on the ground was incredible: while wounded travellers screamed for help, those who were still able were more concerned with taking photographs of the catastrophe! Asseline hauled himself out through the left window of the cockpit, then crawled back in, a few seconds later, to evacuate his copilot.

A simple Air France demo flight had just turned into a tragedy. With 3 dead and 111 wounded, June 26, 1988 was engraved as a black Sunday in the annals of French and European aeronautics.

The human loss, the pain of the families, the inevitable polemics of the post-crash discourse. . . A representative of the powerful national airline pilots' union (the SNPL), loyal on principle to his member Michel Asseline, prudently evoked the possible failure of "an apparatus built to please the engineers". Less cautious, minority trade unions castigated the two-man piloting system. They implied that "if a flight engineer had been in the cockpit, he would have been able to save the plane".

Even the legal institutions seemed to be rearing up. The senior examining magistrate of Mulhouse, German Sengelin, made several statements to the press. Considered "insensitive to the higher reasons of the State", he reproached the public prosecutor for having allowed the "black boxes" to be taken away from Habsheim without sufficient legal precautions. The head of the General Civil Aviation Administration (French homologue of the American Federal Aviation Administration) had actually given these recorders of flight parameters (as they are officially known) to the Office of Investigations of Civilian Flight Accidents, the body that was responsible for determining the causes of the drama, under the guarantee of the Minister for Transport. The procedure was not new; but it is still news. In the heat of emotion, people get carried away. Diving into the fray, some were already talking about "kidnapping", "hijacked black boxes", "destroyed evidence". It must have been "an affair of State", or more precisely a "financial-political lobby" looking to cover up its responsibilities.

There was sadness and consternation at Airbus. This pearl, this A 320 equipped with all the latest technical improvements, they believed in it with all their hearts in Toulouse, Hamburg, Bremen, Filton, Chester, Nantes and Saint-Nazaire, all the cities where the European plane is built. They still believe in it today. Launched in 1984, carried to the baptismal font by Lady Diana, the Princess of Wales herself, this 150-seat middle-distance carrier was coming on line right behind the A 300 and the A 310, earning an unprecedented commercial success: several hundred orders and options already recorded. Would the A 320, a direct competitor to the old Boeing B-737 used by a trifling 200 airlines throughout the world, be the second victim (after its unfortunate passengers) of the Habsheim crash?

The staff of the European consortium fully appreciated the commercial impact this drama would have. In civil aviation, competitors attack at two key junctures. While the plane to be built exists only on the drawing board, early persuasive maneuvers aim to keep customers from getting interested in a model that may never see the day. Thus the rival manufacturer hears a negative echo from its future client base, and the potential market for the plane is weakened on suspicion. This guerrilla operation of psychological warfare is carried out on two fronts, that of the client companies and that of the manufacturer. It has all the more chance of success when the competitor suffers from a lack of credibility — as was the case of the European consortium for so many years.

Several years of lull would follow, but it was the precarious calm before the storm. The test period being finished, the manufacturer addressed itself to various national and international authorities — the FAA in the United States, the DGAC in France, and the JAA for the

European Community. This was another hoop that had to be gotten through: their invaluable "certification" is required before the airlines can bring in a new plane to land at any airport. This crucial moment when sales take off — or don't — signals the start of the second wave of assault. Airbus, duly educated by its difficult experiences with the A 300, staunchly waited.

But it wasn't the competition that struck the first blow against the A 320, it was Destiny herself; there can be nothing more disastrous for a new apparatus than a fatal and spectacular accident like the one at Habsheim. Under indictment, Michel Asseline defended himself like a devil, rejecting all responsibility for the accident. He attacked the A 320 in order to defend himself, involuntarily giving Boeing and McDonnell-Douglas a host of arguments to use against Airbus. According to him, the plane he was piloting was flying at too low an altitude over the aerodrome because of a faulty altimeter. And another technical failure: the in-flight computer delayed the transmission of orders, and, finally, the "black boxes" had been tampered with.

His lawyer went on at length about "lies of the State". But beyond the solidarity (on principle) that one feels for a colleague, it soon became apparent that Asseline had only one sincere supporter among the pilots: his friend Norbert Jacquet. After having stormily quit the SNPL to create a small "dissenting" trade union, the SPLAF, Jacquet took the story one step further in 1994, picking up the always eye-catching topic of State lies, in a book entitled *Airbus, The Assassin Lives in the Elysée*. The only comic note in this whole sorry business: the book was published with the assistance of the Institute of Misinformation Studies!

A Funny Kind of Game

Toulouse was in tears, Seattle and Long Beach were holding their breath. Not wishing to be accused of unfair competition, Boeing and MDD rejected the idea of a making contact with Asseline. The fact remains that this media hurly-burly suited them just fine. The two

161

American firms translated into English (all's fair in love and war) the French newspapers articles that were most critical of Airbus, as soon as they were published — so many instruments of demolition that they could then disseminate amongst pilots and airlines.

The denials of the pilot on trial, added to the French press's passion for "mystery" fanned by the detective-novel episode of the disappearing black boxes, simultaneously weakened the credibility of the fledgling aircraft. It was already catastrophic for the A 320 that Asseline, obsessed with clearing his own name, would blame the altimeter; but when he challenged the control device, the "Fly-by-wire", he struck Airbus right in the heart. It was in this decisive field of innovation that the European consortium hoped to surpass the American manufacturers, whose too-long supremacy had rendered them conservative in technological matters.

The A 320 was proud of two major advances, first of all the electric drives based on innovations in the Concorde. These were revolutionary in their time, and they remain unequaled. Boeing adopted them for its B-777 only in the mid-1990's. Like a nervous system, the network of cables and tubes that connects the cockpit to the innumerable moving parts of the aircraft was replaced by electric cables. And the traditional "joy stick" was also replaced. A simple lever, the side-stick, located at the left hand for the pilot and the right hand for the copilot, provides control over every maneuver of the plane.

And that is not all. A powerful in-flight computer, guarantor of the correct operation of the aircraft, analyzes the instructions from the side-stick, translates them into signals and transmits them to the "actuators" of the ailerons, deflectors, rudders, elevators — in other words, to the plane's "muscles", the electric motors and hydraulic pumps.

It was on the marvelous in-flight computer that Asseline (who should have considered it a natural ally) was trying to pin the blame. He claimed that, like a strait jacket, this ultramodern device prevented pilots from making essential flight corrections. He claimed that this was the principle cause of the Habsheim crash (and other catastrophes to come). These attacks were reiterated and met an unquestioning echo in the public, since they corresponded to a natural mistrust of computers. If the pilots say so, said the *vox populi*, it must be true.

That's a prejudice that the manufacturers, as profit-making machines, do not find amusing. Airbus vainly rebutted the charges, declaring that on the contrary, it is the computer that prevents jerky or exaggerated maneuvers from pilots who might be alarmed by an unexpected incident; that argument ran up against a wall of disbelief. How can you explain to an already unsettled public that the computer limits the risks of crashes precisely because it does not lock up the controls, but adjusts them? How can you get anyone to understand that that is what prevents precisely those sudden yaws that the lumbering, none-too-agile jumbo-jets would not be able to withstand?

When the men from Airbus pointed out that, according to the dialogues recorded by one of the two Habsheim "black boxes", Asseline was reproached for playing acrobatics "to impress the gallery", they scored a definitive success. Thus is life: when overly technical explanations confuse the general public, personal accusations, easier to grasp, catch their attention more readily.

On March 14, 1997, the court sentenced Asseline to 18 months in prison, 6 months without probation; he appealed the decision; and on April 9, 1998 the Court of Appeals increased his sentence to 20 months in prison, 10 without probation. Without going into the rest of the details, we can affirm that by now the facts stack up largely in favor of Airbus. More than one thousand specimens have been sold, and the A 320 has flown for a decade on air routes all across the globe without any sign of becoming a "flying coffin", as its detractors predicted in a long ago era.

An era, admittedly, of a merciless commercial war.

Torpedo the A 320!

The anti-A 320 attacks were able to cause so much damage principally because they were the product of an explosive mixture of deeply-rooted fantasies. After the assassination of President Kennedy, the Vietnam War, the Watergate scandal, the forced resignation of President Nixon, the crisis of confidence with regard to the CIA in the 1970's, and the obsession with "gov-ernment plots" based on lies, the United States was devastated.

This phobia only reached its full force in France later on, in the wake of the contaminated blood scandal, the mad cow uproar and the waves of political-financial scandals that exposed the moral and civic degradation of the public powers. This fear already existed in a latent state, and to the detriment of the European aircraft consortium it combined with the Latin tendency to refuse to admit that — when it comes to aviation — the weak link is more often the human being than the machine. The A 320 entered a very dark period, and with it its manufacturer, too weak to afford a missed opportunity.

What damaged Airbus the most were the flight crews' repeated criticisms of the two-man (rather than the three-man) piloting system on wide-bodies — this was already standard on the smaller passenger. planes, but the public did not know that. The leaders of the European consortium did not forget the combat that had been played out in the shadows between 1978 and 1981. Boeing condemned the two-man piloting formula as too risky. A legitimate concern for the passengers' welfare? Sure. But the Seattle firm had other less noble reasons for its conduct: its B-767 was about to come to market, a long-haul carrier with a piloting team of three, due to come on line in March-April 1983.

Still, the argument "three pilots are twice as good as two" sounded good. Under pressure from the trade unions, Air France had already given in, against its own interests, in favor of the crew of three on the Airbus A 310. That was an expensive decision that threatened the future of the company. Refusing to pilot the future A 320 in teams of two, the unions at Air Inter (the two national aviation companies had not yet merged) won a similar case. The government feared like a plague any upheaval in the nationalized companies.

Airbus could have done without all this professional counter-publicity, for by now its development strategy was on the ropes. Don't forget that, at the time, it was still known as "The French Company". If the French flight personnel, who must have been innately pro-Airbus, were refusing the 2-man piloting scheme for the A 320, why should anyone else go along with it? And so the refrain was heard throughout the world's airports: they are only trying to cut personnel costs, that is why so many companies are considering Airbus's middle-distance carrier. To the detriment, no doubt, of passenger safety.

Safety versus profitability, was it as simple as that? Many of those who opposed the two-man piloting plan were sincerely convinced that it was. But history would prove they were wrong. Boeing ended up giving in to the Airbus standards, not the reverse, including for its larger passenger aircrafts. While the first generations of "jumbo jets" were piloted by three, the 747-400 were piloted by two. This American change of course did not, strangely enough, kick off any protests.

From Seattle with love, Frenchies. We should mention that some of the pilots from Air France and Air Inter were particularly unhappy with the technological upheaval represented by the new European aircraft. The A 320 heralded the "revolution of the cockpits". And with it, the end of an era when the pilots enjoyed an impressive panoply of benefits and statutory privileges, the logical recompense for the key role they played in the event of technical hitches, breakdowns, and even crash landings — a role that the in-flight computer minimized, if it did not cancel it entirely.

Thus, the advent of the A 320 changed the rules of the game, to the psychological and financial disadvantage of the pilots. Gone was the magic wand, the "joy stick", that had symbolized their absolute power. And what had replaced this emblematic accessory — some little lever that looks like a child's toy? And what about the old-timers,

165

veterans who would need to be re-trained on an equal footing with those sharp-fanged "young upstarts" who, in aviation as elsewhere, thought they owned the world?

The anti-Airbus reaction of the French crews, a mix of nostalgia and fear for the future, reinforced the conservatism of a group that is infinitely less open to change than it would like to have us believe. At the same time, it shored up the already dominant trading and industrial position of "Big Daddy". Boeing had a field day, presenting itself as a kind of "wise old man" of aeronautics who knows how to take its time, avoiding any confusion between speed and precipitousness.

From sophistry to paradox. When the European Airbus innovates, it takes the blame. When the American Boeing resists taking technological risks like the ones that led Juan Trippe and Bill Allen toward the extraordinary success of the "Jumbo-Jet", it is crowned in laurel wreathes — short-sightedly giving them a premium on stagnation.

Competition was once the watchword in the civilian aircraft industry, where it had fostered the greatest successes. Had it gone out of style? No, of course not. And the people in Seattle soon realized the extent to which, secure in their position as world leader in aeronautics, they had underestimated their European adversary. Was that an error of the industrial guidance system, or a Comet-syndrome in miniature? Believing that Airbus's reputation had been tarnished irremediably by the post-Habsheim wave of criticism, Boeing focused for two years on the McDonnell-Douglas MD-11, a great advance compared to its B-777 — not realizing that at the same time, the folks in Toulouse were coming back in through the porthole with their new long-distance carrier, the A 340.

Its Majesty, the Internet

In the United States, technological innovation is not always rejected. Especially when a 100% American innovation is pointing its nose — or its false nose — at the dawn of modern communications. In the late 1980's and the beginning of the following decade, as we know, the Internet network virtually exploded. Servers, software, channels, and websites proliferated exponentially, transforming this universal means of connection into a unique theater of economic operations.

Logically enough, several sites cropped up that were dedicated to aeronautical problems. Many of them were intended both for professionals and knowledgeable amateurs, and they offered a wide range of technical information. Looking to encourage interactivity, some also hosted newsgroups, electronic discussion forums — as liable to manipulation as those discussed in the chapter about Total's experiences in Burma.

First to open fire, bombarding the A 320 with sarcastic remarks, was *anon.penet.fi*, a server from remote Finland that has since disappeared. This mysterious "Finn" only primed the pump against Airbus on the Web. With every accident involving an A 320 (the Indian Airlines crash in February 1990 in Bangalore — 90 killed, the Mt. Sainte-Odile catastrophe in January 1992 — 87 victims), the ether rumors took wing, making claims that flew in the face of all the evidence: "The in-flight computer did not function properly" (or the opposite: it functioned too well, preventing any useful intervention by the crew).

This campaign made the A 320 the most attacked aircraft in the entire Airbus "family"; every incident, no matter how small, served as a pretext for the dissemination of erroneous information. The word "campaign" is not an overstatement. Aérospatiale, the Airbus shareholding entity on the French side, conducted an intensive monitoring of the Web and the international news industry, and concluded that A 320 mishaps were given six times as much coverage as the crashes of competing aircraft.

What could top off this mass propaganda wave better than a very targeted batch of misinformation? The electronic in-boxes of the leading decision-makers at the airlines, in government and in the tourist agencies were deluged with e-mails hostile to Airbus, from impossible-to-trace anonymous writers. Many members of the target audience were, as part of their jobs, members of list-serves (electronic mass mailing lists), and were "alerted" by that second avenue as well. In parallel, several websites posted very selective information. When the official report from the French board of inquiry on Habsheim appeared — more than 400 pages detailing the deficiencies of the crew in particular — an American aeronautical site chose to publish only three pages. Those pages — what a surprise — that might be considered to implicate the plane itself.

"Ross" and Co.

Far from being the prerogative of newsgroups alone, the fallacious attacks against the European plane were picked up and amplified elsewhere on the Web. Take "Ross", for example. This enigmatic character slipped like an eel from one chat group to another, distilling the increasingly sour criticisms of Airbus, its electric drives, its in-flight computer, its side-sticks. It was impossible to know who he was, or what he was after! In despair, the leaders Airbus hired a French firm specialized in Web analyses to conduct an investigation.

Here are our cyberdetectives on the trail. They located Ross's signature on the Internet and traced it all over the Web. In just a few weeks, the true identity of Airbus's anonymous foe was revealed. They even got his photograph.

"Ross" was an aviation consultant specializing in crash prevention, living in England. He prided himself on his prestigious customer list: 21 of the biggest American airports and 24 airlines, all British or American. In point of fact, his entire "experience" in fire protection and safety was apparently limited to his role as an auxiliary in a helicopter rescue squad. That rather limited his ability to make peremptory judgments on the A 320.

Newsgroups gone wild, newsgroup gone mad, or newsgroups somehow being remote-controlled? "Ross" was just the most salient member of a whole tribe. Other anonymous pessimists methodically attacked the Airbus technology as "dangerous", "irresponsible", or "inaccurate".

"I am an A 320 pilot," one claimed. "This plane is always on the brink of stalling."

"I literally had to fight with the in-flight computer that was preventing me from controlling the plane. It was like being in *2001, A Space Odyssey*, when "Hal", the computer, tries to take control of the spaceship. With a Boeing 737, nothing like that would have happened", testified another.

"All our colleagues need to know: the A 320 is dangerous", added a third.

"European engineers are not up to this level, especially the French. Since they refuse to admit that, we are heading straight toward another catastrophe", concluded another.

Why this electronic barrage? These unknown personalities, using the Web to mask their identities, presented themselves as qualified experts, professionals. Pilots, they may well have been — but of simple single-engined tourist planes! No professional airline pilot would have taken the risk of releasing onto the Web such aggression against Airbus. The "patriotic task" of denigrating the A 320 thus fell to amateurs or to semi-professionals who were sufficiently familiar with airplane technology to create appropriate illusions and to "feed the debate" in the newsgroups.

As we look to pin down the origin of this gossip, let me observe that the ranks of Web-based A 320 antagonists would expand, eventually, with the arrival of American students recruited from the most famous technology institutes. These young people, aspiring to land jobs with their country's big aircraft manufacturers, wrote their theses on rather astutely selected topics in airplane technology.

Was it their own idea to use the Web to promote their anti-Airbus thoughts as a passport to job interviews? Or did some malignant mind lead them to it? A mystery. In any event, these web-savvy students made up a very resolute group of shock troops, well-versed in the art of virtual guerrilla warfare where you don't need to truly convince anyone so much as to insinuate, to suggest. The ultimate target of this campaign was, still, the actual airline pilots. Many of them, familiar with new technologies, were active on the Internet, discussing their jobs or exchanging impressions with their colleagues throughout the world (English being the international language of aviation). It would be highly advantageous to sow doubt in their minds.

The ATR 72 in A Snare

Airbus was not the only target of these Internet commandos. The other European aircraft that was being built in Toulouse by the French Aérospatiale and the Italian Alenia, the ATR 72 was hit in turn by a storm of repeated attacks. This 70-seat turboprop covered short distance routes. Catastrophe occurred on October 31, 1994: an ATR 72 crashed in Rosebud, Illinois, causing the loss of its 68 occupants. The wings had iced because of an unfortunate pilot error — and not because of any technical failure involving the propellers as suggested by the misinformation campaign, a three month campaign of intensive attacks that started coming as soon as the catastrophe was announced.

Three months? That's just how long it took the FAA to decide to ground the ATR as a precautionary measure. The timing of this forced immobilization proved crucial for various sales contracts that were pending, and the results were soon clear: since that date, orders for the ATR 72 fell by 75%. And the Americans set to work to get their hands on this share of the market for regional passenger aircraft.

Tilting with Rumor Mills

This really hurt. How can you thwart such rumors, other than by attempting to trace as many of the attackers as possible back along the long filaments that they "spin" on the Web? The response may take various forms. Traps are laid. Camouflaged under false identities and using Web addresses based in the United States, one can drop hints via e-mail, messages sometimes sibylline, often more threatening.

That seems to be an effective method. It is derived from standard anti-guerrilla tactics. European Internet users friendly to Airbus tried, for their part, on several occasions to post messages hostile to Boeing on certain manifestly pro-American sites. That was an instructive experiment: their texts were summarily "censured".

In the world of aviation, the war on the Web is waged in waves of attacks centered on precise topics. In 1992-93, for example, Airbus was blamed for its role in a series of crashes. Then it was the ATR's turn. Running concurrently to these indirect trials, head-on criticism like that which is openly practiced on sites honest enough to display the banner "Anti-Airbus" — to cite just one — appears almost trivial.

That did not stop the Europeans from complaining about the spiteful remarks made by the "Boeing professors", as the "fellow travelers" were called — researchers funded by Seattle, in the context of a American private industry that has such close ties with the world of the universities. Or from pointing out that it was not so long ago that Boeing's own official website displayed comparative graphs with honest statistics but dubious color choices: a beautiful blue sky behind the Boeing images, and aggressive red for Airbus, vaguely hinting at crashes and Communism during this Cold War era.

Honesty or realism? As soon as Airbus got its own site up and running, these documents were spontaneously withdrawn.

Tabula Rasa

The Web is like an international inn where some visitors depart wealthier than they were when they arrived; it can also be used as a booster to amplify various maneuvers — maneuvers that look like individual initiatives and would be hard to trace back to the big manufacturer in Seattle.

On November 6, 1997, two American passengers on Sabena's Airbus A 340 flight from New York to Brussels claimed they had suffered a very annoying incident. The hard disks on their portable computers had apparently been erased by magnetic interference due to the presence of a small magnet in the seat-back tray tables. The rumor sped across the Internet like a rocket: the A 340 is dangerous to computer equipment.

This message was posted on one of the most frequently visited aviation sites under the heading, "Warning to international travelers".

> Magnetized tray tables erased the two hard disks. In the particular case of this Belgian flight, the plane was a new model of the Airbus 340, which explains why no one had reported this kind of problem earlier. The problem seemed to come from the seat manufacturer for this specific European plane. U.S. Airways, Northwestern and United Airlines did not intend to use these magnetized tray tables in their new Airbuses. Boeing and McDonnell-Douglas weren't using components made by that firm, and there did not seem to have been any example of similar incidents occurring on other types of planes. The purpose of this note is simply to make travelers aware of the existence of this particular problem, in particular on the Airbus built for use by the European airlines. If the tray table is magnetized (use a paper clip to test it), then let the other passengers know that they should not use their portables on them. Please, pass this message along to travellers on intercontinental flights.

Watch out for your tray tables! The contagion spread like measles. Other sites replicated the warning, newsgroups launched debates. More worrying still, the major international tourist agencies were deluged with alarmist faxes, as though people "more representative" than our two Sabena passengers had been waiting for just such a weapon to renew the battle against the A 340. If Airbus and Sabena did not mount a counterattack very quickly, this would turn out very badly indeed. But once burned, twice shy: the two companies banded together to fend off this new threat.

Thanks to their prompt reaction, the truth was soon restored. For the real story of the "magnetized tray tables" is this. The two passengers from Sabena's November 6 flight demanded compensation for the "damages". And unfortunately for them, the Belgian company already knew that game, as it had already been the target this sort comparable attempt at extortion of money two years earlier. "Your case was presented very well, but your fundamental information is pretty far off base. Our four A 340's are all equipped with seats manufactured in England and they do not have a single magnetized piece", the lawyers explained with a laugh.

Most websites, informed of these adventures by Airbus and Sabena's public relations offices, immediately changed the contents of their messages. The written press found no need to display any corrections: aside from a few travel magazines, the newspapers and magazines had taken care not to pass along these Internet-based assertions without verifying them first. The whole thing collapsed like a cold soufflé. Still, the "magnetized tray tables" episode was an instructive case study. Limited to the Web due to the prudence of the written press, limited in scope thanks to the fast and comprehensive response from Airbus and Sabena, the damage was survivable.

Does this mean that only articles in the newspapers can support or, conversely, destroy the credibility of a given rumor? To answer this question, we would have to widen the debate to take in such events as the Clinton-Lewinsky affair in summer-autumn 1998. There, something broke down that may never be put right again: the role of "filter", of interpreter of the facts, that the newspaper industry has traditionally played. Doesn't that promise a brilliant future for the disinformation specialists of tomorrow!

... and Suction Toilets

As long as it starts from some fact likely to touch a sensitive cord with the general public, a campaign can just as easily be propagated through writing. In December 1996, a nine year old South African, little

Nwabisa, was wedged for half an hour in the toilet seat on a South African Airways A 300. This incident was terribly upsetting for the little girl, as one may well imagine; what caused it was a defective valve. The difference in pressure caused by this technical deficiency literally "stuck" Nwabisa on the seat.

The South African press was moved. The *City Press*, *Pretoria News*, *Mercury*, *Native Witness*, *Citizen*, the *Cape Times*, *Evening Post*, the *Cape Argus*, *Daily Dispatch*, *Daily News*, the *Sowetan*, the *Saturday Argus* all vied with sketches and diagrams to describe this spectacular incident to their readers. Radio and television shows kept pace with them, until the legend was born of the Airbus as "the plane whose toilets suck in the passengers and try to spit them out into space". Terrifying, indeed.

The technical plan makes clear that the toilets cannot spit anyone out the other end; the diameter of the drain is far too small. The rumor disappeared as quickly as it had appeared. But while the good faith of the South African press is not in doubt, its lack of rationality (the result of decades of blockades due to institutionalized racism) is still striking. Given that the first flight of the A 300 took place on October 28, 1972, a quarter century before the spectacular episode on flight SAA 327, and given that more than 600 of these planes have been in service with 80 airlines and no other such incident had ever occurred, the journalists could just as easily have concluded that this had been nothing more than a truly exceptional combination of circumstances.

Nwabisa was the victim of a traumatizing dysfunction that impinged on neither the competence of the airframe manufacturer, nor that of South African Airways. That was established with certainty, and so there remains little room for malignant exploitation of this particular event. But that is not always the case.

Secret Services in the Arena

Is it true that a team from the DGSE* went to Seattle in mid-April 1988 to spy on the testing of the new Jumbo-Jet model, the 747-400, as

*The Directorate General of External Security, headed at that time by an aviator, General François Mermet

investigative journalist Peter Schweizer affirmed in his 1993 best-seller *Friendly Spies* (based on information from the FBI)?

It is entirely possible, although this fellow gets his timing mixed up a bit when he attributes to Boeing the invention of the sophisticated navigation instruments that make it possible "to reduce the technical crew from three people to two". We know that, on the contrary, it was Airbus who initiated the formula of 2-man piloting for wide-bodies, with the A 320; and it was Airbus that suffered through an immense concert of protests from the French pilots (the Habsheim disaster took place on June 26 of the same year).

Even if it could be confirmed by a non-American source, especially a French one, this lively enough episode of industrial espionage would still be just one example among many others of the covert assistance given by the special services of the industrial powers that are grappling in today's economic and commercial conflicts.

Not all of them are related to the civilian aircraft industry. In October 1982, France managed to land a juicy contract to supply 40 combat planes to the Indian Air Force. There can be no doubt that the quality of the jets — especially the Mirage 2000 — had a lot to do with this resounding success. However, that alone was not enough to explain it completely, for without a concerted effort by the DSGE to influence and, frankly, to corrupt the Indian elite, the negotiations probably would not have come to such a satisfactory conclusion for the French manufacturers.

If the matter was left at that, it could only backfire. In January 1985, the French military attaché in New Delhi was kicked out for "activities incompatible with the status of a member of the diplomatic corps" — more specifically, for building a vast spy network within the political and local government circles. At the same time, several Indian nationals were accused of infringing the country's economic security laws. Like their French mentors, it seems they had been denounced by a disappointed competitor.

Under the circumstances, nobody was surprised in October 1985 when Indian Airlines, one of Asia's leading companies, chose to buy 19 A 320's and not the B-757's that "Big Daddy" was hoping to sell it. Seattle considered this decision proof of special ties between Prime Minister Rajiv Gandhi (himself a former Airbus A 300 pilot for Indian Airlines) and the European aviation company but also, and more so, as the effect of "the invisible hand" of the French secret service.

While the Indian press was tackling the Prime Minister's entourage, suspected of corruption (the "sales representation company" chosen by Airbus did, in fact, go through some $150 million in "expense" money instead of the usual $35 million), a judicial enquiry was opened. The case was eventually withdrawn. Twelve years later, Jean Pierson, who preceded Noël Forgeard as the head of Airbus, was satisfied to acknowledge to the TV cameras: "Our sales team had good relations with the leadership groups."

In the face of distrust, you'd better be doubly distrustful. No matter what. In India again, the Group of Industries for Terrestrial Armament (GIAT) lost an important sales opportunity for military combat equipment to the benefit of its Swedish rival, Bofors, in 1987. Persuaded (wrongly or rightly) that there had been some "improper conduct", the DGSE decided to get revenge. At the end of the 1980's, batches of photocopies from the diary of a close relation of Rajiv Gandhi's family appeared, specifying the sums allegedly paid by Bofors to various recipients, designated by their initials; these papers began to be circulated to the newspaper offices of New Delhi. Thus started the "Bofors scandal" that would lead to Gandhi's defeat in the 1989 elections and the success of his former Finance Minister, V.P. Singh, considered to be a resolute adversary of corruption.

Two years later, a mini-incident disturbed the Le Bourget Air Show. When Pierre Joxe made as if to place his hand on the display model of the Lockheed F 117 stealth plane, the marine on guard pushed away the French Defense Minister's arm with a curt gesture and peremptorily barked, "Don't touch, Sir." The Americans, it seems, were afraid that the governmental visitor, acting as an industrial spy, might use the occasion to scrape up under his nails a little bit of the top-secret coating on the plane! What had fed this distrust was the FBI's discovery in 1988 of DSGE "moles" operating at the expense of Boeing and Bell Helicopter, in particular. Thus the frosty climate, which a visit to the United States by the DSGE's new director Claude Silberzahn (in spring 1989) had not significantly thawed.

In April 1993, the U.S.-European war of the skies hit one of its most spectacular moments of turbulence. The scene: back at the Le Bourget Air Show. "Tipped off" by a 21-page secret report written by the CIA indicating that 49 U.S. companies including Boeing, McDonnell-Douglas and the aircraft engine manufacturer Pratt & Whitney would be under close surveillance by French spies, Michael Amstrong, the head of Hughes Aircraft (a GM subsidiary producing missiles, satellites and defense electronics), decided to let it be known that his firm would not be taking part in the demonstration.

Confidence does not reign between ally-competitors, necessary as it would seem to be. The intelligence services entertain fairly good relations with the manufacturers, although that varies depending on the country in question. Whatever is good for Boeing is good for the United States, to borrow a proverb that was coined for the automobile industry. U.S. aircraft manufacturers don't have any trouble getting a meeting with the local CIA representatives stationed at U.S. embassies abroad. Indeed, the federal information agency regards them as both information sources and as allies to be used.

As a multinational corporation, Airbus has more trouble playing the "economic patriotism" card. And our British friends, while they have one foot in the European consortium, still maintain solid commercial and industrial ties with the United States, a heart-wrenching situation that leads them to hold back concerning intelligence activities that could help Airbus. The Germans, finding the mixture of counterproductive, are reluctant to combine politics and business. And as for the French, finally, the Quay d'Orsay [the foreign office] avoids anything that might smell like economic information.

And Governments, Too

The Heads of State and government, the most active politicians, more and more often put in their own oars. The French presidents and their Prime Ministers al made efforts to promote Airbus. As did the Christian-Democrat leader Franz Josef Strauss, "the Bull of Bavaria", in his own way (he was a president of the Board of Trustees of Airbus Industries); by the way, during the Cold War he was one of the KGB Disinformation Department's favorite targets. President Clinton never hesitated to get on the phone and explain to his foreign colleagues and debtors that it would be in their interests to have their respective countries obtain some examples of America's excellent aeronautical technology.

The post-war ballet in the Gulf surrounding the $6 billion contract for the modernization of Saudi Arabia's civilian air fleet must be considered a textbook example of the system of official pressures and counter-pressures. President Clinton himself took part in the hunt, with his Secretary for Transportation Frederico Peña, his Trade Secretary, Ron Brown, Vice President Al Gore, and Senator Murray. Pugnacious salesmen, they had to match their powers of seduction against those of Chancellor Kohl, President Mitterrand, Prince Charles of England, the French Prime Minister Edouard Balladur, Vice Chancellor and Minister for Foreign Affairs Klaus Kinkel, and Alain Juppé, Gerard Longuet and François Léotard.

No one loved the Palestinians more than they did in those days; no one felt so much sympathy for the Bosnian Moslems — but alas for Airbus, the game of musical chairs resulted in a U.S. victory. Boeing pocketed a comfortable profit margin and the signed contracts prolonged the survival of Douglas by a few years.

Little Jokes Among Salesmen

The conditions of international competition are such that the more contracts Long Beach or Seattle sign, the fewer jobs there will be in Toulouse, Hamburg, Bremen, Filton, Chester, Nantes and Saint-Nazaire. That reality is what justifies such dirty tactics in the air transportation sector.

Sometimes it gets rough. After receiving death threats from locals who were "favorable" to the Americans, during a commercial battle in a region close to the Indian Ocean, an Airbus salesman had to head for the French embassy, where he slept in the bed that had recently been used by Prime Minister Michel Rocard. The atmosphere did not quiet down, so our man had to be urgently repatriated to Toulouse, where the climate is less hot and the life is more serene.

One event leads to another. In the next round, a contract hunter from Boeing lost precious time in a certain African country whose regime does not especially resemble what we call democracy. An indigenous police officer, bought by the competition, found that the poor fellow's vaccination certificate was not valid, not at all. "I am citizen of the United States and I don't think this story smells right", protested the Seattle man. Indeed, it reeked. It smelled so badly that the police officer threatened to jail the salesman, purely and simply.

Concerned for his safety, the good fellow decided to head home in order to have his vaccination documents verified by two eminent American specialists. By the time he got back, it was too late: Airbus had already signed a deal.

If there was ever an era when civility prevailed, that time is now over. In the opinion of the two companies' salesmen themselves, the commercial competition sometimes spills over into personal hatred. But isn't it even more striking that these tricks and traps, whether they are perpetrated by secret agents, political leaders or simple sales representatives, are nothing compared to the strategic misinformation that the manufacturers constantly spew about each other?

Aeronautical Misinformation: How-To

As a consumer, the user of air transportation seems to be an exception to normal standards. How many of us seriously inquire about the brand and model of the equipment that we are committing ourselves to travel upon, when we are buying an airplane ticket? One out of ten? The proportion does not go up much — if at all — even when we are boarding the flight. True, it may go up considerably as the number of "air alliances" grows.

Is it strange that we are so uninterested? Not really. Deciding to fly means showing a certain degree of confidence, no matter what type of aircraft is involved. We place this confidence in a given airline depending on what our experience has been, more than on the basis of any information about the various types of aircraft, which we know mostly by hearsay. Besides, most of us would have real trouble identifying on which kind of plane we travelled: was it an Airbus, Boeing, Douglas, Fokker? What difference does it make, as long as we make it to the next airport safely?

This banal point amounts to one thing: unless some specific event gives it a "black eye", as was the case of the unfortunate Comet, and the DC-10 and, temporarily, the A 320 in the immediate aftermath of the Habsheim accident, none of the existing apparatuses causes a spontaneous horror among consumers. "Allied" or not, the airline companies play the role of linking passengers and manufacturers, and all attempts at misinformation that target the general public can only expect to have a limited impact. Such campaigns are, therefore, less and less often seen. They cost too much, are too likely to compromise the perpetrator, and are too unreliable. The only exception to the rule comes with the renewal of concern that naturally follows any crash, opening an appreciable "window of opportunity" to any rumor hostile to the manufacturer in question.

The quality of the airplanes that are manufactured in the U.S. and Europe and the service provided by most airlines are such that accidents are rare. In ordinary times, therefore, the general public is not really part of the battle plan. Rather, it is the decision-makers who must be influenced, the folks inside the companies who are in a position to intervene in the choice of which equipment to buy — purchasing directors of course, and also pilots, financial executives, maintenance directors and the heads of customer service.

As in all fields, nothing stays fixed for long. The importance of these "targets" varies over time. Until the early 1970's, the rival manufacturers' campaigns of mutual discredit were mainly aimed at the pilots. For good reason: they had strong professional positions and the unions were strong; the crews were sensitive to any hint of loss of prestige or change of status; and, as we saw in the case of Air France, they were vulnerable because they were disinclined to change their ways. These were all factors that Boeing was able to exploit to the fullest by forging, within this well-defined sphere, the image of a manufacturer that was not much inclined toward innovation — a reassuring posture. But this strategy was a two-edged sword. It was beneficial in the short run, but in the long run it could play against the originator. "Big Daddy" lost the initiative, and its more innovative European rival got ahead. Boeing would have to fight hard to restore its damaged prestige.

In the mid-1970's and most of the following decade, some of the power passed out of the hands of the flight crews to those of the engineers. And the engineers were more concerned with ease of maintenance than they were with the problems of piloting. At this stage another flurry of attacks began: were they seriously supposed to have confidence in Airbus, a neophyte manufacturer with only one model, the A 300? And how about all the new procedures and the revised training materials that would have to be digested? And the spare parts, which no doubt would be delivered late? The major airlines' maintenance directors were, by nature, hardly more revolutionary than the pilots; they were sensitive to these arguments. And there were so many arguments to choose from, including the possibility of pulling out of the hatbox that eternal argument that "it's a French Company".

"Every time you had an emergency, we managed to get the spare parts and the technicians to you at the appropriate time. The French don't know anything but the heavy state apparatus, it will take them weeks to respond."

"Think of the Comet, the Caravelle, the Concorde. With Europeans, you can never be sure that the manufacturer will still be in business from one day to the next."

"If your company buys Airbus, you're going to have to change everything, you'll need to work from new maintenance manuals and learn all new procedures."

Between the mid-1980's and the mid-1990's, the power would change hands again, this time moving to the financial departments. Mounting costs were the principal danger. The tune was haunting; and the constant refrain was: "Airbus costs too much". First verse: it has no future. Second verse: it eats far too much fuel.

In 1983-84, the imminent emergence of the A 320 threatened the survival of the B-737. To ward off this danger, Boeing tried to knock the European aircraft out of the game. "There's no market for this type of plane", repeated the salesmen from Seattle.

Adding a note of commercial realism, starting from the end 1986, they added the attention-grabbing argument: "Getting stuck with that would be a big mistake. We're preparing to launch a supermodel that's going to make the A 320 a museum piece: wait 'til you see the 7 J 7."

The 7 J 7 — A Coup

It was so beautiful, on the drawing board. The model about to be born was backed up by a thick file of documentation. The 7 J 7 really was marvel: a double travelling track propelled by two General Electric GE-36 pro-fan engines, more efficient and quieter than anyone had thought possible. They could accommodate from 147 to 195 passengers, and offered greater comfort, greater safety, and less noise. Perfect.

Delay followed delay, postponement followed postponement. This airborne cruise ship never saw the light of day. "Big Daddy" announced that it was terminating the 7 J 7 project in 1988-89, the famous years when the commercial launch of the A 320 was confirmed. And that leads to the legitimate question: was the 7 J 7 only a mirage, a skillful "phantasm" created for the purpose of preemptively casting in the shade this overly enterprising European rival?

We'll never know; but in the aircraft industry, the technique of proclaiming the virtual obsolescence of a competitor's airplane is not a new idea. Even Boeing had been hurt by that tactic, while its Jumbo-Jet was still only in the planning stages. To deprive the 747 of market, Lockheed told the airlines that the Boeing model was condemned in advance since Burbank was going to be launching a three-bridge 900-seat super-giant civilian passenger plane, derived from the military C-5 A.

And again, fuel consumption was a big concern. In 1993, a good two years before its direct competitor the B-777, Airbus launched its long-distance twin-jet aircraft, the A 340. It took all the genius and persuasive skills of the European salesmen to counter Boeing's innumerable sales brochures that appeared, one after the other, "proving" with great quantities of distorted technical data that their forthcoming plane was going to be able to fly farther than the A 340 — at a lower cost.

While the music seemed to be the same, the words had changed a bit. The mid-1990's were the sales operations' glory days. Obsessed with profitability and the optimization of cabin configurations, the marketing men scanned every millimeter of the floor plans, examining various ways to "re-distribute" the seats and re-considering the types of services offered. These requirements forced the manufacturers to work upstream with the airlines' marketing executives. Boeing was already doing this before the debut of its B-777, and Airbus used that approach during the planning stages for the A 3XX. (Now known as the A 380, this jetliner had its "commercial launch" in June 2000, lining up 50 orders and 42 options from six world-renowned customers in just six months; that enabled the Airbus supervisory board to give the go-ahead to its industrial launch on December 19, 2000).

The reader may find it surprising that aviation history should conform to such clear cut timeframes: the 1960's, 1970's, 1980's and 1990's. The truth is, this calendar reflects the evolution of the most modern companies, and in fact evolves at a different pace in different countries. The further behind they are in terms of equipment, management practices, and internal processes, the more the airlines depend on old criteria. Thus the influence of the pilots is still very powerful in many Third World airlines companies.

Those who are in a position to decide which types of aircraft will be purchased (planning directors, often) are quite naturally the chief targets of the most subtle and most persistent stratagems for persuasion and seduction. When this is not enough, there are always other tricks to consider, especially direct personal cultivation. Given the international prestige enjoyed by American universities, one of the most effective techniques used in the Third World countries is to let drop a casual suggestion like the following:

"I am glad I met your son. He' a smart boy. Why not give him an extra chance? I happen to have a good friend at New York University (or Berkeley, or Georgetown, or Massachusetts Institute of Technology). I have already spoken with him about this: he can accept him within his own department. And I have some ideas as to where he can stay."

Studying in the United States means a future, social promotion, personal fulfillment — all weighty arguments. Certain salesmen may even be tempted to go further. No one among the airframe manufacturers has forgotten the head of purchasing, at a big national company in a Third World country, who left his desk one Friday and on Monday walked into a new job at Boeing.

Being Number One worldwide has its advantages but it has drawbacks, as well. Especially when a challenger like Airbus is coming up behind you at full speed. For years, on the basis of its position of authority, Boeing used and misused one particular form of argument that basically consisted in pounding into the heads of the airlines executives the mantra that its rival's plans were asinine: "Dangerous." "Not profitable". "There's no market for that." "The Europeans aren't going to get anywhere with this". "If you go that route, you'll lose your wallet". "Airbus is crazy". But in the end, these arguments have lost their impact. The time for that kind of arrogance is over.

Finally Alone Together, in the "Clear Blue Sky"

"The salesmen from Douglas were gentlemen, compared to the others. They never would have said that a DC-1030 could fly non-stop from Asia to Europe, and they never would have alleged that the MD-80 was the ideal cargo plane", wrote Richard Stirland, editorial director at the specialized journal *Orient Aviation*, in August 1997. His article was symbolically entitled "It's Time to Get Tough with the Manufacturers".

Stirland is not a man to mince his words. "Boeing continues to regard purchases from Airbus as a personal affront. This is aberrant behavior that invites a reprimand from the airlines, to make it to change its style."

He didn't spare Airbus either, which, according to him, shared some guilt in this area; but this professional who was broadly recognized for his impartiality translated into elegant terms the "dissatisfaction" of many airlines executives who were tired of being considered dunces every time they decided to buy anything but a plane made by Boeing. And his remarks related to more than Airbus alone. When McDonnell-Douglas was still flying under its own power, Boeing representatives had "flogged" the MD-11 as a vulgar freak. In their book, you would have to be more or less mentally deficient to buy that plane. Only, nobody likes to be called an imbecile and, by the way, the MD-11 was a good three years ahead of the B-777.

"It is high time for the airlines to let the manufacturers know that denigrating their competitors is not a viable sales method; it is even counter-productive", asserted Stirland — in case anyone had missed his point the first time around.

Counter-productive and dangerous for the profession as a whole. By insisting too much on the rival manufacturer's possible culpability in the event of a fatal catastrophe, you could easily sow doubt about the aviation industry altogether. And such a policy was all the more absurd since the planes that Airbus and Boeing were manufacturing were safe enough so that travellers were not afraid to fly. Thus, neither of the two competitors who shared the world market could find it beneficial to set off a wave of fear in the general public, and neither could the airlines.

"Boeing's aggressiveness has decreased appreciably in the last two years", they privately concede in Toulouse, and the impression is confirmed in Seattle. Can we conclude that the hatchet has been buried in the overhead storage bin forever? Not when you consider what is at stake. According to Airbus, 16,700 planes with 70+ seats are expected to be purchased in the twenty next years (Boeing sets the figure a little higher: 17,650) to replace 8,500 obsolete aircraft, and world traffic patterns face an average annual growth rate of 5%. Three thousand one hundred of these new planes will either be bought used, or leased, so that the remaining potential market would be some 13,600 units, for a theoretical sum of $1,000 billion.

Five billion per annum! A nest egg like that has got to capture the attention of any manufacturer, whether we are talking about the Boeing Company, credited with 53% of the market for 1998 (44 in the name of Boeing itself and 9 for MDD), or the Airbus consortium (in the process of privatization), which conquered 47% the same year. *Homo aeronauticus* will always be a wolf, among wolves. The future will no doubt bring further evidence of that.

And that will be a future where misinformation will play a growing role in every field of economic life. It will affect not only the consumer but also the conservationist, the foes of nuclear power, those who oppose chemical additives, genetic modification and irradiation of foods, and those who are against alcohol and tobacco. You, me, we are all in this, since these will be the real "targets" tomorrow.

CHAPTER 7

ECOLOGISTS AND CONSUMERS,
THE NEW BATTLEGROUNDS

In December 1994, Greenpeace International decided to focus its attacks on Cogema (the commercial subsidiary of the French nuclear power commission, the ECA) and its partner BNFL, British Nuclear Fuels. These two companies were about to send a convoy of 28 containers of "vitrified" Japanese radioactive residues to the reprocessing plant in La Hague. The waste was then to be shipped back to Japan by sea. This was to be the first of a long series of convoys, since the operation would take until 2003 and perhaps even longer to be completed.

Cogema and BNFL were transporting wastes on behalf of some of Japan's top companies, Tokyo Electric Company and Kansai Electric, in accordance with the terms of the contracts, signed in 1978. Japanese nuclear waste started being reprocessing in La Hague in 1990. The shipment of a ton and half of plutonium back to Asia on board the Akatsuki Maru had already been the target of many hostile demonstrations in 1992-93.

Greenpeace planned to repeat that process. "Greenpeace" has treated France with particular enmity since 1973, when the Mururoa atomic tests were first singled out for recrimination by this organization of "ecologists" — we'll have to place that term in quotation marks since, in this case, the high degree of political engagement renders it disputable. And France reciprocates the feeling. Before 1985, the Service of Documentation and Counter-Espionage, the DGSE's predecessor, carried out 29 extremely discreet operations (without human loss) ranging from the mini-sabotage of boats flying the rainbow pennant to infiltration agents under false identity, going as far as mixing purgatives into the crew's food supplies. These conflicts turned tragically for the worse on July 10, 1985,with the scuttling of the Rainbow Warrior and the death of the Portuguese photographer Fernando Pereira. Since then, Greenpeace has considered France its principal adversary.

How could they ignite the desired public outcry in response to the planned transport? This question was feverishly discussed at the Greenpeace headquarters in Amsterdam. It was going to be harder to mobilize public opinion against the Cogema-BNFL joint operation than it had been for the Akatsuki Maru event. This time, the cargo to be transported was not plutonium but simple residues from the reprocessing process — dangerous products that cannot be recycled, but which are militarily useless. The British company Pacific Nuclear Transports Ltd was commissioned to convey the containers to their final destination.

I was aware of this issue early on, since I was head of the Paris office of the *Asian Seas Newsletter*, which focused on Europe-Asia maritime and para-maritime problems. Ecological groups like the Nuclear Control Information Center were already mobilizing in Japan. Under these conditions, I had little choice but to contact Greenpeace.

Operation "Smile"

Damon Moglen, a recent arrival from Amsterdam, was designated "Coordinator - Plutonium Campaigns". This initially pleasant enough young man directed the local activities of Greenpeace France, on rue Petites-Ecuries in Paris. He seems to be of Anglo-Saxon origin, and that is the principal source of the prestige that surrounds him. The

French members of "Greenpeace", who clearly suffered from an inferiority complex with regard to the Anglo-American world, waited on him hand and foot. Aside from Jean-Luc Thierry in Cherbourg, they were all bit players in the anti-Cogema operation.

A high-ranking personage in the Greenpeace hierarchy, Moglen wasted no time with folding flyers and mailing letters; that task was delegated to a group of dedicated young Frenchwomen in a dim room in the apartment that served as the Greenpeace headquarters in France. The French participants whirled around their Anglo-Saxon "big boss" with an astonishing enthusiasm. A young woman served us coffee and disappeared without a word.

Nevermind the minor details; Moglen adores journalists. I sensed that our Coordinator - Plutonium Campaigns was fascinated by the relationships that exist between members of the press and the authorities, a small coterie of people who may hold key information that Greenpeace, dependent on the success of its media operations, desperately needs.

Pacific Nuclear Transports has a flotilla of ships designed for transporting radioactive waste: the Pacific Crane, Pacific Pintail, Pacific Sandpiper, Pacific Swan and Pacific Teal. However, Greenpeace has neither the human nor the material resources to monitor these ships individually, much less to keep five different teams battle-ready. The only thing that could help them was good luck, but no one at rue des Petites-Ecuries had any faith in that. Or else some serious research work: the rainbow warriors absolutely had to find out in advance which of the boats from "the Club of Five" would be responsible for ferrying the waste from La Hague to Japan. Without that basic information, there could be no spectacular demonstration against Pacific Nuclear Transport, British Nuclear Fuels or Cogema. No cameras, no colorful images broadcast throughout the world — in short, no sign of "the Greenpeace Touch".

Unless one good-hearted journalist would lend a hand. A small gesture would be welcome. Without the game being described to me in quite such vulgar terms, I was not long in coming to understand what was up. If, by chance, I should happen to find out the name of the ship, the date it was to leave port, and its exact route, Greenpeace would not show itself ungrateful. I would earn the immense privilege of joining the list of "friendly journalists". In exchange for the information they deliver and for the amplification they give to the "Greenpeace" message, these "friends" are the first ones alerted to any new operation that is started.

Journalistic complicity — no, thank you! That's not for me. I decided to abide by the basic rules of the profession, informing the public of the respective positions of the protagonists of the controversy and, generally, of the problems related to shipping radioactive waste to Asia.

Pirates on the Asian Seas

The *Asian Seas Newsletter* was not especially worried about the apocalypse that Moglen and his friends described in advance, on the basis of a report from an (American) self-proclaimed independent scientist (a classic technique that had been much in use in the late Eastern bloc). We were more concerned with the risks of an attack on Pacific Nuclear Transports ships by the pirates that were lurking about near strategic traffic lanes including the straits of Malacca. The notion was not at all eccentric: these modern pirates shoot first, forcing their quarry to stop, and they open discussions later. Should a group of them fire on a vessel charged with nuclear waste, it could lead to an ecological catastrophe.

"Do you seriously think that you need to provide military protection for tankers transporting chemicals like ammonia?" one of the leaders of Cogema, Jean-Pierre Laurent, responded with irritation.

I had not suggested anything of the sort but, with the increasing audacity of the Asian pirates (until then known only to specialists) and the quality of their equipment — speedboats, automatic weapons, rockets, missiles — I thought that the idea did deserve more than superficial consideration. Was I way out of bounds? Time would prove me right: maritime piracy threatens to become a severe problem.

I had in mind the exclusive information that we were to publish, after verifying the details, fifteen days later on January 19. Back in 1970-71, Palestinian attacks were a risk not only for the luxury cruise ship, *Le France* — still flying the tricolor pennant — which was escorted by a destroyer every time it left port. The public authorities took further precautions as well: fake tourists and real marine commandos acting incognito, a handful of "civilians" equipped with the necessary arms were posted on board the ship. They never had to go into action. A quarter century later, shouldn't we take their example as a starting point?

"Radioactive waste is not as sensitive as plutonium. It isn't very interesting. Consequently, terrorist operations or acts of war not really to be feared", stated Jean-Louis Ricaud, director of the "Reprocessing" branch of Cogema.

This attitude was nothing new. It was summed up by a silver-tongued pundit who observed that, "In France, it is impossible to get the supervising authorities to tell us what they are doing. It is congenital. The French cannot be taught to communicate. The French civil servant considers himself the proprietor of any information he holds. And in a big company, too, it is difficult to keep this mentality from becoming entrenched."

Pierre Guillaumat knew what he was saying. The son of a general in the Great War, an engineer from the Mining Corps, a Gaullist resistance fighter and member of the information services for the French troops in Algiers, he belonged to that special species of major State entrepreneurs. Guillaumat had been head of fuel commission at the Industry Ministry, had been head of Gaz de France, had served as the State's managing director for the Commissariat for Atomic Energy, was boss of the Office for Petroleum Prospecting, had commanded armies, chaired the EDF, and founded Elf-Aquitaine before heading up the National League Against Cancer.

…and "Eco-Guerillas"

If I am recollecting the atmosphere that prevailed during the Greenpeace-Cogema confrontation in early 1995, it is because as time goes by, one can begin to see what a good lesson it was. The adversaries, obsessed by their respective goals, pursued their two irreconcilable logics to the utmost.

Let's set the scene. On the "ecologist" side, we have hard-core ideologues proclaiming themselves to be the builders of a radiant future under the banner of clean technologies. Skillful demagogues, they appealed to the diffuse fears of a public that was already anxious and, in the case of the French, less inclined than ever to believe the reassuring words of the authorities.

"Greenpeace exploits people's anxiety by creating confusion between plutonium and radioactive waste", was the conclusion of the Japanese Power Reactor & Nuclear Fuel Development staff. At the receiving end of all this controversy, they were eager to analyze the eco-guerillas' *modus operandi*. Dramatic, exaggerating, anxiety-provoking, under-informing and over-communicating, the Greenpeace method has proven to be fairly effective. They offer simple truths to a public that is disconcerted by the complexity of the modern world. In order to inform the public in a clear and penetrating, yet objective, way, about the risks inherent in an industrial society? Not in the least. On the contrary, by intentionally exaggerating the dangers, Greenpeace sucks in our fellow-citizens, creating a negative mindset that has cult-like overtones. We are surrounded by evil, and only a handful of pure souls are defending us.

Should one lie for a good cause? It happens. In any case, Hans Jonas, the philosophical guru of certain ecologist movements, wrote these worrisome lines: "Under certain conditions, the best opinion is a false opinion, by which I mean: if the truth is difficult to maintain, then a white lie must intervene. We would need a new Macchiavelli, one who would propound his doctrines in a rigorously esoteric way."

Esoteric. And why not millennarist? That's strong medicine. On the other side, the nuclear industry pours out rivers of tepid messages that one would think had been invented by Doctor Coué, the French prophet of self-persuasion: everything will be okay because we need everything to be okay, everything will be okay because we want it to be, everything will be okay because everything will be okay.

As long as nobody bothers us, we who are in the know. We, the inflexible guardians of the nation's energy resources. My contacts at Cogema, accustomed to dealing with a scientific, parliamentary and journalistic lobby and strongly supported by one of the most influential feudal systems within the Republic — the Mining Corps — were evidence of this. They clearly were irritated and uncomfortable whenever anyone raised new questions.

Until the clouds blew towards us from Chernobyl, respectfully stopping short of the French border! This technique of under-informing and de-dramatizing an issue is the exact opposite of the eco-warriors' approach.

Greenpeace announced with great fanfare the imminent catastrophe, knowingly mixing the true and the false. Cogema denied that there was any risk. The "anti's" offered pre-fab scoops to the press; battened down in their citadel, the "pro's" tried to use the press as a simple spokesman to disseminate its reassuring spiel. Which method is more likely to resonate with the public? This dilemma doesn't relate to Greenpeace and Cogema alone.

To be convincing, your message has to be consistent. Cogema minimized the dangers but at the same time said that it was taking added precautions. This kind of language can only stir up concerns and confirm its detractors' allegations. If there was no danger, why waste time fine-tuning unnecessary protective measures? If, on the contrary, such measures were needed, then there must be some danger. This is a contradiction which many other branches of industry — such as chemistry, pharmaceuticals and food processing — are falling into every day.

However, when it comes to making people worry, nobody can

beat Greenpeace! Quick to make analogies, astute, sharp as a knife, the "eco-guerillas" long held the high ground. Hair blowing in the wind, little boats tossed on the waves and bravely flying the rainbow insignia, they played on people's need for adventure and the desire for purity. They were helped by the obstinacy and inflexibility of their adversaries, when an intelligent and measured response easily could have forced them to act with more moderation.

The Kings of Agitprop

Greenpeace was said to be manipulated by the Eastern bloc. That was never proven. But I myself might well see this as one of the last misadventures of the Leninist model. The founder of the Soviet Union and his trusty sidekicks identified two types of militancy: agitation, by which they meant raising on high an entirely minor incident in order to rouse the crowd ("present one single idea or a few ideas to a great mass of people"), and propaganda, in which a smaller number of people is exposed to the general ideology of the Party ("present many ideas to a few people"). By combining these two factors, agitprop could ignite the revolutionary spark at the right moment.

This was a dialectic that Greenpeace, British-American as it may be, brilliantly transposed to the troubled world at the end of the millennium. "Greenpeace" agitprop! With its left hand it sows anguish, using one-sided arguments and wildly false statistics; with its right hand, it fosters the fundamentalist vision of the "Khmers green" where man, a malevolent being that disturbs the natural order of life, ends up becoming an intruder on earth. Leninist, too, is the extreme importance attached to questions of money. From recently opened Soviet archives, we know how obsessed the creator of Bolshevism was with financial questions; he made them a key element of his strategy for seizing power. Lately, we've become accustomed to seeing Greenpeace as a "money pump" marching under the slogan: Fight the capitalists with weapons provided by the capitalists.

194

Lenin invented the concept of "useful idiots" (also called "innocents") — as my own uncle, the painter and cinema costume designer Iouri Annenkov made known in the West — and formulated the basic techniques of manipulating "fellow travelers". Stalin, a perfectionist, took this technique to its extreme in his concern to equal and then to exceed his master. But let's imagine for a moment the two dictators witnessing the masterful performance of "Greenpeace". Vladimir Ulianov and Iosif Djugashvili would both be impressed by these practices of journalistic complicity that make dupes of some of their pals and accessories of many others. Experts in disinformation, our satraps of yesterday would taste nectar in the acid words of Paul Watson, a one-time pillar of the "Eco" movement: "For Greenpeace and for McTaggart*, it is not the truth that counts, but what people take for the truth."

At least, we can speak of this all in the past, for Greenpeace's star is no longer at its zenith. Six months after the anti-Cogema campaign, the end of summer 1995, sounded if not the death knell, then at least the hour when the "ecologist" organization was partially demystified.

At the height of their campaign against the last series of French nuclear tests in Mururoa, Greenpeace first stumbled by publicly failing to thwart the response of the French naval services on the information and counter-information front. Having learned through a long series of bad experiences, the Navy destroyed its adversary's reputation of media infallibility. An annoying ignorance of international maritime law deprived the rainbow warriors of their logistics infrastructure. Because its helicopter violated French airspace, the "ecologist" flagship MV Greenpeace was confiscated by the Green Berets.

After this first setback, "Greenpeace" suffered another blow, one that was more seriously damaging to its credibility. Having overestimated the hydrocarbon contents of a Shell oil platform, the *Brent Spar*, Greenpeace United Kingdom was obliged to eat crow and publicly apologize to Shell on September 5, 1995. In the purest form of wooden

* its founder

195

language — for which they had so successfully denounced their adversaries — the eco-guerillas uttered something about "regrettable errors of analysis". This was a constrained and forced strategic retreat: apparently, Shell had declared itself ready to pursue an impressive array of legal remedies.

Greenpeace suffered a new humiliation in summer 1997, this time in its own birthplace, British Colombia, one of the Canadian provinces most dedicated to protecting the environment. Howling against the destruction of forests, the rainbow warriors associated with a swath of American ecologist groups opposed the construction of new roads through the area. They flooded North American and European companies with mailings calling for a boycott of products containing wood cut in British Colombia.

"Environmentalists who choose to work together with U.S. interests in opposition to our industry and our jobs are enemies of British Colombia", Glen Clark declared. For the province's Prime Minister to suspect complicity between certain ecologists and the American timber industry was nothing new. What was new was that he said it loud and clear. Ten years earlier, Clark would not have been able to permit himself such leeway. And for good reason: nothing could be more harmful to a politician than to develop a reputation, right or wrong, for being weak on conservation questions. The ecologists — anxious (with some reason) over the degradation of our natural environment, plant lovers and friends of animals — have gained increasing influence in public opinion. Thus, they have evolved into a sounding board that can be played effectively by astute disinformation artists. The new Sanofi episode of the "damned monkeys" was a good example.

Sanofi and Its "Damned Monkeys"

In 1992, Elf's pharmaceutical subsidiary, Sanofi, started the long process that leads to bringing a new drug to market. First, the new product has to undergo preliminary trials on animals.

Sanofi sought permission from the Senegalese government to start breeding monkeys. Soon, several French, Dutch and American animal protection associations popped up. This was a fine opportunity to catch everyone's attention, with photographs of miserable-looking primates, their craniums gaping open. At the same time, all sorts of rumors were flying in Senegal. There are people who eat monkeys' brains — a rumor that is as shocking in Africa as the leaflets that denounce the horror of vivisection in Europe and America.

There was no mystery as to the objective of this opinion campaign. They wanted to force the local authorities to turn down Sanofi's request. Certain powerful American companies in Dakar exerted their own pressures on the Senegalese government at the same time. "Animal protection leagues are threatening to boycott us if we continue to have economic relations with you", they claimed. "It would be better to stop exporting your monkeys." Spelled out in such clear terms, the message was received loud and clear. The Senegalese were in a bind; they soon gave in. The French industrial firm had to find other primates to conduct its experiments, in Gabon, where people are more understanding of the needs of the Elf Group's pharmaceuticals subsidiary. . . Take our monkeys, and let's not hear anything more about it.

It is not for the reader's entertainment alone that I have chosen to relate this anecdote. It illustrates in a very concrete way how the ecologist groups and environmentalists have cropped up right in the middle of the economic battlegrounds, a phenomenon that is spreading. Even in Russia, where the security directors of certain firms (all veterans of the KGB) claim, in private, that several pharmaceutical factories have had to close, following demonstrations by ecologists who were "manipulated by foreigners". In the United States, supported by environmental protection organizations in Washington, a handful of Green extremists managed to force companies that were considered to be polluters to relocate to the hinterlands, where the regulations are looser, thus risking a weakening of the big cities and depriving the workers of some of their union-guaranteed rights.

Another Elf subsidiary, Atochem, was targeted for its use of chlorine; now, it keeps a close eye on Internet sites dedicated to ecology and environmental defense. At the same time, the "Chlorophiles", a work-ers' group from Belgian industries linked to chlorine, opened a website that violently attacked Greenpeace, which was very actively engaged in anti-chlorine activities. These trade unionists, anxious to protect their jobs, created the picturesque character of "Greenocchio", whose nose gets longer every time the rainbow warriors propagate an untruth.

In the information war and counter-war, the battle is raging. Ecology extremists are not the only ones involved. The opposing camp, the industrialists, have their own experts in the manipulation of facts and figures. This is a skill set that has been admirably exploited by the tobacco international lobby over the years; and will no doubt continue to exploit.

One Butt, What Difference Does It Make?

The session opened early in the morning on March 31, 1983. Sev-enteen men and women were seated around the long oval table, the first ten representing all the major players in the American tobacco in-dustry: Arthur Stevens and James Cherry, of Lorillard Tobacco; Josiah Murray, of Ligett Group; Sam Witt of R. J. Reynolds; Fredric Newman, Alexander Holtzman and Tom Ehrensfeld, of Philip Morris; Ernest Pep-ples, of Brown & Williamson Tobacco; Horace Kornegay and Samuel Chilcote, of the Tobacco Institute. The other participants were all law-yers, including Janet Brown, from the office of Chadbourne & Park, Manhattan.

This deliberative group from the Tobacco Institute (Committee of Counsel) had the same question on their agenda as ever: what to do with the "special plans" of the Tobacco Institute Research Committee, the TIRC?

The TIRC, an American invention. In 1954, the U.S. tobacco in-dustrialists, realizing that their fun-loving ads founded on nothing but the exaltation of the pleasures of cigarette smoking were starting to wear thin, made a brutal change of direction. A proclamation entitled:

"An honest declaration to cigarette smokers", published at their expense in 448 newspapers (totaling some 40 million copies throughout the United States), was the first major sign of change of attitude.

With a cunning prudence, our industrialists admitted the obvious, for the first time: yes, tobacco does present health risks. This "realistic" attitude quickly sparked sarcastic comments by analysts who maintained that the cigarette industry was committing suicide through negative slogans: "Can you imagine a whisky ad, where they confidentially whisper, "Watch out for cirrhosis of the liver", or "Research conducted over a ten-month period by leading doctors has indicated no clear case of serious or chronic alcoholism"?

TIRC, a "research" organization, was created in 1958; in fact, its purpose was to promote tobacco — a dubious and debatable strategy. In 1964 Addison Yeaman, a counselor at Brown & Williamson, drafted a report denouncing this mutation of the TIRC into a "public relations" organization. According to him, it would be better to replace this obsolete and counter-productive mechanism with a genuine research institute. Financed by the tobacco industry, the new organization would be subjected to inspection by the official public health organizations. This oversight would guarantee its independence and therefore its credibility.

Yeaman was annoying, far ahead of the times. No one listened to him. And following the tried and true methods of yore, they settled for changing the sign without changing anything inside the store. The TIRC became the CTR, the Council for Tobacco Research. Time past, and criticism of nicotinism increased. On September 10, 1981, Mr. Stevens, a representative of Lorillard, stepped into the breach at a plenary meeting held in at the Chadbourne & Park offices. If we keep working with one restricted group of pro-tobacco scientists, always the same ones, "they will lose all their credibility and ours", he said.

The minutes of the CTR meeting, taken by Frank K. Decker, a legal consultant of Ligett Group, are edifying:

"If you have a doctor, he should be kept busy or he will lose interest", objected a lawyer from Medinger & Finnigan. What did he mean, that as soon as one succeeds in buying people, one should keep them as profitable as possible?

"I understand perfectly well that there are times where we need to put money in the hands of a researcher, but I would prefer not to take on meaningless projects", retorted Stevens, who was not born in yesterday's puff of smoke.

"These projects don't bother us", murmured another lawyer, adding to the Lorillard representative's irritation.

"If the research work is worthless, that poses a problem for me", stated Stevens. He was convinced that by doing nothing but corrupting minds and people, the cigarette industry was driving itself into a quagmire. America was no longer living in the era when businessmen made the sun shine and the rain pour. They had to take changing attitudes and the need for transparency into account.

This realistic argumentation got him nowhere. Law firms are savage adherents of the status quo. And Stevens reminded them of the prophetic report his former boss Curtis H. Judge, president of Lorillard Tobacco, had presented three years earlier: "We have once again given up the conduct of the industry's scientific research to the law men. . . Lorillard's management is against having the entire future of the industry in the hands of the Committee of Counsel." Smoke rings, carried off by the winds of irrational profit-seeking!

"Smoke, Smoke, Smoke that Cigarette"

"Smoke, smoke, smoke that cigarette", sang Eddy Mitchell in the mid-1970's, drumming away with nonchalant humor the constant message of "tobaccization", whose future was still strong. Today, the tobacco industry goes on, imperturbable. It relies on its traditional pillars: support by the tobacco-producing states of the South, such as North Carolina and Virginia; massive but legal payments to the political parties ($4.1 million in 1995, including $2.4 for the Republicans) and more discreet contributions to specific "friendly" politicians.

In 1992 and 1993, thirteen American researchers paid by the Tobacco Institute peppered the scientific journals with articles and letters casting discredit on a report from the Environment Protection Agency that had established that 20% of lung cancers in nonsmokers are caused by passive nicotinism. For their support for the noble cause, these specialists earned some $709,000. Among them were well-known academics, highly reputed American medical celebrities and some "independent" researchers. The memoranda attesting to these payments include, in fine print, messages indicating that the "papers" had been read over by the legal consultants of the tobacco lobby.

In spite of these financial efforts, modest as they may have been, the industry ran into trouble with the Clinton administration. Another special interest group had been created in the meantime: the anti-smoking lobby. Like any lobby, it has its extremists, its crusaders driven by moral semi-fanaticism, and it has realistic members who may be members of various associations, the health commissions of big American cities and the Food and Drug Administration. This FDA has compared nicotine to a drug. But out of concern for effectiveness, it favored a moderate prohibition that would mostly aim at limiting young people's access to tobacco, through a regime of tax measures.

Money talks. And so does the law. The Attorneys General of 37 states filed a class action suit, seeking to compel the industry to compensate states for medical expenses related to tobacco use. The lawyers of the big groups, Philip Morris, NJR Nabisco, Brown & Williamson, and Lorillard, set to work to come up with a less radical solution. On June 27, 1997, a first agreement was reached. Interrupting the ruinously expensive trial procedures, the tobacco people agreed to pay a fine of $368 billion over 25 years. This tidy sum would be used to finance the treatment of diseases linked to cigarette smoking, to compensate private individuals, to develop prevention campaigns and to open research centers worthy of the name.

This agreement was questioned by the industrialists but even more so by the militant faction of the anti-tobacco lobby; it touched off new debates within the FDA and the Justice Department. Anti-tobacco crusaders were playing an increasing role, stepping up the pressure; they enjoyed the clear support of the public, whose views had been fashioned by a kind of American "fundamentalism" that would wake up and show itself more strikingly later on.

The attorney general of the State of New York, Christine Gregoire, secretly negotiated a new text with the professionals. On November 20, 1998, the great tobacco groups signed a second accord with 46 states. Contrary to appearances, it is much more favorable to them than the 1997 version. But the princes of tobacco had lost the first battle, just the same. From now on, their empires would be under close watch. And Bill Clinton could say, during his State of the Union address, that "the taxpayers should not bear the cost of lung cancer, emphysema and other diseases linked to tobacco; the cigarettes manufacturers should".

The predictions of Ralph Nader, the American herald of consumerism, have been at least partially fulfilled. By becoming organized, the consumers have become a force that the big industries must indeed take into consideration: by seducing, if possible, and by manipulating through subtle and sometimes unexpected processes. Surprise attacks on the Web, for example, an innovative technique a perfect example of which is the ongoing wrangle between Europeans and Americans over genetically modified foods.

On the Transgenic Soy Front

Genetically Modified Organisms, the famous GMO, are a worry. Still, our perplexity should not make us blind. The introduction of these disputed products to the market raise questions in the areas of food, the environment, medicine and others. Fruits of conflicts of interests between the powerful multinational agro-alimentary groups and certain sectors of European, French agriculture in particular, they are highly strategic in nature. This characteristic undoubtedly explains why the techniques implemented to ensure their promotion rather often concern the pure and simple disinformation.

The remark particularly applies to soy. In its natural form, this

202

annual plant of the legume family has already enjoyed a fantastic 25% expansion of cultivation, from 125 million acres in 1979 to 157 million in 1996. In 1996, still, the United States produced more than 63 million tons of seed, more half of the world's total, Brazil 20%, China and Argentina approximately 10% each, and Europe. . . 1%!

"Our livestock breeding is almost completely dependent on protein imports, a situation of dependency very much like that which we are experiencing in the energy sector", declared Edith Cresson, Minister for Agriculture in 1981. . . twenty years ago. This dangerous situation has not improved since, to put it mildly. In 1997, France spent some $130 million to import soy and the unified Europe of Fifteen spent $2.7 billion.

Convinced (rightly) of the strategic importance of "Green Power" (the agroalimentary industry), American producers — united in two powerful professional organizations, American Soybean Association and the National Soybean Processor Association — literally managed to "hook" the European pig breeders on soybeans. As a result, the protein- and lysine-rich soybean became the basic food of pigs and poultry. What else could they do? Short on ideas, the European agricultural strategists came up with just one alternate route by which to evade this general offensive from the U.S., and it was the worst: the systematic and uncontrolled use of bone meal.

Until now, we have only spoken about the natural forms of soy. But the invention of genetic engineering complicated matters. Since 1944, researchers have been working on ways to transfer desoxyribonucleic acid, the "instructions" that pass along hereditary features. In 1953, Watson and Crick discerned the helical structure of DNA. In the mid-1970's, the methods of DNA "recombination" gave birth to "genetic engineering". In 1978, finally, specialists at Genentech, a Californian company, first applied this technology to agricultural products in order to make them more resistant to the combined ravages of time, microorganisms and insects. The method spread; today it is used on more than 800 products, especially soy. Among other effects, biogenetics makes it possible to considerably increase the lysin content of soy.

As one might suspect, the American soy producers, always on the lookout for any innovation that might strengthen their hand with the European market, were quick to understand the importance of these discoveries. To preserve their competitive advantage, they were eager to implement them. And so they did! In summer 1996, 1,000,000 acres of good American soil was already sown with soybeans; and this expanse was increased to 37 million acres just two years later.

At the same time, powerful groups like Monsanto, the "Microsoft of food" based in St. Louis, Missouri, and Genentech wove close ties with the Clinton administration during the 1996 presidential campaign. So close that Monsanto and other biotechnology companies would donate, perfectly legally, several hundreds of thousands of dollars in soft money to the Democratic camp (contributions that are not subject to the dollar limits that apply to direct gifts). And so close that, shortly thereafter, Genentech would co-finance the festivities around Bill Clinton' second inauguration.

This kind of generosity deserves some payback. After the second electoral success of the ex-governor of Arkansas, Marcia Hauls, who had handled intergovernmental relations for the Clinton campaign, was promoted to the role of coordinator of Monsanto's Britain strategy. Later, the 1997 presidential speech on the State of the Union would pay homage to the group from St. Louis. After all, what's good for American biotechnology is good for the United States, isn't it?

Under the circumstances, it's no surprise that a consumer advocate like Ronnie Cummins, director of the Pure Food Campaign, says that the bio-techno-pharmaceutical-agro-commercial complex "is now competing with the oil industry in terms of revenue as well as influence". In the United States, the extent of this influence is indicated by the fact that the Food and Drug Administration, which is responsible for oversight of the food industry as well as pharmaceuticals, hired Margaret Miller, a former Monsanto research worker. In Great Britain, Ann Foster — former director of Scottish Consumers Council, and a member on several key commissions such as the Committee on Medical Aspects of Food and Nutrition — was hired as a lobbyist. By Monsanto.

"Web-maneuvers"

The European producers, already very weak, sought to protect themselves as best they could against the inexorable advance of this biotechnology steamroller. In June 1996, people were beginning to talk about transgenic soy, just when certain lobbyists related to European interests were working the halls of government throughout the Old Continent; especially the Brussels Commission. These agents of influence were trying to get the European Community authorities finally to authorize their employers to cultivate and to market GMO on the territory of the EEC.

Such demands met a rather chilly reception in Brussels; and chillier yet with the consumer advocacy groups and various types of ecologists. Reinforcing the arguments of those in the resistance, a wave of information hostile to GMO's in general and to transgenic soy in particular began to circulate on the Web. Some of these warnings were picked up by the press, some not; but overall, the efforts of the European pro-transgenic soy lobbyists were hampered at a critical moment.

Where were these data coming from? From just four sources. And they were all related to one single content provider, a British institute that makes a profession out of defending nature against its predators, as was soon confirmed through the monitoring work carried out on the Web by the French company Datops.

We met this high-tech firm during the Total affair in Burma. Its big program, Périclès, measures the intensity of information being circulated on certain well-defined topics, identifies their sources, and performs statistical analyses. By calculating the ratio of the number of targets (opinion-leaders, decision makers, journalists) and the number of sources, you can detect signs of an orchestrated manipulation. In this case, the results were startling.

Let's take a closer look. There had been a lull since mid-July 1996; then, according to the graphs generated by Pericles, it shot up abruptly in September. The general outline was similar to what had been going on in the early summer. The British primary source, already identified by Datops, would publicize a set of data, and it would be picked up and amplified by its four usual "loudspeakers", passing the information from the Web to the newspapers.

The attacks did not bother to go into the possible health risks to consumers; they concentrated on the damage that growing genetically modified soy could do to the environment. Why this subtle discrimination? That will soon be seen. And let's not overlook the timing: in just a month, Monsanto was due to deliver to Europe its first cargoes of genetically modified soy, a move that was staunchly being resisted by organizations hostile to GMO's.

On October 10, Datops felt confident that it could advise its customer that a campaign of information/disinformation about transgenic soy was, indeed, underway; this campaign, it seems, was targeted only to the countries of the European Convention. Its concrete results appeared soon afterwards on the European markets, when the market for transgenic soy temporarily collapsed.

The British source then ceased its emissions while, at the end of October, the press echoed the attacks against modified soy more and more loudly. These were accelerating, under their own momentum, when Greenpeace launched its own anti-transgenic demonstrations at the beginning of November when the first cargo of American modified soy arrived on board the U.S. ship, the *Ideal Progress*.

No one could have suspected that "Greenpeace" was in collusion with the American "Green Power". On the other hand, its demonstrations against *Ideal Progress* were foreseeable (after all, they were planned in advance), so that the anonymous attacker on the Web could easily integrate them as a factor of acceleration in its campaign of psychological warfare. In November-December, impressed by the battery of arguments that just happened to mention only the dangers to the environment, Germany, Austria, France and the Netherlands officially opposed the production of genetically modified soy.

The health risks to the consumers having been "overlooked", the marketing of transgenic soy was not hurt by these measures. While the European agricultural lobby was pondering its failure, distributors on the Continent placed enormous orders with U.S. producers in order to satisfy their customers. American "Green Power" won that round.

During this period, our British environmentalist institute sank into a strange lethargy: the more urgent the threat to nature, the more catastrophist information it disseminated via the Internet. Had it now fallen into the big sleep? Apparently.

The European agricultural lobby re-grouped, and went on the offensive again in September 1997. This renewal of activity was dictated by the calendar: transgenic soy is planted at the beginning of autumn. And that was precisely the time when the British "source" awoke from its slumber: there were new questions raised, renewed warnings posted on websites, troubling new press releases distributed . . . and new postponements on the decision whether to authorize the growing of genetically modified products in European countries. The American producers had just won the second round, one would be tempted to conclude: another year of commercial monopoly for them, another year lost by their European competitors who were already struggling. The day when the Continent would be self-sufficient in terms of food production was a long way off, and not getting any closer. The Commission found no objection to the paradoxical notion that a GMO may be dangerous to cultivate but not to consume, and that in the final analysis, the American "Green Power" was the beneficiary!

In matters of hygiene, Brussels was more active in 1990 when it was a matter of preserving British agricultural interests in the name of the sacrosanct rule of community communal unanimity, when the "mad cows" scandal was starting to come alive.

"We must adopt a cool attitude, in order not to cause unfavorable reactions in the market. There should be no more talk about BSE*. This point should not appear on the agenda", required a brief internal

* The Brussels acronym for Bovine Spongiform Encephalitis, "mad cow disesase".

note from the Commission on October 12.

For those who might not have gotten the hint, the memorandum writers dotted the "i" later on: "Generally speaking, this matter must be minimized by practicing *disinformation*. It is to better to say that the press has a tendency to exaggerate".

A healthy European philosophy founded on lies and manipulation! And today, we see the results: greater distrust from consumers, outbreaks of panic, and perhaps avoidable deaths. In September 1997, while the American agriculture industrialists were triumphing on the transgenic soy front, the Luxembourgian writer of this note continued to walk the carpeted corridors of the Brussels offices of the EEC.

Community ways hardly seem to have changed. In January 1999, an unsigned internal memo from the executive staff in Brussels recommended on two pages "not to be obnubilated" by "transparency" in contacts with the press. "A certain amount of cynicism — and sometimes of hypocrisy — in the manner of disseminating information is sometimes necessary", it specified, since, "vis-à-vis certain particularly clever journalists, we unfortunately must be resigned to being (temporarily) attacked".

Really!

Phobias, Fantasies and Manipulations

"As a rule, disinformation requires an amplifying factor, which it usually finds in the media and sometimes in the activities of special interest groups, whether their interest is financial or other", notes Jean-Jacques Duby, scientific adviser to the National Institute of Risks and the Industrial Environment, in a collective work on *Food Risks and Fears*, published under the direction of Prof. Marian Apfelbaum.

That is true enough, even if it glosses over the role of the public powers whose opacity is, as we have seen, particularly harmful. Duby contrasts certain dangers that are underestimated because they are so familiar — the car, for example — to "new risks introduced by the development of the agroalimentary industry, which are highly susceptible to being over-estimated". He considers GMO's and "mad cows" to be among the best candidates for exaggerated risks.

Unfortunately, it is not very hard to manipulate consumers. No specialist is likely to forget the "Villejuif brochure". Typed by unknown hands and disseminated for the first time in 1976, this document was presented as a warning from the Gustave-Roussy de Villejuif Institute, a center universally known for cancer treatment. A list of additives authorized in the foodstuffs followed the false claim. Many of these products were arbitrarily denounced as "carcinogens", others were called "suspect", and the rest were labeled "innocuous". This leaflet was photocopied by private individuals and reprinted without any fact-checking by hundreds of magazines, even cited extensively in a book on "popularized medicine"; it was still circulating nine years later. Jean-Noel Kapferer, author of a reference book on *Rumors*, estimates that 7 million French citizens have been "deceived by its credible and scientific appearance".

A typewriter, some eager volunteers, and a rudimentary distribution network are all it took to get this false memorandum the backing of the print media. Because, these days, anything that has to do with health and safety has become a "sensitive" issue that lends itself to fantasies — and thus to manipulation.

Perrier — Bubble Troubles

For example, it's hard to believe that the barrage of attacks in the American press against the French water purveyor, Perrier, at the very beginning of 1990, was inspired only by a legitimate concern to educate consumers. On January 19, a laboratory in Charlotte, North Carolina, supposedly detected benzene in certain bottles of carbonated water. Perrier investigated and, after eliminating the idea of any pollution at the mineral water's source, put forth the suggestion that there may have been some human error at the factory. This line of defense calmed neither the press nor the public, so it became necessary to consider radical countermeasures. On February 12, the embattled French firm withdrew 3 million cases from the American market — worth some

$40 million. Two days later, Perrier's chairman, Gustave Leven, ex-tended this decision to 160 million bottles worldwide, an expensive precaution that did not prevent ten lawsuits from being filed in the U. S..

How could any foreign element have gotten into the water? What could have gone wrong, and why? How bad was it? The worrisome discovery by the experts in Charlotte could not have hit at a worse time; Perrier was already struggling with a legal controversy with the giant Pepsi-Cola, since 1989, in connection with a licensing agreement that was already 25 years in existence. The episode still remains shrouded in mystery. In addition to taking a spectacular fall on the stock market (-16.5% for the period of February 9-14), it cost between $100 million and 150 billion for a company that was already being rocked by unprecedented financial and commercial difficulties.

The benzene had not caused any irrevocable harm to Perrier con-sumers, fortunately, but the rumors did irrevocable harm to the com-pany's reputation, driving the French non-alcoholic beverage maker toward a painful end. Bad-mouthed by the Americans, including at least one major industrial group (not Pepsi-Cola), Perrier ended up throwing in the towel. In 1991, an outsider — the Swiss company Nes-tle — bought this crippled contender. But even the change of owner-ship did not put an end to the soft drinks war.

Deadly Summer

The summer of 1993 was expected to be a scorcher in the United States, and all the soft drinks manufacturers were rubbing their hands over the prospect of making heaps of money.

All the "soda-pop makers" except for Pepsi-Cola, the world's sec-ond largest cola producer. They were the 15th largest American com-pany in terms of income, but the brand was having serious image prob-lems. The ultra-orthodox rabbis of the world were furious that Pepsico was sponsoring the rock group Guns n' Roses, and the singer Michael Jackson, both of whom were on their black list. The international media was trumpeting the rabbis' request that the faithful buy Coke instead.

At this juncture, on Wednesday, June 9, 1993, Earl Triplett, a consumer in Tacoma, Washington, made known to the authorities that he had just discovered a half-milliliter hypodermic insulin syringe in his can of Diet Pepsi. The following day, the Food and Drug Administration opened an investigation. . . and within twenty-four hours they learned that a consumer in Seattle had had a similar experience. This time, the syringe had a one milli-liter capacity.

In Somers, NY, the Pepsi headquarters, the company leadership was obsessed with fear over a possible link with AIDS. But by Saturday, the Food and Drug Administration officially published the results of the tests conducted by its experts. These examinations showed that the two syringes were not contaminated. The acidity of a drink like Pepsi-Cola, the FDA pointed out, would eliminate most bacteria and viruses. All the same, Karl Behnke, the chairman of AlpacCorp (Pepsi-Cola's bottler and distributor), suggested as a precaution that consumers to empty their cans into a glass before drinking.

Was there any more danger? On June 13, three new complaints were received by the FDA, thus triggering the law of the series that encourages the media to take a greater interest. And on June 14 came the avalanche: lawsuits came tumbling in from the four corners of the United States, Cleveland, Monticello, Rock Springs, Los Angeles, New Orleans.

Pepsi Counterattacks

Was this some concerted offensive? A collective hallucination? In any case, some response was necessary. A crisis meeting was led by Craig Weatherup, Pepsi-Cola's chairman for North America. In addition to this former trucker, the group comprised nine people: Rebecca Madeira, VP for Public Relations; Dr. James Stanley, VP for product safety; Anne Reynolds Ward and Andrew Giangola, from public affairs; Steve Rapp, the legal adviser; Cathy Dial, Director of Consumer Relations; Sheila Sackman, Director of Risks and Insurance; Dave Gabriel, Director of Development and Negotiations; and Phil Faxlanguer, Director of the Rapid Response Service. These four women and six men would organize the counter-offensive, with the support of several specialized communications companies: Video Public Relations Newswire, Medialink, Robert Chang Productions, North American Network Radio News Service and Ad/Sat.

The response had to be fast, heartfelt, well-planned and well-worded. Making a wrong move at a time like this would be disastrous. The Perrier business was on everyone's mind at Pepsico. Because of their emblematic value, the recurring difficulties of Procter & Gamble were also borne in mind. Since 1981, the detergents multinational had been the butt of a malignant and obstinate rumor in the southern states — Alabama, Arkansas, the Carolinas, Florida, Georgia, Indiana, Kansas, Kentucky, Louisiana, Mississippi, Missouri, Oklahoma, Tennessee and Texas, and also in Great Britain and France — linking it to . . . satanic cults.

Pepsico started by setting up a toll-free number, 1-800-433-COLA, where twenty-five duly briefed "operators" were ready to reassure anxious customers. They received some 5,100 calls between June 14 and 21. Craig Weatherup, for his part, stepped up his communication with Doctor David Kessler, the top FDA official following this case, and thus Pepsi-Cola was informed on June 16 that FDA agents had made their first arrests for false declarations.

Learning through an intermediary that the surveillance videotape in a Denver mini-market had caught a woman placing a syringe inside one of the cola cans, the shopkeeper did not hesitate one second. In spite of its technical defects, the document was sold to the highest bidder and was shown the next day on CNN World News, then on all the American channels. In addition, thanks to 403 relay stations, a television audience of 186 million viewers was bombarded with a flurry of "educational" images: how Pepsi bottles are filled, and why it is impossible to get a syringe inside during that operation. Craig Weatherup was a great success on the talk-show circuit, where he answered consumers' questions on a call-in line, and so was the advertising campaign designed by the BBDO agency — every day the newspapers delivered this ironic message: "Pepsi is pleased to announce . . . Nothing".

Rapid, muscular, multifaceted, this media response was not long in bearing its first fruits. Figuring that it was giving them honest information, consumers retained their respect for the company. Far from dropping, Pepsico's stock price remained stable. Sales went down, but only by an acceptable margin: some $15 to 20 million. And finally, the overall revenue for that year increased by $3 billion compared to 1992.

The fact remains that it had been close to a complete catastrophe. Without this fast, effective counter-attack, the company could very likely have experienced the kind of disaster that befell its chief enemy, Coke, six years later: the pure and simple suspension of its products from the Belgian and French markets in spring 1999, as a "precaution".

Or worse yet, a generalized boycott.

Story of a Boycott

This term is more than a century old. It was coined in 1880 in the Irish village of Neale, in the county of Mayo, by the village priest, the good Father O'Malley. Fed up with centuries of English occupation, spoliation and massacres, his parishioners engaged in a new form of revolt that year. Disputing an annual custom imposed by force, Father O'Malley's flocks refused the drudgery of the potato harvest ordered by Captain Boycott, the British landowners' local agent. The peasants folded their arms and waited, praying to God.

Their courageous resistance was not in vain; it opened the path of nonviolent action later enshrined by Gandhi in India, and in the southern United States by the pastor Martin Luther King.

What a scandal it caused! Those Irish devils were making trouble yet again! Journalists from all over converged on Neale to observe the phenomenon. The "media event" was created.

This incident came to the attention of independence leader Charles Stuart Parnell. He appealed for widespread "boycotting" to disrupt the country. The English, looking to de-fang the dangerous Parnell, orchestrated a concerted maneuver against this Irish "king without a crown". He was a Catholic, with the beautiful Kitty O'Shea as his mistress — his enemies played on that in order to discredit him.

So, the word "boycott" was associated right from the start with human rights, and it is used more and more to mobilize people throughout the world. Since the years of the Vietnam War and especially of the battle to end antiapartheid, the weapon of boycotting showed its power throughout the Anglo-Saxon world and in northern Europe, where consumer arguments are given a consistently better reception than in Latin lands: France, Spain, Italy. In the U.S.A, Germany, Sweden and Great Britain, the effectiveness of the campaign against Outspan oranges, cultivated in South Africa, is still remembered; however, in the Latin countries, its impact was almost nil.

The phenomenon has become so widespread that two specialized publications exist now in the United States, the *National Boycott News* and the *Boycott Quarterly*. These periodicals gave full coverage of the campaign against Nike sporting goods in 1998: a 39% drop in revenue following revelations in the press of the poor work conditions in its subsidiaries that had been relocated to Asia and South America. "Now that the informed consumer is king, no company can afford not to listen. No company can afford to make a bad choice", concluded a report from Faith Popcorn, one of American business's best-loved consultants.

Seeing which way the wind was blowing, those businesses preferred to take the initiative. Firms as emblematic as Walt Disney and Wal-Mart let it be known that they were voluntarily adopting codes of moral self-discipline. Taking the ball even farther, Reebok created its own foundation for the defense of human rights, in close partnership with Amnesty International. Jeans-maker Levi-Strauss & Co. enacted a code of good conduct in 1992, stipulating that the company would deal only with companies that prohibited child labor, did not use forced labor, guaranteed heath and safety conditions in their factories, respected legal obligations (especially in regard to work hours) and strictly observed their workers' rights of association. The clothing manufacturer withdrew from China, somewhat spectacularly, in 1993 in the name of these very principles. It announced its return via sub-contractors in January 1999.

In Europe, C & A, Auchan, Promodès, Marks & Spencer and Ikea announced that they were adopting similar rules. At about the same time, international standards such as SA 8000 appeared, a certification of good social behavior invented by the Council of Economic Priorities, a conglomerate of American associations. This goodwill ended up leading to a proliferation of outcomes, sometimes overtly contrary to the expressed goal: 215 social codes were listed in 1998 by the International Office of Labor; less than half of them had to do with child labor, one quarter prohibited forced labor and only 15% referred to trade-union freedom. This led Michel Hansenne, general manager of the ILO [International Labor Organization], to remark to *Le Monde*: "Nothing guarantees their perenniality. And we are not sheltered from manipulation, either."

Such maneuvers may be promulgated by companies seeking to mask their turpitudes as well as dishonest contractors looking to charge their competitors with imaginary infractions. It's one more trap. Given the lack of rationality and critical thinking on behalf of consumer associations and human rights groups, nothing would be simpler than to launch an unfounded attack on perfectly innocent industrial and commercial companies, just by ridiculing them. Let's not forget that the German television producer Michaël Born, tried by the court of Coblentz in December 1996 on sixteen counts of falsified reports, had delivered a particularly "moving" documentary on the exploitation of Indian children by the wretched carpet manufacturers.

What can we learn from all this? Not to confuse legitimate indignation and distorted information. In 1997 OCB, the leading French cigarette paper company, a member of the Bolloré Technologies group, was shaken by a series of rumors. OCB supposedly was financing the

National Front. Without looking for any proof, a few radio stations carried away by their enthusiasm repeated this accusation. "One of the FN's subsidiaries is called OCB; don't help them", sang a rap group. Polygram pulled their CD off the shelves. But it was already too late; the rumor (whose origin is a matter of curiosity) had a severe impact on the company's revenues.

Vigilance and sagacity are so essential if we are to avoid sinking into paranoia and credulity. Sometimes, what is at stake has been so well masked that it is hard to discern. The distinctions between truth and falsehood are like the differences between dogs and wolves; and disinformation is not only refining its techniques, it is broadening its field of application.

In the 20th century, it was a weapon in political war; at the dawn of the new millennium, disinformation is transforming itself into one of the most effective weapons of economic war.

CONCLUSION

In the age of CNN, satellite dishes and the Internet, the techniques of mass persuasion that were developed during the Cold War have not lost one iota of their impact. Only their field of application has changed. Today's great industrial and commercial confrontations are played out to a great extent in the semi-real, semi-virtual arena of psychological manipulation and disinformation.

There was a time when the Kremlin and its sidekicks used an exhaustive array of slogans ranging from the antifascist and socialist to the anti-imperialist. The West responded with "freedom". These ideological confrontations, the fruits of a whole new approach to the conquest of minds, were an inextricable mixture of truth and lies. Only the objectives were clear. Each protagonist spelled out its concepts, its terminology, and its vision of the world in such a way as to back its adversaries into a corner, making it a prisoner of its own inflexible dogma.

Dezinformatsia was a major theater of operations. It is not by chance that some of its most astute practitioners — the Russians, known for their prowess at chess, and the Chinese, virtuosos in the game of Go — assimilated long ago the strategies of encirclement, of infiltration, of the most complex mystifications. And it's not by chance either that their most adept counterparts in the West have been the British, experts in multifarious machinations — the glory of Sherlock Holmes, Hercules Poirot and George Smiley.

The most diabolic weapon in the world can only do so much. Leninist, Stalinist, Khrushchevian, Brezhnevian, Andropovist and finally Gorbachevian disinformation could not prevent the collapse of the Berlin Wall nor the dissolution of Communism into nothingness. But history has more than one trick up its sleeve. Using a logic that is hardly less powerful than yesterday's ideologies, today's industrial and commercial quarrels will also be played out principally as a war of semantics.

Imposing your own vocabulary is half the battle. From "walkman" to "wargame", "teenagers" to "fast-food", "management" to "benchmarking", the Americans seem to have won the first round. In the face of such profusion, how many globally-accepted terms can the Japanese claim? None but "karaoke" — and the Europeans, zero. And it is due to this increasing linguistic impregnation that the American-British cultural influence has extended to three quarters of the world. From the leading elites to the tertiary sectors to the advance troops of the "battalions" of the common man, it has been spread throughout the average people.

A war of words, and a war of images. Here, too, the United States has scored invaluable points. For decades, movies and above all television series have been imposing on the whole world the standardized canons of the American way of life and the American dream. What a way to foster a confusion of identifications, aspirations and plans, laying the groundwork for an actual "cultural takeover". The ultimate goal of the offensive is to "sell" the American-style personality throughout the world. The recent fashion of celebrating Halloween is just one more example of fully-formed commercial mythologies that can be passed along.

The Americanization of the vocabulary and the imagination encourages the Americanization of patterns of consumption. Thus, this nearly global cultural phenomenon serves as one of the most effective tools by which U.S. companies can penetrate profitable markets. The "Yankees" have a genius for associating with their economic strategies the powerful impression that they give of themselves: young, dynamic, relaxed, professional, technically proficient.

Any war, commercial or otherwise, is a psychological war first and foremost. In this game, our competitors across the Atlantic have accumulated quite a collection of trump cards. One of the most significant is their extraordinary capacity to "universalize" the products of their industries. The ten most evocative brand names on the planet are, in descending order: McDonald's, Coca Cola, Disney, Kodak, Sony, Gillette, Mercedes-Benz, Levi's, Microsoft and Marlboro. Eight Americans, one European and one Japanese. And that's not counting such outstanding industrial objects as the DC-3 Dakota, "the freedom plane" that broke the Berlin blockade in 1948-49 under the aegis of the U.S. Air Force (11,000 specimens were sold), and the B-747 "Jumbo-Jet" that still makes the rules at the major airports, the Coke can, the pack of Marlboros, the "Big Mac". And in the world of computers, it's Personal Computers from "Big Blue" (IBM), Macintosh, and software from Microsoft.

Make them dream/make them buy: and it's not limited to civilians. Not such a long time ago, a media campaign was presenting the American Apache helicopter as "the weapon of peace" in Kosovo, using the Balkans conflict to some extent as "display window" to market these "tank-killers" stuffed with electronics. Representatives of the (American) Indian nations protested against the tasteless use of the name, but they were ignored. The Apache did not live up to expectations, so Boeing shoved another model, the Comanche, onto the market. Everything becomes a good opportunity to make a sale. . . although it is kind of hard to imagine the French naming combat machines the "Cathari" or the "Camisard"!

The close bonds linking industrial development, commercial expansion, cultural penetration and modern forms of disinformation are far from coming apart; they are only changing their forms. Among other skills, American-British partnership has developed a pragmatic approach to the analysis of economic and social functions, seeing them as the results of conflicts of interests, rather than the product of a royal order imposed from above. Far from denying contradictions inherent in modern societies or, worse, seeking safety in archaism, they put up with these difficulties in the hope of reaching the point of ideal equilibrium: that which optimizes their successes. This worldview enables them alternately to resort to brute force, to appeal to international legal authorities (which are largely impregnated with the Anglo-Saxon sense of law) and quite simply to resort to the usual tricks. Those on the other side can often muster no opposition but impotent rage, the modern version of yesterday's "anti-imperialism".

Such flexibility in interpreting events and conduct gives the Anglo-Americans a head start in the Info War — to borrow the trendy Americanism. The term is fairly recent and it encompasses several complementary categories. First comes simple information, absolutely stupid and absolutely honest. Then over-information, an intensive "bombardment" of the media, the decision-makers and the public with a deluge of data that is mainly favorable to those who are putting it out. Counter-information (a specialty that seems to have a rosy future based on the ambient commercial aggressiveness) blends art and the techniques of self-defense, by taking apart the unfavorable bulletins point by point with objective and verifiable facts. Lastly, although it is rarely acknowledged so openly, pure and simple disinformation is used as a supplement to the entire panoply.

As the reader may have noted, while reading these pages, disinformation is not at all a psychological blitzkrieg that is dreamt up and deployed on a moment's notice. Disinformation is, on the contrary, a sustained action, using technical, financial and human resources in an orchestrated campaign.

Based on that fact alone, the use of disinformation can only be a deliberate choice; no one ever puts out disinformation by chance. Any "cyber-detective" knows that there is as much difference between one specific inaccuracy asserted by a subaltern and a genuine disinformation campaign conceived by the bosses as there is between a fatal blow delivered in a fit of rage and a crime committed with all the coolness of premeditation.

The Internet, born of a convergence between the brains of the U.S. Army and those of certain big universities, has become one of the essential tools of the Info War. The quintessential globalizer, this network has been responsible for an extraordinary advance in communications, and it has also fostered the birth of an avant-garde of little computer geniuses. Young (mostly in the 12 to 25 age range), capricious, looking for kicks, and quite self-centered, this recent aristocracy of knowledge exhibits a considerable degree of amorality: to them, all's fair, even the most underhanded tricks.

Such a mindset has something in common with those of the perverted intellectuals who, in another time, threw in their lots with Nazism and Communism. Without losing a sense of proportion, it should be noted that intelligence services the world over attach the greatest importance to controlling, recruiting, and even manipulating the deviant members of the "new wave" of high-tech marginality.

These exceptionally gifted young folks have a promising future in the design, programming and the deployment of "intelligent agents". These artificial systems fist appeared on the network two years ago, and they have been proliferating since then. They sweep pre-selected chat groups, catching any occurrence of a certain acronym, company name or brand, and bombard the newsgroups at once with all sorts of messages attacking the product in question: X cars are dangerous. . . Y vacuum cleaners cause pollution . . . Z food is full of toxins.

In order to make the good-faith Internet user confuse these prefabricated texts with genuine contributions by dissatisfied users, dissatisfied consumers, the propaganda software constantly refreshes the word choices, changing about the sentences and altering the angles of attack. Short and incisive enough to give a convincing illusion, these missives sometimes blame the quality of the company "to be demol-ished", sometimes they impugn the reliability of the goods. There is plenty of ammunition: anything that can hurt the rival, on any grounds. And these cybernetic lies are so widespread today that some specialists have coined a new acronym, CAT, for "computer-assisted threats".

How much computer assistance is there? According to some sources, American users of "intelligent agents" get technical support from the National Security Agency, which supervises and even controls a substantial share of the Internet traffic. Unlike the CIA, which is even more avid for publicity since its official budget is always in danger of being cut back, the NSA, the federal agency officially in charge of "electromagnetic interception", likes to maintain an aura of mystery. Only one serious book has been published on the NSA . . . in 1982. On the other hand, many movies and novels exalt its omnipresence, usually in a rather worrying context. The military power — only entity that can really craft a strategy for the United States — uses the "Cyber War" as a war horse to enhance its might.

Technological revolution, psychological upheaval. The develop-ment of the Internet is wreaking havoc with the traditional methods of disinformation. Everything happens fast on the Web, which is itself developing at amazing speed.

Beyond its indisputable utility for companies, governments, and private individuals, the fascination that the Web exerts on our societies is gaining in significance. As long as the phenomenon only touched a fraction of the population, it wasn't a big problem; the written word — more reliable, less transitory — was still what mattered. But that might change, in the future.

A danger exists. This is no reason to become "Internet-paranoïacs" but it is one more reason to understand that with every passing day, we will need to get better at learning how to live between truth and falsehood. Disinformation has a grand future ahead of it, and only our vigilance, our realism, and our technical skills have kept it from overflowing the bounds of the acceptable thus far.

If things start to go the other way, the economic cold war could start to heat up. And the consequences could be dire.

ACKNOWLEDGEMENTS
and
BIBLIOGRAPHICAL SOURCES

To avoid overburdening my tale with an endless stream of footnotes, I have chosen to identify my principal sources (oral, written and audio-visual) at the end of the work, chapter by chapter. Concerning the newspaper industry, I have limited myself to citing major articles. In order to avoid redundancies, I have generally abstained from giving the full citation for articles when their sources are already identified in the text.

Given the particularly sensitive nature of the information revealed in this book, the reader will understand that it is impossible for me to cite by name all the many individuals who agreed to assist me. For various reasons having to do with their professional activities, these witnesses preferred anonymity. They have my fullest gratitude. To all, I wish good reading.

And finally, a hearty thanks to my friend Alain Dugrand, who supported this project from start to finish with all his usual enthusiasm.

Chapter 1

Interview with Joseph Daniel and Michel Delaborde, of Total, as well as with Eric Dénécé, Louis Gay and Klaas Kooy. My thanks also to those who asked not to be named.

Books

Francis Christophe, *Birmanie, la dictature du pavot*, Paris, Philippe Picquier, 1998.
Pierre Péan, Jean-Pierre Séréni, *Les Emirs de la République, l'aventure du pétrole tricolore*, Paris, Le Seuil, 1982.

Anthony Sampson, *Les Septs Soeurs*, Paris, Alain Moreau, 1976.

Barbara Victor, *La Dame de Rangoon, Aung San Suu Kyi, une Nobel en prison*, Paris, Flammarion, 1997.

Daniel Yergin, *The Prize, the Epic Quest for Oil, Money and Power*, (2 volumes) New York, Simon & Schuster, 1991.

Antoine Zichka, *La Guerre secrète pour le pétrole*, Paris, Payot.

Various:

Papers from the UDF and ACFCI conference: "La France en guerre économique : quelles ripostes, quelles armes, quels acteurs [France at economic war: what responses, what weapons, what actors?]", Paris, National Assembly, Wednesday February 26, 1997.

Christophe de la Chapelle, *Guerre de l'information, intelligence économique et géostratégie du monde atlantique : Le cas de l'entreprise Total en Birmanie dans les années 90*, A DEA memorandum on contemporary history, Université Paris-Sorbonne (Paris IV), under the direction of Prof. Georges-Henri Soutou, printed by the Association of veterans of the special services for national defense (ASSDN). [The War of information, economic intelligence and geostrategy in the Atlantic world: The case of Total in Burma in the 1990's,].

Eric Dénécé: *L'Action de Total en Birmanie, une entreprise française confrontée aux nouvelles stratégies concurrentielles anglo-saxonnes dans le cadre d'un marché emergent* [Total's Actions in Burma: a French company confronted with the new Anglo-Saxon competitive strategies in the context of an emerging market.] An unpublished study of new economic intelligence, June 1996.

Beatrice Laroche and Anne-Christine Habbard, *La Birmanie, Total et les droits de l'homme, dissection d'un chantier* [Burma, Total and human rights, dissection of a building site], a status report for the International Federation of the Leagues of Human Rights, October 1996.

Collection from the *International Dispatch on Drugs*, a monthly newsletter in French, Spanish and English published by International Dispatch on Drugs, Ltd. N°19075463 Paris cedex 10. Very detailed on the Burmese narcodictatorship.

Press:

Aline Basela, Georges Dupuy, "L'encombrant chantier de Total en Birmanie", *L'Express* ["Total's troublesome building site in Burma"], April 28, 1997.

Emmanuelle Boullestreau, Patrice Picquard and Xavier Thomas, "Dossier Birmanie", *L'Evénement du Jeudi*, December 19, 1996.

Rémi Kauffer, "La Guerre de l'ombre. Cela s'appelle l'intelligence économique. Un combat sans règles où, pour saper l'ennemi, on infiltre, on dégrade son image, on débauche son personnel. Enjeu : la conquête des grands marchés. Récits. Total dans le guêpier birman. Les cadeaux intéressés de Stockholm à la Namibie. D'étranges Japonais dans le Poitou" [The Shadow War. It's called economic intelligence. A war with no rules, in which, to get their enemy, they infiltrate it, they degrade its image, they corrupt its employees. At stake, the biggest markets. How it's done. Total in a Burmese trap. Tainted gifts from Stockholm to Namibia. Strangers from Japan in Poitou." *Challenges* n° 112, March 1997.

Remi Kauffer, "Klaas Kooy, le survivant de la rivière Kwaï" [Klaus Kooy, survivor of the River Kwai], *Historia* N °630, June 1999.

Chapters 2, 3 and 4

My public thanks to Pierre Chirac, from the magazine *Prescrire*. And my private thanks to all those individuals who, unlike Pierre, preferred not to use their names.

Remi Kauffer, "Klaas Kooy, Survivant of the Kwaï river", *Historia* N °630, June 1999.

Books

Prof. Marian Apfelbaum, *Vivre avec du cholestérol* [Living with Cholesterol], Paris, Le Rocher, 1992.

Prof. Marian Apfelbaum (under the direction of), *Risques et peurs alimentaires* [Food Risks and Fears], Paris, Odile Jacob, 1998.

Yves Audève & Gerard Delteil, *La Médecine malade de l'argent* [Medicine: Made Sick by Money], Paris, Les Editions de l'Atelier, 1994.

Marc Dem, *Fric santé, le scandale* [Cash, Health, and Scandal], Monaco, Le Rocher, 1992.

Bruno Donatini Dr., *L'Intox, quelques vérités sur vos médicaments* [Mindgames: some truths about your drugs], Cormonteil-France, 1997.

Charles Harboun, *Le Marketing pharmaceutique*, Paris, ESKA, 1995.

Prof. Dominique Jolly (under the direction of), *Politiques de santé en France, quelle légitimité pour quels décideurs?* [Health policies in France, how legitimate, according to which decision-makers?], Paris, Flammarion Médicine-Sciences, 1997.

Prof. Dominique Jolly (under the direction of), *Quelle place pour les médicaments génériques en France ?* [What role should generic drugs play in France?] Paris, Flammarion Medicine-Sciences, 1996

Prof. Dominique Jolly (under the direction of), *Médicaments et médecines, les chemins de la guérison* [Drugs and medicines, ways of healing], Paris, Flammarion Medicine-Sciences, 1996.

Philippe Meyer, *La Révolution des médicaments* [The Drug Revolution], Paris, Fayard, 1984.

Maurice Punch, *Exploring Corporate Misconduct, Analysis and Cases*, London, Sage Publications Inc, 1996.

Mutualité française, Les Enjeux du médicament [French insurance; what's at stakes with medication], Paris, Mutualité française, 1997.

Prof. Edouard Zarifian, *Le Prix du bien-être, psychotropes et société* [The Price of Well-being, Psychotropics and Society], Paris, Odile Jacob, 1996.

Press

"If You Are Depressed About Being Obese, New Drug May Cure Both Your Problems", *Wall Street Journal*, May 22, 1986.

"Omeprazole and Genotoxicity", *The Lancet*, February 17, 1990.

"US FDA Warned Glaxo on Omeprazole", *Scrip*, May 2, 1990.

"Glaxo's Genotoxicity Study Flawed", *Scrip*, October 16, 1991.

"Will Glaxo Adjust Viewpoint over Rival Drug", *Pharmaceutical Business News*, October 18, 1991.

"Eli Lilly Chairman Focuses His Vision on Europe", by Daniel Green, *Financial Times*, August 23, 1995.

"Controverse sur les inhibiteurs calciques dans le traitement de l'hypertension artérielle : les inhibiteurs calciques sont-ils nos amis ou nos ennemis ? [Discussion on calcic inhibitors in the treatment of arterial hypertension: are calcic inhibitors our friends or our enemies?"], *La Lettre du cardiologue* N ° 251, January 1996.

Le Monde, Dossiers et documents N °40, February 1996, "L'industrie pharmaceutique veut la liberté des prix" ["The pharmaceutical industry wants price free-dom"], by Dominique Gallois.

"Deception in Medical and Behavioral Research: Is It Ever Acceptable?" by Dave Wendler. *The Milbank Quarterly* vol. 74, number 1, 1996.

"The Goodwill Pill Mess", by Andrew Purvis, *Time*, April 29, 1996.

"How a Drug Firm Paid for University Study, Then Undermined It", by Ralph T King Jr, *Wall Street Journal*, April 26, 1996.

"Inhibiteurs calciques : une utilisation trop fréquente pour des médicaments mal évalués" ["Calcic inhibitors: a too frequent use for drugs that haven't been properly evaluated"], by Emmanuel Dumont, *Prescrire*, April 1996.

"The Elvis of Pharmaceuticals", by Carl Elliott, *BMJ*, volume 313, October 12, 1996.

"Thyroid Storm" by Drummond Rennie, *Journal of the American Medical Association*, April 16, 1997.

"Le marketing pharmaceutique est-il (encore) spécifique ?" ["Is pharmaceutical marketing (still) specific?"] by Martine Gaillard and Christian Dussart, *Décisions Marketing*, May-August 1997.

"Les accros du Prozac" ["Hooked on Prozac"], by Jean-Michel Bader, *Marianne*, September 29, 1997.

"Conflict of Interest in the Debate over Calcium-Channel Antagonists", by Henri Thomas Stelfox, Grace Chua, Keith O' Rourke and Allan S. Detsky, *New England Journal of Medicine*, January 8, 1998.

"Les labos, rois du cash-flow" ["Laboratories, Kings of Cash-flow"], by Gene-vieve Dupoux-Verneuil, *Le Nouvel Economiste*, March 27, 1998.

"Traitement amaigrissant : le médicament qui a déjà fait 30 morts" ["Slimming treatment: the drug that has already killed 30"], Eric Giacometti, *Le Parisien libéré*, March 28-29,1998.

"Pharmaceutical marketing: which evolutions?", *Marketing Magazine* N °28, March 1998.

"Anorexigènes: gérer le risque de valvulopathie et d'endocardite" ["Growth regulators: managing the risks of valvulopathy and endocarditis"], by Eric Giacometti, *Prescrire*, April 1998.

"Is Good Marketing Bad Medicine?" , *Business Week*, April 20, 1998.

"Biotechnologies, le réveil européen" ["Biotechnologies, the European alarm clock"], *Les Echos*, May 27, 1998.

Capital, June 1998: dossier sur le pouvoir des lobbies en France, partie concer-

nant les personnels de santé [a file on the power of lobbies in France, concerning personal health]. "On ne peut pas intervenir sans réfléchir sur un
processus comme l'appétit" [One cannot intervene, without reflecting, in a
process like the appetite"], interview of Dr. Lucien Abenhaïm by Jean-Yves
Nau, *Le Monde*, October 14, 1998.

"Les journaux scientifiques sont menacés par la concurrence d'Internet" ["Scientific journals are threatened by competition from the Internet"], *Le Monde*, January 22, 1999.

"Enquête exclusive medicaments" [Exclusive investigation on drugs], *Sciences &
Vie*, March 1999, N °978.

Audio-visuals

Envoyé spécial [Special correspondent] October 8, 1998 on A 2. *Des Racines et des
ailes* ["Roots and wings"], October 14, 1998. *Un Autre journal* [Another jour-
nal], Canal +, April 19, 1999.

Chapters 5 and 6

The episode at the Truite Saint-Honoré was related to me by Pierre Clostermann himself. My thanks as well to Pierre Carpent, Wolfgang Didshun,
Robert Elizard, Michel Guerard and Barbara Kracht, to Bernard Violet;
and to all the others.

In reconstructing this account, I relied on the following works,
in English:

Alec Dubro & David Kaplan, *Yakuza, the Explosive Account of Japan's Criminal Underworld*, London, Futura Publications, 1987.

John J. Fialka, *War by Other Means, Economic Espionage in America*, New York, W.W.
Norton & Company, 1997.

Matthew Lynn, *Birds of Prey, The War Between Boeing and Airbus*, London, Heine-
mann, 1982.

John Newhouse, *How the Great Aircraft Manufacturers — Boeing, Lockheed, McDonnell
Douglas, Airbus — and the Extraordinary Men Who Run Them Play What They Call*

the *Sporty Game*, New York, Alfred Knoff, 1982.

Arthur Reed, *Airbus*, London, Norden Publishing House, 1991.

Maria Schiavo (and Sabra Chartrand), *Flying Blind, Flying Safe, the Former Inspector General of the US Department of Transportations Tells You Everything You Need to Know to Travel Safer by Air*, New York, Avon Books, 1997.

Peter Schweizer, *Friendly Spies*, New York, The Atlantic Monthly Press, 1993.

Ira Winkler, *Corporate Espionage, What is Happening in Your Company, What You Must Do About It*, New York, Prima Publishing, 1998.

In French:

Pascal Andrei, "Approche de l'intelligence économique et de la veille stratégique à travers la production d'information élaborée. Applications à l'aide à la décision dans les domaines de l'Aéronautique et de l'Espace" ["The economic intelligence and strategic surveillance approach through the production of information. Applications as an aid to decision-making in the fields of Aeronautics and Space", a doctoral thesis defended on January 25, 1997, Université de Marne-la-Vallée.

Lofti Belhassine, *Le Ciel confisqué, les relations incestueuses d'Air France* [Confiscated Sky, incestuous relations of Air France], Paris, Albin Michel, 1997.

Lew Bogdan, *L'Epopée du ciel clair, de Lindbergh à l'Airbus* [The Epic of the Clear Sky, from Lindbergh to Airbus], Paris, Hachette, 1988.

Frank Bouaziz, *Air France*, Paris, Plon, 1998.

Norbert Jacquet, *Airbus, l'assassin habite à l'Elysée* [Airbus: the Assassin Lives at the Elysée], Paris, Première ligne, 1994 (work published with the assistance of the Institut d'Etudes de la Désinformation).

Henri Mézière & Jean-Marie Sauvage, *Les Ailes françaises, l'aviation marchande de 1919 à nos jours* [French Wings, commercial aviation from 1919 to our days], Paris, Rive droite, 1999.

Jean Picq, *Les Ailes de l'Europe, l'aventure de l'Airbus* [Wings of Europe, the Adventure of Airbus], Paris, Fayard, 1990.

Anthony Sampson, *Les Empires du ciel, les dessous des grandes compagnies aériennes* [Empires of the sky, the underside of the major airlines], Paris, Calmann-Lévy, 1986.

Bernard Violet, *Attachez vos ceintures* [*Fasten your seat belts*], Paris, Plon, 1990.

Press

"Why Boeing Doesn't Have the All-Clear Yet", by Dori Jones Yang, *BusinessWeek*, May 11, 1992.

"Reinventing Boeing", by Dori Jones Yang and Andrea Rothman, *BusinessWeek*, March 1, 1993.

"Boeing-Airbus, le match du siècle [The match of the century]", by Etienne Gingembre and Loïc Grasset, *Capital* magazine, January 1995.

"La Guerre mondiale de l'espionnage économique [The World War of Economic Espionage]", a report by Jean Guisnel and François Vey, *Capital* magazine, February 1995.

"Aerospace Prognosis 1998" by Seanna Browder, *Business Week*, January 12, 1998.

"Time to Get Tough with Planemakers", by Richard Stirland, *Orient Aviation*, August-September 1998.

"Boeing se remet en cause [Boeing is in trouble again]", by Nadine Bayle, L'Usine nouvelle, September 3, 1998.

"Boeing-Airbus, la guerre du ciel [War of the Skies]", by Rémi Kauffer, *Le Figaro-Magazine*, September 19, 1998.

"Can a New Crew Buoy Boeing?", by Andy Reinhardt and Seanna Browder, *Business Week*, September 14, 1998.

"Airbus conçus en ingeniérie simultanée", by Nadine Bayle, *L'Usine nouvelle*, September 17, 1998.

"Toulouse, comment Airbus dope les PME [How Airbus misleads the SME]" by Laurence Lafosse, *Le Nouvel Economiste*, September 18, 1998.

"Boeing cloué au sol [nailed to the ground]", an investigation by Sylvain Courage, special correspondent for *Capital* magazine in the United States, November 1998.

"Cleared for Takeoff: Another Turnaround", by Andy Reinhardt and Seanna Browder, *Business Week*, November 9, 1998.

"Année faste pour l'industrie aéronautique et spatiale française" [A Promising year for the French aircraft and space industry", by Thierry Gadault, *Le Tribune*, March 9, 1999.

Audio-visuals

"Capital", M 6, September 20, 1998.

Chapter 7

Books

Prof. Marian Apfelbaum (under the direction of), *Risques et peurs alimentaires* [Food Risks and Fears], Paris, Odile Jacob, 1998.

Pierre Harisson, *L'Empire Nestlé* [The Nestle Empire], Lausanne, Pierre-Marcel Favre, 1982.

Jean- Noël Kapferer, *Rumeurs, le plus vieux média du monde* [Rumors, the oldest medium in the world], Paris, Le Seuil, 1987.

Ralph Nader, *Main basse sur le pouvoir* [Grabbing Power], Paris, Lattès, 1973.

Vance Packard, *La persuasion clandestine* [The Hidden Persuaders], Paris, Calmann-Lévy, 1984, foreword by Marcel Bleustein-Strainer.

Jean-Paul Picaper & Thibaud Dornier, *Greenpeace, "l'écologie à l'an vert* [Ecology in the green year]", Paris, Odilon-Media, 1995.

Michel de Pracontal, *La Guerre du tabac* [The Tobacco War], Paris, Fayard, 1998.

Rencontres internationales Médias-défense [International meetings, Media-defense 95 (a collective work). *Les Manipulations de l'image et du son* [Manipulations of image and sound], Paris, Hachette-Fondation pour les études de la Défense, 1996.

David Riesman, *L'abondance, à quoi bon?* [What good is abundance?], Paris, Robert Laffont, 1969.

Michele Rivasi and Helene Crié, *Ce nucléaire qu'on nous cache* [This nuclear power that they are hiding from us], Paris, Albin Michel, 1998.

Patrick Romagni, *La Communication d'influence, lobbying, mode d'emploi* [The Communication of influence, lobbying, how-to], Paris, Les Presses du management, 1995.

Olivier Vermont (pseudonym), *La Face cachée de Greenpeace* [Greenpeace's Hidden Face], Paris, Albin Michel, 1997.

Documents

Missions d'information commune sur l'ensemble des problèmes posés par le développement de l'Encéphalopathie spongiforme bovine, a report submitted to the National Assembly, Paris, 1997, volume 1. Report, volume 2. Hearings.

Erik Mistler-Level, *La Planète soja, un enjeu mondial* [Soy planet: A world at risk], ᵗ

Université de Marne-la-Vallée, diplôme d'Etudes Supérieures Spécialisées, Ingénierie de l'intelligence économique, 1997

"Phil", *La Face cachée de Greenpeace (une organisation écologiste au-dessus de tout soupçon* [The Hidden face of Greenpeace (an ecologist organization above all suspicion?)]. A publication of "Chlorophiles", an association of workers and sympathizers of the industries related to chlorine and to PVC, Brussels, 1996.

Asian Seas Newsletter issues from January 5 and 19, February 2, 1995.

Senate Report N °440: "Transgéniques, pour des choix responsables" [Transgenics, for responsible choices"], for the Commission of Economic Affairs and Planning, by Jean Bizet, 1997-1998.

Press

"Produits transgéniques, quand la publicité s'invite au débat [Transgenic Products, when advertising invites a debate]", by Daniel Aronssohn, *Alternatives économiques*, March 1999.

"Les entreprises face aux droits de l'Homme [Companies confronting human rights]", by Laure Belot, *Le.Monde*, December 12, 1998.

"Stanching the Flow of China's Gulag Exports", by Amis Borrus and Joyce Barnathan, *BusinessWeek*, April 13, 1992.

"Inside Big Tobacco's Secret War Room", by Mike France, *BusinessWeek*, June 15, 1998.

"Guerre et contre-guerre de l'information économique [War and counter-war of economic information", by Pascal Jacques-Gustave, *Echanges* N °108 — 4th quarter 1994.

"Pepsi-Cola, l'été de tous les dangers [The summer of all dangers]", by Jean-Marc Lehu, *Décisions marketing* N °4, January-April 1995.

"Des responsables politiques si influençables [Political leaders so easy to influence]", by Mark Pertschuk, *Le Monde diplomatique*, June 1997.

"La Rumeur qui a déstabilisé OCB [The Rumor that destabilized OCB]", by Estelle Saget, *L'Expansion*, October 23, 1997.

"La dictature alimentaire [Food Dictatorship]", *Courrier international*, February 19, 1998 — a summary of an investigation in the British daily *The Guardian*, which ran many articles on problem of the pro-GMO lobby, in particular in on December 16, 1997.

"Les organismes génétiquement modifiés [Genetically modified organizations]", *Enjeux*, March 1998.

Conclusion

Books

James Adams, *The Next World War*, New York, Simon & Schuster, 1998.

Richard d Aveny with Robert Gunther, *Hypercompetitive Rivalries*, New York, Free Press, 1994.

Guy Durandin, *L'Information, la désinformation et la réalité* [Information, disinformation and reality], Paris, PUF, 1993.

Jean Guisnel, *Guerre dans le cyberespace* [War in cyberspace], Paris, La Découverte, 1995 and 1997.

Alex Inkeles, *L'Opinion publique en Russie soviétique, une étude sur la persuasion des masses* [Public opinion in Soviet Russia, a study on persuasion of the masses], Paris, les Iles d'Or, 1956.

Richard H. Shultz and Roy Godson, *Desinformatsia, mesures actives de la propagande soviétique* [Disinformatsia, active measures of Soviet propaganda], Paris, Anthropos, 1985.

Press

"Brand Warfare", *Information Strategy*, April 1997.

"CNN, il lui faudrait une bonne guerre [CNN needs a good war]", by Isabelle Durieux, *L'Expansion*, December 4, 1997.

"MAO", by Angela Minzoni-Déroche, *Veille, le magazine professionnel de l'Intelligence économique* N °24, May 1999.

Also from Algora Publishing:

CLAUDIU A. SECARA
THE NEW COMMONWEALTH:
FROM BUREAUCRATIC CORPORATISM TO SOCIALIST CAPITALISM

The notion of an elite-driven worldwide perestroika has gained some credibility lately. The book examines in a historical perspective the most intriguing dialectic in the Soviet Union's "collapse" — from socialism to capitalism and back to socialist capitalism — and speculates on the global implications.

DOMINIQUE FERNANDEZ
PHOTOGRAPHER: FERRANTE FERRANTI
ROMANIAN RHAPSODY — An Overlooked Corner of Europe

"Romania doesn't get very good press." And so, renowned French travel writer Dominique Fernandez and top photographer Ferrante Ferranti head out to form their own images. In four long journeys over a 6-year span, they uncover a tantalizing blend of German efficiency and Latin nonchalance, French literature and Gypsy music, Western rationalism and Oriental mysteries. Fernandez reveals the rich Romanian essence. Attentive and precise, he digs beneath the somber heritage of communism to reach the deep roots of a European country that is so little-known.

IGNACIO RAMONET
THE GEOPOLITICS OF CHAOS

The author, Director of Le Monde Diplomatique, presents an original, discriminating and lucid political matrix for understanding what he calls the "current disorder of the world" in terms of Internationalization, Cyberculture and Political Chaos.

TZVETAN TODOROV
A PASSION FOR DEMOCRACY – BENJAMIN CONSTANT

The French Revolution rang the death knell not only for a form of society, but also for a way of feeling and of living; and it is still not clear what we have gained from the changes. Todorov examines the life of Constant, one of the original thinkers who conceptualized modern democracy, and in the process gives us a richly textured portrait of a man who was fully engaged in life, both public and private.

MICHEL PINÇON & MONIQUE PINÇON-CHARLOT
GRAND FORTUNES – DYNASTIES OF WEALTH IN FRANCE

Going back for generations, the fortunes of great families consist of far more than money—they are also symbols of culture and social interaction. In a nation known for democracy and meritocracy, piercing the secrets of the grand fortunes verges on a crime of lèse-majesté . . . Grand Fortunes succeeds at that.

JEAN-MARIE ABGRALL
SOUL SNATCHERS: THE MECHANICS OF CULTS

Jean-Marie Abgrall, psychiatrist, criminologist, expert witness to the French Court of Appeals, and member of the Inter-Ministry Committee on Cults, is one of the experts most frequently consulted by the European judicial and legislative processes. The fruit of fifteen years of research, his book delivers the first methodical analysis of the sectarian phenomenon, decoding the mental manipulation on behalf of mystified observers as well as victims.

JEAN-CLAUDE GUILLEBAUD
THE TYRANNY OF PLEASURE

A Sixties' radical re-thinks liberation, taking a hard look at the question of sexual morals in a modern society. For almost a whole generation, we have lived in the illusion that this question had ceased to exist. Today the illusion is faded, but a strange and tumultuous distress replaces it. Our societies painfully seek a "third way", between unacceptable alternatives: bold-faced permissiveness or nostalgic moralism.

SOPHIE COIGNARD AND MARIE-THÉRÈSE GUICHARD
FRENCH CONNECTIONS –
The Secret History of Networks of Influence

They were born in the same region, went to the same schools, fought the same fights and made the same mistakes in youth. They share the same morals, the same fantasies of success and the same taste for money. They act behind the scenes to help each other, boosting careers, monopolizing business and information, making money, conspiring and, why not, becoming Presidents!

VLADIMIR PLOUGIN
RUSSIAN INTELLIGENCE SERVICES. Vol. I. Early Years

Mysterious episodes from Russia's past – alliances and betrayals, espionage and military feats – are unearthed and examined in this study, which is drawn from ancient chronicles and preserved documents from Russia, Greece, Byzantium and the Vatican Library. Scholarly analysis and narrative flair combine to give both the facts and the flavor of the battle scenes and the espionage milieu, including the establishment of secret services in Kievan rus, the heroes and the techniques of intelligence and counter-intelligence in the 10th-12th centuries, and the times of Vladimir.

JEAN-JACQUES ROSA
EURO ERROR

The European Superstate makes Jean-Jacques Rosa mad, for two reasons. First, actions taken to relieve unemployment have created inflation, but have not reduced unemployment. His second argument is even more intriguing: the 21st century will see the fragmentation of the U. S., not the unification of Europe.

ANDRÉ GAURON
EUROPEAN MISUNDERSTANDING

Few of the books decrying the European Monetary Union raise the level of the discussion to a higher plane. European Misunderstanding is one of these. Gauron gets it right, observing that the real problem facing Europe is its political future, not its economic future.

CLAUDIU A. SECARA
TIME & EGO – Judeo-Christian Egotheism and the Anglo-Saxon Industrial Revolution

The first question of abstract reflection that arouses controversy is the problem of Becoming. Being persists, beings constantly change; they are born and they pass away. How can Being change and yet be eternal? The quest for the logical and experimental answer has just taken off.

PHILIPPE TRÉTIACK
ARE YOU AGITÉ? Treatise on Everyday Agitation

The 'Agité,' that human species that lives in international airports, jumps into taxis while dialing the cell phone, eats while clearing the table, reads the paper while watching TV and works during vacation – has just been given a new title. "A book filled with the exuberance of a new millennium, full of humor and relevance. Philippe Trétiack, a leading reporter for Elle, takes us around the world and back at light speed." — *Aujourd'hui le Parisien*

PAUL LOMBARD
VICE & VIRTUE — Men of History, Great Crooks for the Greater Good

Personal passion has often guided powerful people more than the public interest. With what result? From the courtiers of Versailles to the back halls of Mitterand's government, from Danton — revealed to have been a paid agent for England — to the shady bankers of Mitterand's era, from the buddies of Mazarin to the builders of the Panama Canal, Paul Lombard unearths the secrets of the corridors of power. He reveals the vanity and the corruption, but also the grandeur and panache that characterize the great. This cavalcade over many centuries can be read as a subversive tract on how to lead.

RICHARD LABÉVIÈRE
DOLLARS FOR TERROR — The U.S. and Islam

"In this riveting, often shocking analysis, the U.S. is an accessory in the rise of Islam, because it manipulates and aids radical Moslem groups in its shortsighted pursuit of its economic interests, especially the energy resources of the Middle East and the oil- and mineral-rich former Soviet republics of Central Asia. Labévière shows how radical Islamic fundamentalism spreads its influence on two levels, above board, through investment firms, banks and shell companies, and clandestinely, though a network of drug dealing, weapons smuggling and money laundering. This important book sounds a wake-up call to U.S. policy-makers." — *Publishers Weekly*

JEANNINE VERDÈS-LEROUX
DECONSTRUCTING PIERRE BOURDIEU — Against Sociological Terrorism From the Left

Sociologist Pierre Bourdieu went from widely-criticized to widely-acclaimed, without adjusting his hastily constructed theories. Turning the guns of critical analysis on his own critics, he was happier jousting in the ring of (often quite undemocratic) political debate than reflecting and expanding upon his own propositions. Verdès-Leroux suggests that Bourdieu arrogated for himself the role of "total intellectual" and proved that a good offense is the best defense. A pessimistic Leninist bolstered by a ponderous scientific construct, Bourdieu stands out as the ultimate doctrinaire more concerned with self-promotion than with democratic intellectual engagements.

HENRI TROYAT
TERRIBLE TZARINAS

Who should succeed Peter the Great? Upon the death of this visionary and despotic reformer, the great families plotted to come up with a successor who would surpass everyone else — or at least, offend none. But there were only women — Catherine I, Anna Ivanovna, Anna Leopoldovna, Elizabeth I. These autocrats imposed their violent and dissolute natures upon the empire, along with their loves, their feuds, their cruelties. Born in 1911 in Moscow, Troyat is a member of the Académie française, recipient of Prix Goncourt.

JEAN-MARIE ABGRALL

HEALING OR STEALING — Medical Charlatans in the New Age

Jean-Marie Abgrall is Europe's foremost expert on cults and forensic medicine. He asks, are fear of illness and death the only reasons why people trust their fates to the wizards of the pseudo-revolutionary and the practitioners of pseudo-magic? We live in a bazaar of the bizarre, where everyday denial of rationality has turned many patients into ecstatic fools. While not all systems of nontraditional medicine are linked to cults, this is one of the surest avenues of recruitment, and the crisis of the modern world may be leading to a new mystique of medicine where patients check their powers of judgment at the door.

DEBORAH SCHURMAN-KAUFLIN

THE NEW PREDATOR: WOMEN WHO KILL — Profiles of Female Serial Killers

This is the first book ever based on face-to-face interviews with women serial killers. Dr. Schurman-Kauflin analyzes the similarities and differences between male and female serial killers and mass murderers.

RÉMI KAUFFER

DISINFORMATION — US Multinationals at War with Europe

"Spreading rumors to damage a competitor, using 'tourists' for industrial espionage. . . Kauffer shows how the economic war is waged." — *Le Monde*

"A specialist in the secret services, Kauffer notes that, 'In the CNN era, with our skies full of satellites and the Internet expanding every nano-second, the techniques of mass persuasion that were developed during the Cold War are still very much in use – only their field of application has changed.' His analysis is shocking, and well-documented." — *La Tribune*

CARL A. DAVIS

PLANE TRUTH — A PRIVATE INVESTIGATOR'S STORY

"Raises new questions about corporate and tribal loyalties, structural engineering, and money and politics, in a credible scenario that makes my flesh creep. . . I think I'll take a train, next time. Or walk." — Western Review

"Takes us around the world and finds treasure under stones that had been left unturned After reading these 'travels with Carl,' (or is he Sherlock Holmes?), my own life seems very flat." — Book Addicts

JENNIFER FURIO

LETTERS FROM PRISON — VOICES OF WOMEN MURDERERS

Written by incarcerated women, these incredibly personal, surprisingly honest letters shed light on their lives, their crimes and the mitigating circumstances. Author Jennifer Furio, a prison reform activist, subtly reveals the biases if the criminal justice system and the media. The words of these women haunt and transfix even the most skeptical reader.

COPING WITH FREEDOM

CHANTAL THOMAS

40 million American women of marriageable age are single. This approachable essay addresses many of their concerns in a profound and delightful way. Inspired by the author's own experiences as well as by the 18th century philosophers, and literary and historical references, it offers insights and the courage to help us revel in the game of life, the delight of reading, the art of the journey, and the right to say "no" to chains of obligations and family.